THE PLATING

OF THE

PENNY BLACK POSTAGE STAMP

OF

GREAT BRITAIN,

1840.

THE PLATING
OF THE
PENNY BLACK POSTAGE STAMP
OF
GREAT BRITAIN,
1840.

With a description of each individual stamp on the eleven different plates, affording a guide to collectors in the reconstruction of the sheets.

BY

CHARLES NISSEN

(IN COLLABORATION WITH

BERTRAM McGOWAN).

WITH A NEW FOREWORD BY

CHARLES W. GOODWYN LLB, RDP, FRPSL

Keeper of the Royal Philatelic Collection

REPUBLISHED BY

STANLEY GIBBONS, LTD

LONDON AND RINGWOOD, 2008.

ISBN 10: 0 85259 701-0
ISBN 13: 978-085259701-9

This edition is taken from the 1922 edition published by Chas. Nissen & Co. Limited.
Produced and printed in Great Britain by Pardy & Son (Printers) Ltd., Ringwood, Hampshire.

FOREWORD.

"The Plating of the Penny Black Postage Stamp of Great Britain 1840"

The original book by Charles Nissen, in collaboration with Bertram McGowan, published by Charles Nissen and Co. Ltd., in 1922, has stood the test of time. Together with Volume I of the Stanley Gibbons Great Britain Specialised Catalogue, it remains the yardstick for plating the Penny Black.

Twelve years of research resulted in the photographic reproduction of 2,880 different stamps from 11 plates – or 12, if you regard the two states of plate 1 as being separate plates, 1a and 1b. Apart from the written descriptions of each stamp with its corner letter and further distinguishing features, the study includes details of all the 'double letters' and re-entries.

I am delighted that this classic work is to be reprinted and be available to modern students.

Charles W. Goodwyn LLB, RDP, FRPSL
Keeper of the Royal Philatelic Collection

November 1998

FOREWORD.

THE cult of the "Penny Black"—and no true British philatelist is so pedantic as to call the first postage stamp the "Black Penny"!—has so spread amongst, and is now so highly specialised by, many collectors, that, from being a side-line of philately, it has become almost a "country" in itself.

Where the old-time collector was content with one or two copies of the famous Penny, the modern specialist aims at the completion of a made-up sheet of stamps from each of the eleven plates, from which printings were made in black. And, as most, if not all, of these plates existed in one, two, or even three "states"—due to touching-up, repairing or strengthening—the eleven sheets may well be only the beginning of a collection numbering many thousands of stamps, all in the familiar sombre hue, a veritable study in black and white.

For even the wealthy and leisured specialist, an absolutely complete collection of the Mother of all postage stamps is well nigh an impossibility: Plate 11, as is now well known, would prove a practically insurmountable difficulty; for how comparatively few stamps from the 700 sheets printed in black can have escaped destruction!

What then of the limited specialist, or even the "each plate, one stamp" man? His fate is, or rather was, to be pitied, for, unless he sought the aid of some more fortunate brother-philatelist, how was he to tell from which plate came each of his little collection of "Penny Blacks", all of similar lettering, but varying in the details inseparable from hand-work?

Now, the possessor of even a single copy of our first Postage Stamp will, with the aid of this work, be able to say, "It is from plate —", let us hope the rare 11.

Mr. Charles Nissen, who has devoted many years to the study of British postage stamps, has had through his hands probably more "Penny Blacks" than any other man, collector or dealer; and several highly specialised accumulations of this popular stamp have been acquired by him.

Some years ago, probably ten or twelve, Mr. Nissen took up the study of the "Penny Black", and gradually, at first with many slips and mistakes, built up portions of sheets of stamps, obviously from different plates though of similar letterings. But then difficulties arose: who has not, in making up a sheet even irrespective of plate, found the last few stamps elusive to a degree which has ended almost in despair?

Multiply this by eleven, and then give a thought to re-entered, strengthened and recut stamps. The labour was enormous; and only a keen student, sacrificing his time, damaging his eyesight, and working for the love of the task—never, perhaps, to be capable of completion—would have carried on for years, gradually building up the material for his finished work.

I, knowing something of this gradual building-up in matters philatelic—an addition, perhaps, of one short item as the result of days, or even weeks, of close application—appreciated the immensity of Mr. Nissen's labour of love, when he first broached the subject to me; and, when he passed on to me the manuscript of this work, with a request to see it through the trials and dangers of the "press", I was able to more fully gauge the care, devotion and thoroughness with which my friend had realised his ambition.

I have written thus out of a sense of duty, and the students from among all the philatelists to whom I commend this work will, after a critical test of the result of my friend's labours, confirm my belief that I have not been unduly eulogistic.

A. B. CREEKE.

PREFACE.

FROM my youth up, the "Penny Black" postage stamp of Great Britain has with me always been a favourite subject for study. It was issued on the 1st May, 1840, to be used for prepayment of postage five days later: the very first to be printed, the "Mother of Postage Stamps" possesses a beauty and dignity not surpassed, and rarely equalled, by any one of her numerous descendants.

During the last twenty-five years, persistent hunting, coupled with a certain amount of luck, has enabled me to handle, and frequently to acquire, large numbers of the "Penny Black", good, bad and indifferent, according to the manner of their early severance from the sheet and their subsequent course of existence. Collectors, desirous of parting with their "Blacks", have, knowing my predilection for the stamp, brought their dusky treasures to me; and, for a similar reason, I have generally had the first refusal of any highly-specialised accumulation of the stamp, which its owner had made up his mind to dispose of. I mention this, not in any boasting spirit, but merely to give some indication of the vast numbers of the "Penny Black" necessary to afford a reasonable hope of selecting two hundred and forty sets of eleven stamps each—all of each eleven at first sight exactly similar to one another, and yet so differing in the minute details of certain portions of the design that they could be separated from each other.

Now the specialist comes into his own, for, without the pairs, strips and blocks which he has steadily accumulated, the selection of the right stamp from each batch of eleven, so that they might all be brought together into one large sheet of two hundred and forty, would have been impossible.

Ten or twelve years ago, working with the optimistic zeal of the comparatively ignorant searcher after truth, I determined to try my hand at building-up, or "plating", as it is more generally termed—the eleven plates of 240 each, a grand total of 2,640 stamps. Prodigious! And even that expressive word does not sufficiently indicate the task of hunting through hundreds, or even thousands of similar stamps, in order to fill, perhaps, one space on an otherwise completed sheet.

With me, the labour—and I use that word intentionally—has been one of love, and the task has given me very many hours of most pleasurable, if difficult, occupation.

My work is now concluded. I do not say "completed", for it may well be that some of my readers will find some slips or errors; but their criticisms will be welcomed and given every consideration—in fact, criticism is invited.

First and foremost, I thank Mr. BERTRAM McGOWAN *for his help in checking the 2,880 plated stamps as photographed, and in describing the position of the corner-letters, which I subsequently checked; and I much appreciate the willingness with which he came forward.*

To the following philatelists also my thanks are due, for the loan of stamps and for suggestions:—Mr. G. Alston, Mr. H. C. V. Adams, Mr. E. D. Bacon, M.V.O., Mr. R. F. Bayford, K.C., Mr. Percy C. Bishop, and Mr. L. A. Burd.

My readers will find, in the "Preliminary" text, some excellent reproductions of Re-entries, Double Letters etc. These are from drawings specially made, originally for the British Philatelist *and incidentally for this work, by Mr. J. Seymour, to whose skill and care my appreciative thanks are recorded.*

It seems hardly necessary to state that I have consulted, and derived help from, not only the leading philatelic journals and the numerous excellent articles contributed from time to time to the British Philatelist, *but also the various works on the postal issues of Great Britain, especially "Wright and Creeke"* and Mr. E. D. Bacon's magnum opus† on the line-engraved issues.*

Lastly, my thanks are given to my friend, Mr. A. B. Creeke, for correcting the proofs and seeing my work successfully "through the press"—an undertaking which calls for skilled and careful application, and is far from being so easy as it may appear to a non-journalistic reader.

MAY, 1922. *CHARLES NISSEN.*

---

* *"A History of the Adhesive Stamps of the British Isles", by Hastings E. Wright and A. B. Creeke, Jun. London, 1899.*

† *"The Line-engraved Postage Stamps of Great Britain, printed by Perkins, Bacon & Co.", by E. D Bacon, M.V.O. London, 1920.*

CONTENTS.

"The Mother of All Postage Stamps"

THE PLATING
OF THE
PENNY BLACK POSTAGE STAMP
OF
GREAT BRITAIN,
1840.

PRELIMINARY.

CHAPTER I.

HISTORICAL.

THE name of Rowland Hill will always be associated with the adoption of Penny Postage and the introduction of stamps, or "labels" as they were originally called, as a means of prepayment of letters. In February, 1837, he published a Pamphlet entitled "Post Office Reform: its Importance and Practicability", in which he was able to show that the cost of conveyance of a letter was very little, as compared with the cost of its collection and delivery, and that accordingly it would be quite fair to all parties to charge a uniform rate of postage irrespective of distance.

His Pamphlet created a great amount of public interest, and a Committee of the House of Commons was appointed to enquire into the rates and modes of charging postage with a view to their reduction. The Committee reported in favour of Hill's proposals, and a Bill was introduced which received the Royal assent on 17th August, 1839. By this Act the Lords of the Treasury were authorised to fix the rates of postage and regulate the manner of their collection, whether by prepayment or otherwise.

Their Lordships after full consideration decided, by Minute dated 26th December, 1839, that, so far as practicable, the postage of letters should be prepaid by means of "stamps", which included, in addition to adhesive stamps, stamped envelopes and covers.

They stated that stamps would be prepared with the least possible delay, and when ready due notice of their introduction would be given. Meanwhile, it was decided, from and after the 10th January, 1840, to introduce a uniform rate of postage for all letters transmitted by post between places within the

United Kingdom, without reference to the distance they were conveyed, beginning at 1d. in the case of letters not exceeding ½oz. Prior to this, the Treasury had published a Notice in *The Times,* in which they invited suggestions from "artists, men of science, and the public in general", as to the manner in which the stamps might best be brought into use; but, although suggestions to the number of over 2,600 were sent in, none was considered suitable.

Accordingly, Messrs. Perkins, Bacon and Petch, of Fleet Street, well known as high-class engravers and steel-plate printers, with whom Mr. Hill had been in touch previously, but who had not replied to the invitation of the Treasury, were approached with a view to their constructing the necessary die and plates for the production of the adhesive stamps. Satisfactory terms having been concluded, a Notice was issued on 25th April, 1840, to all postmasters and sub-postmasters, stating that postage stamps would be brought into use on 6th May, 1840. This was followed on 29th April by another Notice, enclosing two specimens of the penny adhesive label, along with specimens of the 1d. and 2d. stamped covers and envelopes.

Printing of the stamps had commenced on 11th April; and it was originally intended that the stamps should be issued to the public on 1st May, but it was feared that a sufficient supply would not be ready, and accordingly the date was postponed. However, according to Mr. Hill's diary, stamps were issued to the public in London on 1st May and, although not officially available, it is evident that a few were actually used, as stamps, duly postmarked, are known on letters posted on 2nd May, 1840.

CHAPTER II.

THE DIE AND PLATE.

The accepted design consisted of a diademed profile of Queen Victoria to the left, upon a background of ornamental lathe-work. A drawing was made by Henry Corbould, an artist of repute, of the head of the Queen taken from the obverse of a medal by William Wyon, engraver to the Mint, struck in commemoration of Her Majesty's visit to the City of London on Lord Mayor's Day, 9th November, 1837. The die was prepared by Messrs. Perkins, Bacon and Petch, and the method is thus described by Mr. E. D. Bacon in his *magnum opus**:—

> The background first of all selected for the stamp was that of the last of the three essays we have described. An impression of this was transferred from the stock roller on to a flat piece of steel and the exact size of the background required for the stamp and a space for the head were outlined on this die. An impression was then taken up on to another roller, the parts of the pattern outside the indicated marks were removed, the space for the head was cleared, and the background required for the stamp

* "The Line-engraved Postage Stamps of Great Britain, printed by Messrs. Perkins, Bacon & Co.", by Edward Denny Bacon, M.V.O. London, 1920. Page 16.

was then transferred to another flat piece of steel, which became the actual die of the stamp. The die was then handed, with the drawing made by Henry Corbould, to Charles Heath for the engraving of the Queen's head.

Although the die was handed to Charles Heath, it is probable that the actual cutting of the Queen's head was done by his son Frederick under his father's supervision. After the head was completed the die was returned to Messrs. Perkins, Bacon and Petch who, after carefully removing a small portion of the background at the top and bottom, added the inscription "POSTAGE" at the top and "ONE PENNY." at the bottom, along with the four blocks in the corners which were at first left blank. Subsequently a white cross *pâté* was engraved in each of the upper corner-blocks. The die was then hardened and became capable of almost endless reproduction.

To transfer the die to the plate required an intermediate process. This was done by means of a steel roller, previously softened, which was put in a transfer-press and rolled under great pressure backwards and forwards over the hardened die, until the design on the die was transferred to the roller in a reversed form. Each of the rollers used bore from four to eight impressions of the die. The impressions were placed lengthways on the surface of the roller, and were rolled into the plate from top to bottom.

The plates employed for printing the stamps were fine oblong pieces of steel, each plate being large enough to contain 240 impressions, in 20 horizontal rows of 12, of the facial value of £1. After the plates were cut to the exact shape required, they were softened and faint lines were made on them as guides, so that the workmen might transfer the impressions from the roller in proper alignment. The impressions of the engraved die taken upon the rollers were then transferred to the plate. The number of the plate was then added in the four extreme corners, and the following inscription made at the top, bottom and each side of the plate:— "*Price 1$^{d.}$ Per Label. 1^{s}/- Per Row of 12. £1—"—" Per Sheet. Place the Labels ABOVE the Address and towards the RIGHT HAND SIDE of the Letter. In Wetting the back be careful not to remove the Cement*". This inscription varies slightly in its position on the different plates.

The lower corner-blocks of the impressions were, as previously mentioned, left blank. This was for the purpose of inserting check-letters. These were intended as a safeguard against forgery, as it was thought that, if every stamp on a plate had a different lettering, forgeries would likely be of one particular stamp only, and any considerable sale or use of stamps all of the same lettering might attract attention and lead to enquiry. The letters were inserted by means of hardened steel punches, each bearing a letter in relief, which were transferred to the plate in recess, resulting in an inked impression of the letter on the finished stamp. The letter in the left-hand corner denoted the number of the horizontal row in which the stamp was, and the letter in the right-hand corner its place in that row. Thus the stamps in the first row were lettered "AA", "AB", "AC", to "AL"; those in the second row "BA" to "BL"; and so on to the twentieth row, in which the lettering was from "TA" to "TL".

CHAPTER III.

PRINTING THE STAMPS.

Before the plate was printed from, the "burr" between the impressions was cleaned off as far as possible, and also the guide-lines, and any touching-up that was thought necessary was done. The plate was usually hardened before being printed from, though some of the early plates were not hardened when first used, as the printers were pushed to get on with the printing of the stamps before there had been time to harden them.

The paper for these stamps was manufactured at Rush Mills, Hardingstone, a village about two miles from Northampton, by Mr. Stacey Wise.

It was watermarked with a Small Crown repeated 240 times, so that one watermark would appear in each of the stamps when printed. The margins of the paper had the word "POSTAGE" watermarked in outlined roman capitals, once at the top and at the bottom of the sheet, and twice at each side. The paper was hand-made from wire-woven moulds, and the "bits" to form the watermarks were composed of cylindrical wire curved and bent by hand to the required pattern: it was greyish white and, like all hand-made paper, varied considerably in texture and thickness. The black stamps are occasionally found on paper showing a slight tinge of blue, perhaps occasioned by imperfect washing of the rags from which the paper was made after they had been bleached.

The stamps were printed at hand-worked copper-plate presses. The plate was mounted on the bed of the press, and ink dabbed over the whole face of the plate. The plate was then carefully wiped, so that the ink was left only in the incised lines forming the design. A sheet of the paper previously damped was then laid smoothly on the plate. The workman then turned the wheel of the press, pulling the bed, on which were the plate and paper, between two cylinders which squeezed out the ink from the engraved lines on to the paper. After printing, the sheets were gummed and then dried. This gum was made from potato starch and was deficient in adhesive qualities, and large numbers of stamps became detached from the postal matter in the course of transit. It varies in colour from nearly white to brownish yellow.

The colour of the stamps was at first a deep black, becoming less intense as the plate began to wear. Stamps printed from plates before they were hardened are, as a fact, usually found in a greyish black shade, though the plate not being hardened was not a factor in producing the greyish shade.

It is useful to note that stamps from plate 1 in the greyish black shade are nearly all from the first state of that plate. A little discrimination is necessary, as occasionally a worn stamp from the second state of the plate is in a somewhat similar shade.

Plate 2 is often found in the greyish black shade; also most of the other plates occasionally, but more particularly plates 3 and 7. It will thus be observed that the shade of the stamp is of some little assistance, towards arriving at its identification.

At a later date the colour was changed to red, but reference will be made to this in another chapter.

CHAPTER IV.

"PLATING" THE STAMPS.

The stamps were printed from eleven plates numbered respectively from 1 to 11. The distinctive number of each plate was engraved in arabic numerals at each of the four corners of the plate, and consequently appeared at the four corners of the sheet as printed. The stamps themselves have not the plate-number indicated in any way in their design, as is the case with some of the later issues of line-engraved stamps. Stamps of the same lettering from each of the different plates can, however, be separated by the position of the check-letters in the lower corners, which, as previously explained, were inserted by means of punches on the plate itself after it had been made. The letters, being punched in separately by hand, are not found in precisely the same position on any two stamps of the same lettering from different plates. The idea, doubtless, was to have the letters exactly in the centre of the corner-squares, but this evidently was a difficult matter; and the position of the corner-letters, fortunately for "plating", varies very much, with the result that there is not a great deal of difficulty in separating the stamps of any particular lettering. There are, indeed, very few stamps where the position of both letters in two different plates is at all similar. For the purposes of study, the best way to arrange a collection of these stamps is according to lettering—that is to say, to take first the stamps lettered "AA" of each plate, then those lettered "AB", and so on. It is of great advantage to have all the stamps of each lettering arranged on the same page.

Although the separation of the individual stamps is not a matter of very great difficulty, once all the stamps of a particular lettering have been obtained, this was not the initial difficulty that confronted students who first attempted to reconstruct sheets of the stamps from each plate. Their difficulty was that, though all the stamps of the same lettering might be separated, it was impossible to tell from what plate each stamp came. Fortunately, there was a certain amount of material available upon which it was possible to make a start. First there were in existence a certain number of stamps cut from the *imprimatur* sheets, registered at Somerset House, upon which the plate-number had been carefully noted. Then there were a few blocks of stamps or portions of sheets, showing the plate-number in the corner of the sheet. Photographs were taken of as many other blocks and strips of stamps as could be obtained. By carefully comparing the stamps in these photographs with stamps that had been identified, it was found possible to fix the plate-number of some; and gradually to connect other blocks, strips and pairs to those which had been plated, with the result that the sheets of the different plates were gradually built up, until now it is believed that the identity of every stamp has been satisfactorily established. In some cases this result was arrived at by a process of elimination—that is, by proving that the stamp in question could not belong to any other plate.

State of Plate.—Before proceeding to discuss special distinguishing characteristics, it may be as well to mention that this term is used when a plate, after being printed from as originally prepared, is wholly or partly touched up or re-cut; and it is probable that plates 1 to 10 were printed from in two or more such states. Plates 1, 5, 6, 8, 9 and 10 have only so far been noted in more than one state. Plate 1, for instance, is found in two distinct states, which are known to collectors as "1a" and "1b". Many of the roller impressions on the plate were re-entered, and a large number of the corner-letters were re-cut in the second state. "Re-entering", as is now generally known, is a second impression from the roller, which should be, but frequently is not, exactly coincident with the first. A third state of plate 1 is known, to which a reference is made later; but stamps from it have not been found in black, and it is probably confined to the later printings in red.

Plates 5 and 6 are each found in two states. In the second state, several stamps have been retouched by strengthening the side lines, which apparently had the effect of causing one or other or both of the check-letters and stars in the upper corners to become faint. These stamps are noted in the tabular list appended. Plate 5 occurs in a third state, in red as well as in black, as the stamp lettered "PB", besides being found sometimes with strengthened sides, is also found with a re-entry through the value and "B" square. This stamp probably comes from the provisional printing in black, as it is very rare and fully as scarce as stamps from plate 11.

Plates 8, 9 and 10 are also each known in two states, in the second of which the "O"-flaw referred to later has been corrected. The particular stamps occurring in the two states in black are noted in the tabular list. It should be noted, however, that several more stamps from these plates are found in the two states in red, and probably there is a third state of plate 8 found in red only, as stamps from this plate lettered "AH", "AI", "AJ", and "AK" are known with a distinct duplication of the bottom line of the "A" square, and without any trace of the "O"-flaw.

We are inclined to think that plate 11 exists in a second state also, but we are not sure whether in each colour or in red only.

As the work proceeded, it was found that certain peculiarities were characteristic of certain plates, and, once this was established, matters were much simplified. The chief of these peculiarities or distinguishing features are what are known as "Roller-flaws". As has been previously indicated, the roller used for laying down the impressions on the plate had more than one impression of the die upon it; and two at least of these roller impressions had well marked flaws, which are constant and appear (with a few exceptions, caused perhaps by retouching by hand after the plate had been laid down) on every impression of the plate or plates or portions thereof, for which they were used.

RAY-FLAW.

The first of these roller-flaws is known as the

"*Ray-flaw.*"—This is found on the cross pâté in the top left corner of the stamp, and consists of a break in, or almost total absence of, the uppermost of the three short rays on the left-hand side; and this flaw is constant. Stamps showing this flaw must come from either plate 1 or plate 2, as the roller impression with this flaw was not used to lay down any other plates.

All the stamps from plate 1 have the flaw except those lettered "CL", "RL", "SL", "TK" and "TL". In the first state of plate 1, there is generally practically no trace of the missing ray, whilst in the second state as a rule there is some indication of its presence; and, apart from other characteristics, this feature can be relied upon in a general way to distinguish the two states of the plate.

In the case of plate 2, apparently two different roller-impressions were used, as the stamps bearing the letterings "CI" to "JL" inclusive do not show any indication of the flaw, whilst the rest of the stamps on the plate have it. As the probable intention was to use the same roller-impression for the whole of the plate, it is possible that, beginning with the stamp lettered "CI", another impression was inadvertently used; and the workman, so soon as he discovered his mistake, completed the plate with the roller-impression originally used.

"O"-flaw.

The other roller-flaw is known as the

"*O"-flaw.*—It consists of a short, but generally distinct, white line or mark between the letters "O" and "N" of "ONE", extending to the bottom margin of the stamp; it was probably caused by a speck of metal getting on to the die when the roller was made. The stamps in the first six (and less distinctly those in the next two) rows of plate 7, those in the first 15 rows of plate 8, and nearly all the stamps of plates 9 and 10 show this flaw. In the case of plates 7 and 8, apparently two roller-impressions were used, as the remaining stamps of both plates are normal and do not show any trace of the flaw in question.

"K D" FROM PLATE 9.
HORIZONTAL GUIDE-LINE.

"*Guide-lines*".—Next, the stamp should be examined to see if it has any trace of guide-lines. These may be either vertical or horizontal. Vertical guide-lines are found principally in the top right square parallel to the right side line, and may be described for convenience as very close to, close to, or wide of, frame; "very close" meaning that the guide-line is very close to the side line of the square, "close" that it is comparatively farther away, and "wide" that it is much farther off the side line. Sometimes, the line shows in the right-hand letter-square, especially in the case of stamps from plate 9. These vertical lines are found in stamps from all the plates except plate 3, but they are more frequent and more distinct on plate 9, followed by plate 8, whilst, though not uncommon on stamps from other plates, they are often very indistinct. Horizontal guide-lines are found through the lower portions of the value and letter-squares, and occasionally, as in the case of plate 2, along the top and bottom; and similar, but vertical, guide-lines are to be met with on the side margins of the stamp.

"S E" FROM PLATE 2.

"S L" FROM PLATE 2.

On this plate, well-marked guide-lines are found in the "S" row, "SL" being the best example, showing a vertical guide-line on the right side of the stamp, a horizontal line above the top of the stamp, and a short line joining the bottom of the vertical line to the outside corner of the "L" square.

Several stamps from the "J" and "K" rows of the second state of plate 1 have, through the upper portions of the letter-squares, horizontal lines which are not visible in the first state. It is doubtful whether these are really guide-lines, though it is possible they may have been made on the original plate and afterwards burnished out, reappearing on the plate after its repair. A number of the stamps show more or less horizontal scratches in the upper, lower and side margins: these appear to be constant and to be found more frequently on stamps from plates 5 to 7.

Marginal and Frame-lines.—There are several other points to which attention should be directed, when the plating of a stamp is being attempted. It is of importance to note whether the marginal lines on the sides of the stamp, particularly on the left side, are complete or irregular. It is said that these lines were engraved on the plate just prior to its completion. Be that as it may, it is a curious fact that a large number of stamps from several of the plates (more particularly plates 4, 5 and 6) have the margin on the left side very irregular, and occasionally almost non-existent. This is a constant characteristic in certain stamps in their first state, which occurs in a second state with the line subsequently strengthened, but this must not be confused with the weakening of these lines caused by wear of the plate. Possibly, the plates referred to were laid down by a roller-impression having a weak side line; and the fact that some stamps of these plates have a distinct line may be accounted for by retouching, as evidence of retouching is apparent in the case of many stamps in respect of the line round the corner-squares. The stamps from the other plates have, as a rule, the side lines fairly complete, and plate 1 in its second state shows a strengthening of the left side line in the case of several stamps. Plate 11, however, is an exception, as a large majority of the stamps have the marginal line on the right side irregular or wavy, more particularly the lower half thereof. This characteristic seems to be peculiar to certain stamps of plate 11, and can be relied upon with some confidence as a means of identifying many stamps from this scarce plate.

Then the marginal lines of the corner-squares should be examined, as certain deductions can be made from them. In plate 3, the bottom lines of the letter-squares, particularly that on the left, are very thin, whilst in plate 4, the same lines are often particularly heavy, especially the line at the bottom of the right letter-square: this often contrasts strongly with the line on the right of the square, which appears to be much thinner. Stamps from plates 5 and 6 often have the top line of the top left square weak or thin, and many stamps from plate 5 have the side line of the top right square weak or defective.

We have now to consider Re-entries and Double Letters, all well-marked varieties, and easy to plate as they have all been identified.

Re-entries on Plate 1.—Plate 1, put to press on April 11th or 15th, 1840, was, owing to excessive wear, temporarily withdrawn for repair after some six weeks' use, and put to press again on 25th May, 1840. Many impressions were re-entered, and some stamps show the double entry, the result of inaccurate registration. The plate was generally touched-up, frame-lines deepened in some instances and the check-letters retouched, some of them being completely re-cut. The faint dot often found in the left margin (opposite the mouth) in the original plate, seldom occurs in the later states—it apparently disappeared at this period in the cleaning up.

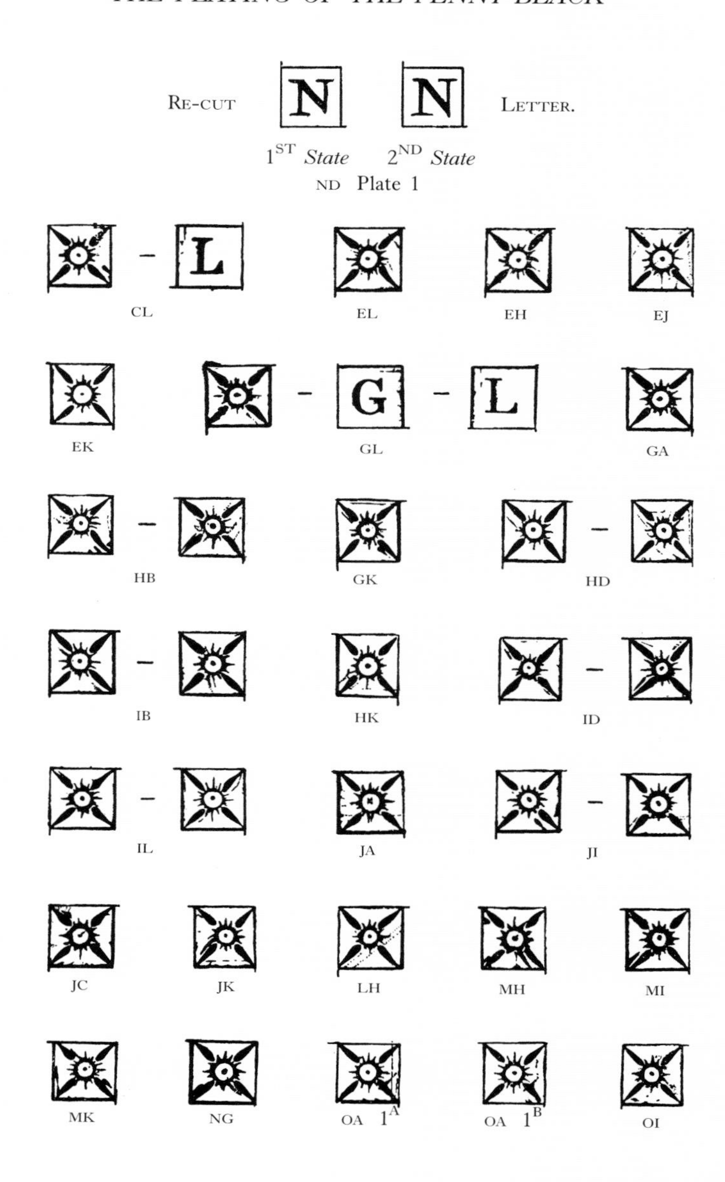

The position of the re-entry on the stamps is indicated by the inside extension of the frame-lines.

The double-entries on "HB", "HD" and "OA" appeared on the plate in its original condition, and therefore can be found in both states.

A special reference should be made to the stamp lettered "TC", showing a re-entry in the upper left square and through "ONE" of the value, and the letter "C" faint, which is from a third state of plate 1. This stamp has not, however, been found in black, and it is probable therefore that the repair to the plate was not effected until the change to red ink took place. Two other stamps only in this third state have been discovered, namely "AK" with the corner of the "A" square complete (broken in the second state) and "RK" with a distinct horizontal line running through the "R" square, towards the top of the square.

Re-entries on Plates 2 to 11.—The foregoing and following illustrations are made from very carefully-executed sketches by Mr. J. B. Seymour, and have recently appeared in the *British Philatelist.*

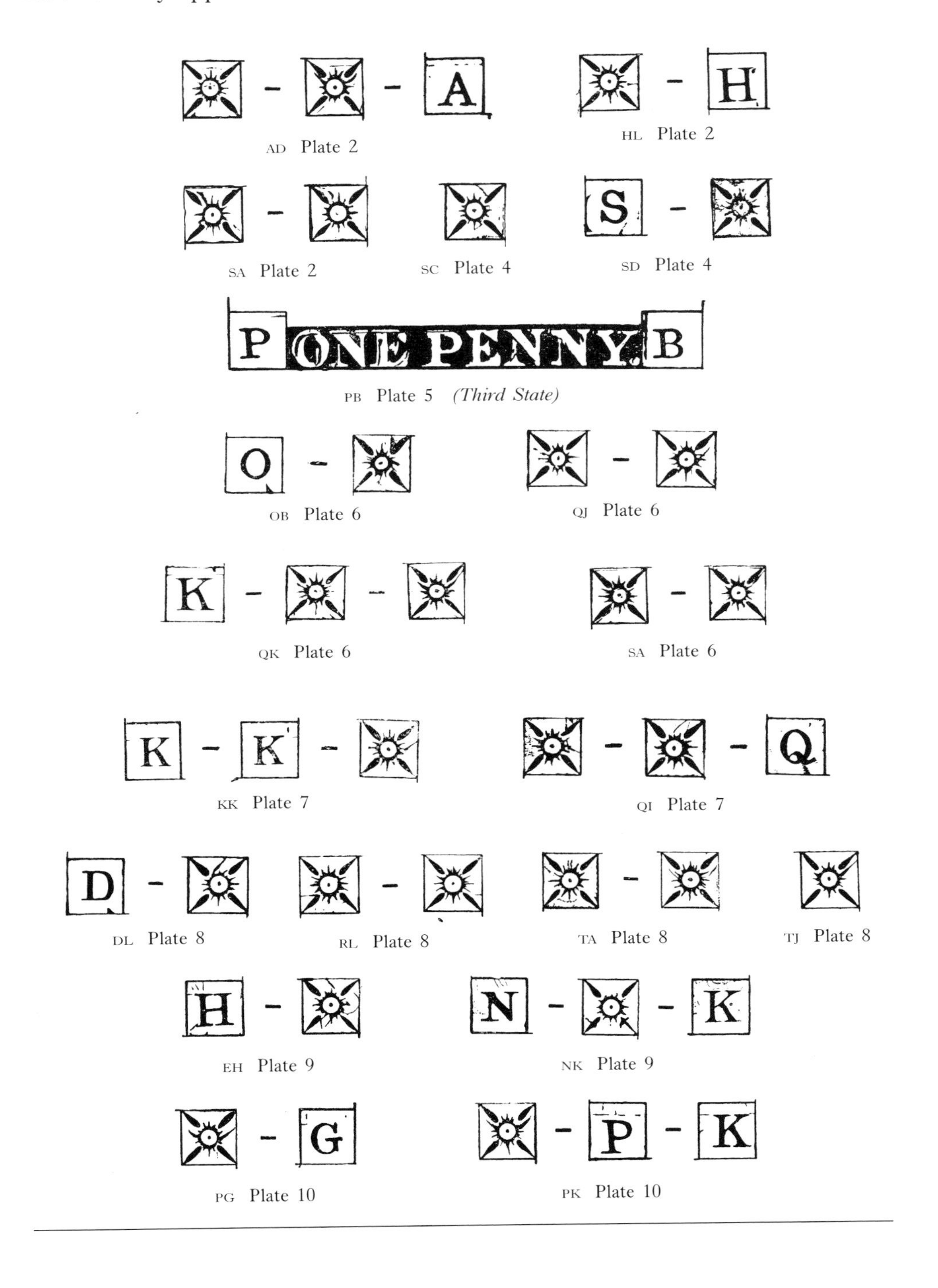

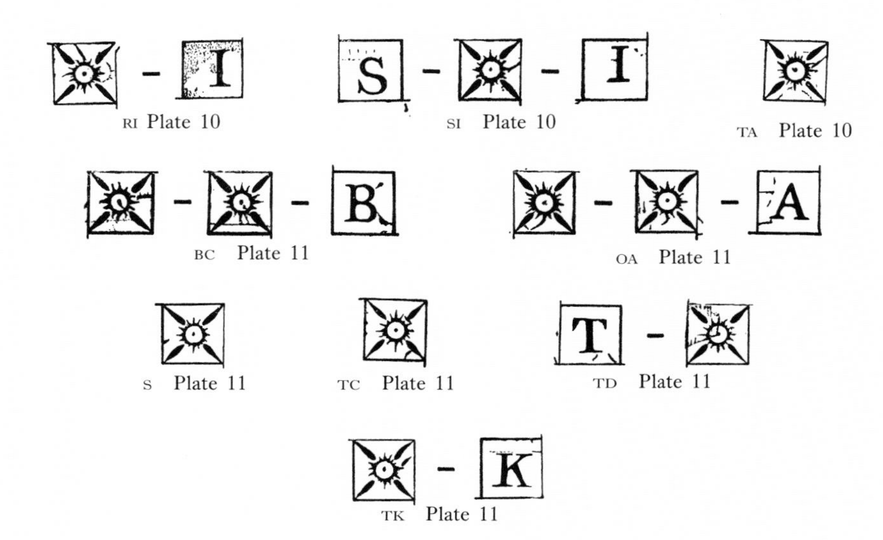

The above show a very large proportion of the re-entries on the Penny Black, and a study of Mr. Seymour's excellent drawings will be worth far more than pages of descriptive letterpress.

Double Letters.

Double Letters.—These duplications—which also are re-entries—are caused by the wrong letter being punched in the first instance, or by a correct letter being inserted far out of its proper position in the square, and then the necessary correction being made. Some of these varieties, for example where the serif of a letter shows double, are probably caused by the punch moving slightly after it had been first struck with the hammer.

On the early plates, a considerable number of letters were incorrectly punched or misplaced, but they were all corrected, though traces of the incorrect or misplaced letter can in many cases be detected; and these corrected mistakes form valuable guides to plating the stamps.

"N E" Joined.

"NE" joined.—Several stamps show the "NE" of "ONE" joined, or nearly so, in the second state of plate 1, though quite normal in the first state. Two or three examples are also found in stamps from plates 2 and 3.

"Star-angle" Variety.

"Star-angle" variety.—Some stamps show a most conspicuous variety in the upper left angle, and such are very easily identified as from plate 2. The left bottom "Ray" in the left square is thick and clumsy, and seems to lean over more towards the right.

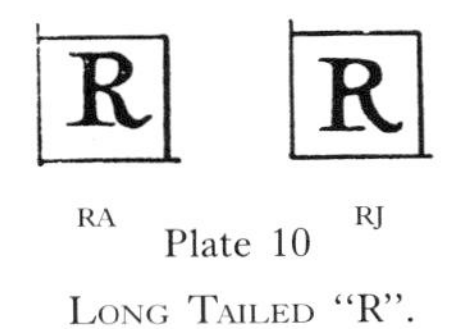

RA Plate 10 RJ

Long Tailed "R".

Special type Check-letters.—A few of the check-letters are of a special type, peculiar to one or more plates, but as a rule the shape of the letter is not of a great deal of assistance in plating.

The letter "R" on plate 10 has a long tail, and cannot be confused with any other. The row containing stamps of this lettering was probably wrongly lettered "P" throughout, that letter being converted into an "R" by hand, as every "R" varies considerably in shape. The letter "H" on this plate is short and squat and easily recognisable, and the "Q" has a short tail and slopes down. The letter "J" in plates 10 and 11 is square-footed, whereas in the other plates it has a round foot. Plate 9 has a type of "J" inclined to be square-footed which, however, cannot be confused with the square-footed "J" of plates 10 and 11, if the letters are carefully compared. The letter "D" in the horizontal row of plate 2 is of a large wide type peculiar to the plate, although this letter on plate 1 has a somewhat similar appearance. If it be remembered that the stamps on plate 1 in the "D" horizontal row have the ray-flaw, whilst those on plate 2 are normal, there is little difficulty in separating them. Probably the letter "E" varies most, and is of some assistance in plating. Plate 1 has a large type of letter, with the lower portion apparently produced farther out than the upper; plates 3 and 4 have a somewhat similar type, but without this peculiarity; on plate 2 the letter is not so wide; plates 5, 6, 7, 9 and 10 have a narrower type; the "E" on plate 8 is usually smaller and can be separated from similar stamps on plate 7 by this characteristic. Plate 11 has a short broad variety which can hardly be confused with that on any other plate. On plate 3 the "M" is small, the "P" has a narrow loop and several of the letters "K" are narrow and blurred. Several letters on plates 10 and 11, in addition to "J", are very much alike—such as the "I" very tall, "L" straight with short foot, "M" with extra long serifs, "N" tall and narrow and "T" short and squat. The stamps, however, cannot be confused, except in a few instances, as those from plate 10 normally have the "O"-flaw, whilst none from plate 11 has it.

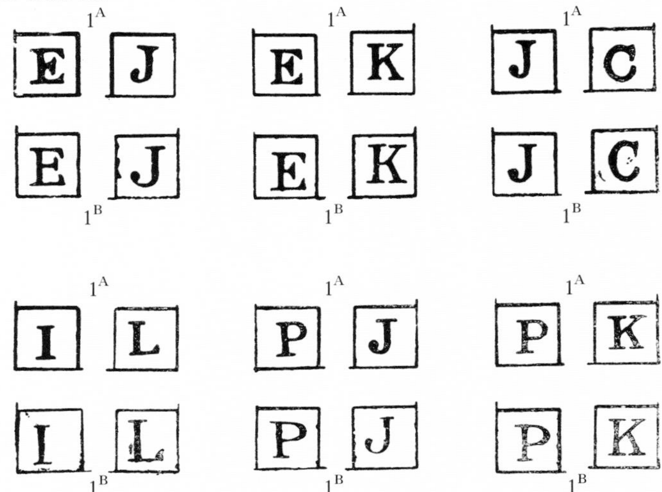

Recut Letters on Plate IB. Compared with the Original Letters on Plate IA.

The difficulty of differentiating between the two states of plate 1 is lessened by the fact that some of the corner-letters were recut.

In some instances, the recutting was very drastic, not only the appearance, but even the position, of the letter being altered.

Recut Letter-squares.

Letter-squares recut.—Many stamps have the marginal lines of the letter-squares recut, and extending into the margin of the stamp on the right or left side; or into the margin at the bottom of the stamp, in the case of the side lines. These are of importance to note, as many stamps can be identified by this characteristic. They are not, however, confined to any particular plate, but are found most frequently on stamps from plate 4, followed by plates 5, 6 and 8. Many stamps from the upper rows of plate 11, have a weakness at the extreme left corner of the top right square, and this appears to be a good characteristic for distinguishing certain stamps of this plate.

"Double Bottom".

"Double Bottom."—The stamps lettered "SL" and "TL" on plate 1,

first state, show the lower line of the frame cutting through the base of the value; but in the second state this is hardly appreciable. A similarly clear variety is found on other plates, especially "RK" and "RL" of plate 10. This variety is also found, but not so distinctly or showing at all, in heavily-printed stamps from Plates 1b to 11.

"Spots."

Spots or Dots.—Many stamps from various plates show occasional dots, which are constant. These dots are more numerous on two of the plates, namely 4 and 6, which had certain portions pitted or marked with small, shallow holes, showing as spots or dots on the prints. These dots are generally found on the margins of the stamps, on the value or in the corner-squares. The spotted stamps of Plates 4 and 6 can generally be identified. It is curious that two of the plates should have these spots, and the suggestion is that they are the result of rust, through the plates not having been put in a thoroughly dry place before being brought into use.

"*Plate-dot.*"—A short reference must now be made to what has been called the "Plate-dot": A close examination will show that quite a number of stamps have a tiny dot on the left margin, just about opposite the Queen's mouth. Certain writers have suggested that all stamps having the dots are from plate 3, and that the dot is a distinguishing characteristic of that plate. This does not appear to be the case, as stamps from several other plates have this dot, though it may be that it is rather more evident in the stamps from plate 3. It does not, however, occur in all stamps from that plate, so it is not a characteristic upon which too much reliance should be placed; and for this reason to give it as a guide would only mislead the plater.

"B L" Plate 8 "T L"

Abnormal Markings.—There are a number of stamps showing what are apparently accidental marks or scratches, which are usually quite constant, although occasionally they only appear in a later state of the plates. Series of faint parallel scratches often occur on plate 6, some of which are peculiar to the second state.

CHAPTER V.

THE PRINTINGS.

The plates, with the exception of plate 11, were printed from first in black ink, commencing with plate 1 on 11th April,* 1840; followed by plate 2 on 22nd April; plate 3 on 12th May; plate 4 on 28th May; plate 5 on 8th June; plate 6 on 15th June; plate 7 on 26th June; plate 8 on 31st July†; plate 9 on or about 9th November; plate 10 on or about 8th December, 1840; and plate 11 on 29th January, 1841.

In their passage through the post the stamps were obliterated by a hand-stamp bearing the design of a Maltese Cross. The ink used for the obliteration was at first red in colour, but very soon attempts were made to clean off the postmark, for the purpose of again utilising the stamps for postage.

Experiments were made with various kinds of ink, and it was eventually decided to use black letter-press printer's ink. The substitution of black for red ink took place towards the end of August, 1840, and a notice appeared in *The Times* of 3rd September that, within the then last few days, black ink had been used instead of red ink for obliterating stamps passing through the post.

The introduction of black ink for the purpose was, however, confined in the first place to the London "Twopenny Post" offices, for letters for delivery in London or the suburbs. Very few stamps used on letters from London to the country, or in the provinces, are known obliterated in black previous to February, 1841, when the stamps themselves were issued in red, and a new black obliterating ink introduced. About the end of August, 1840, experiments were made with a view to changing the colour of the penny stamp, and shortly afterwards it was decided that stamps of this value should in future be printed in red.

Accordingly, on the 24th December, an order was given to this effect, and printing in red began on 30th December, 1840. The printing in the new colour was interrupted, from January 22nd to February 3rd, 1841, by a provisional printing of 10,200 sheets in black ink. This was necessary owing to the new obliterating-ink for the red stamps not being ready, and the unwillingness of the Post Office authorities to issue them until a supply of ink was available. When the printing in red was commenced, plate 3 was not in existence, having been destroyed in the preceding month of October; and on the 9th January three more plates were destroyed, namely plates 4, 6 and 7. They had apparently become too worn to give satisfactory printings. No impressions in red have ever been found from any of these four plates, so it is reasonable to conclude that they were not used for printing the red stamps. Plates 1, 2, 5, 8, 9 and 10 were all used, and plate 11 afterwards as we shall see. It is impossible to say from the evidence available, if all of the first five mentioned plates were printed from in red at the end of December, when the first printings in red took place. Mr. Bacon is able to show that when the provisional printing in black was made, five presses, for part of the time at

* Mr. Edwin Hill, in his Diary, gives 15th April.—*British Philatelist*, X, 42.

† And for this, 3rd August.—*British Philatelist*, X, 50.

least, were at work, and that certainly plates 5 and 11 were used. If only five plates were used for the provisional printing in black, we are inclined to think that the other plates were 8, 9, and 10. Our reason for so thinking is that certain stamps from these plates, which all have the "O"-flaw normally, are found sometimes with the flaw and sometimes without it, both in black and in red. We are of opinion that the presence or absence of this flaw constitutes two states of the plate, and, if this be so, the fact that stamps from these plates occur in two states, in each colour, would seem to indicate that a printing from them had been made in black subsequent to a red printing. On the other hand, our experience of plate 1 (which Mr. Bacon thinks was probably one of those used for the provisional printing in black) is that certain stamps in red are always found with one or other of the corner-letters faint, but the similar stamps in black never show this peculiarity. We are unable to say anything about plate 2, except that the stamps from it and plate 1 in red are about equally scarce, and very much scarcer than stamps in red from the other plates; and it appears possible that they were brought into use for the original printing in red, but discarded before the provisional printing in black was made. Plate 11 was first printed from in red, the date being 29th January, 1841. It was provisionally printed from in black on 1st and 2nd February— the last "black" Warrant was on the 26th January—after which printing in red from it was resumed. No printings from any of the others were made subsequent to March 23rd, 1841, but plate 11 continued to be used for some time afterwards.

According to the figures, as given by Mr. Bacon, 283,992 sheets (or 68,158,080 stamps) were printed in black: of these 8,453 sheets were spoilt and destroyed. An estimate, based on the relative scarcity or otherwise of the stamps from the different plates, gives the following as the total number of sheets in round numbers printed from the various plates, in black; and we take the opportunity of stating the respective dates of approval of the plates and the earliest known date of use of stamps from each; to complete the table, we repeat the dates of going to press already given at the beginning of this chapter:—

Plate.	*Approved.*	*Put to Press.*	*Sheets printed.*	*Earliest Date*
1a	27.4.40	11 (or 15) . 4.40	42,000	6.5.40
1b	28.4.40			12. 6.40
2	27.4.40	22.4.40	32,000	2.5.40
3	9.5.40	12.5.40	20,000	18.5.40
4	18.5.40	28.5.40	28,000	31.5.40
5	1.6.40	8.6.40	36,000	17.6.40
6	17.6.40	15.6.40	38,000	1.7.40
7	6.7.40	26.6.40	24,000	8.7.40
8	31.7.40	31.7 (or 3.8) 40	30,000	11.9.40
9	6.11.40	9.11.40	16,000	18.11.40
10	2.12.40	8.12.40	8,000	6.1.41
11	21. 1.41	29.1.41	700*	15.2.41

* As given by Mr. Bacon.

From these plates in red possibly about 90,000 sheets were printed in something like the following proportions:—

Plate 11, 25,000; plate 9, 20,000; plate 8, 15,000; plates 5 and 10, 10,000 each; and plates 1 and 2, 5,000 each.

The identification of stamps in red from the "black" plates is not always an easy matter, except in the case of stamps showing the "O"-flaw, which is conclusive. Stamps from plates 1 and 2 having the "Ray-flaw" are not so distinct when in red, and besides there appear to be stamps from later plates which may be confused with them, but with a little practice there is not much difficulty in distinguishing them. Stamps from plate 5 generally show the weakness in the side line of the upper right square. As a rule, stamps in red from the "black" plates can after some practice be identified by their colour, which is of a lightish or indistinct yellowish-brown shade, not easy to describe, but which the eye is soon able to discriminate, and the stamps can then be carefully compared with stamps of a similar lettering in black which have been identified. The colour of stamps of plate 11, however, is generally a deep red, in which shade stamps from some of the other early plates subsequent to 11 are also found. Several of these plates can, however, be distinguished by the weakness or absence of the top line of the upper right square. For instance, stamps from plate 12 (except in the case of those in the last horizontal row), have a distinct though short break in this line. In plate 13, the break is larger; in plate 14, it is still larger; whilst in plates 14 and 15, the line is almost completely absent.

In conclusion, we may say, for the guidance of platers, that all extensions of lines which are given in the following chronicle are constant: there are others which are not constant, and these are not given.

Again, in the "Further Distinguishing Characteristics", comparatively few tests are given, because it is useless to describe them unless they are absolutely constant. This applies particularly to plate 11, the very large majority of the impressions from which are in red—the black prints are extremely scarce—and it is known that (for instance) guide-lines showing on the black stamp are absent from, or practically invisible in, similar impressions in red.

It has been a constant aim not to give a description, unless it assists in differentiating a stamp from its fellows; and many apparent peculiarities will on comparison be found either unnecessary or useless—hence their omission.

We have much pleasure in stating that any further information as to the "Plating of the Penny Black", which will be welcome, will be published in the *British Philatelist,* and a copy of the journal sent to all subscribers to, or purchasers of, this present work.

CHAPTER VI.

PLATE 11.

As stamps in black from this plate are exceedingly scarce (the number known used being probably well under 1,000) it may be useful to summarise any distinctive characters with a view to assisting collectors to identify any stamps from this plate, which they may be fortunate enough to come across. In the first place, it may be mentioned that Plate 11 is very rarely found with the Maltese Cross postmark in red, and accordingly it is much more likely that stamps from this plate will be found among stamps having a black postmark. The colour of the stamp is often fairly distinctive, as those from plate 11 are generally met with in a deep greyish black colour, which possibly characterises many stamps from the provisional printing in black, as stamps from other plates are occasionally found in a like shade. Many stamps from Plate 11 have a distinct blur just outside the left letter-square, others again show a kind of blur through either or both letter-squares. Some from the upper portion of the sheet have a distinct weakness at the left-hand corner of the upper square. One of the best characteristics is to be found by examining the margin on the right-hand side of the stamp, which usually appears to be wavy, especially towards the bottom half of its length. Many of the corner-letters are characteristic, though some of these are of a type similar to those found in plate 10, but the absence of the "O"-flaw enables stamps of plate 11 to be differentiated. The letters "A" and "B" in the horizontal rows are of a short variety and generally slope down, as do the letters in the "C" and "D" rows. The "E" in both horizontal and vertical rows is quite distinct and easily recognised, being short and broad. The "F " is tall and inclined to slope down. The "G" nearly always slopes evidently down, and this is a marked feature when a comparison is made with stamps from other plates with this letter. The "H" is not tall, and sometimes shows a weakness on the left side. The "I" is distinctly tall, and the "J" is square-footed. The "L" is straight, with a short foot, the "M" has distinct serifs, the "N" is tall and narrow, and the "T" short and squat. The "S" slopes down, but stamps from this row can readily be identified by the re-entry in the upper right square. As only some 700 sheets of plate 11 were printed in black, it follows that the stamps are many times scarcer than those from other plates, probably at least ten times as scarce as those from plate 10, which is the next best plate, and they in turn are possibly five times as scarce as stamps from the more common plates, such as 1, 5 or 6. A comparatively large printing was, however, made in red and, as it is really an impossible task to make up the plate in black, collectors are advised to endeavour to do so in red, but of course to obtain as many of the black stamps as possible. Several blocks of the plate in black in an unused state are known, which probably came from the same sheet which at some time or other had been cut up. These include a block consisting of the first three rows showing the plate-number, and including the interesting stamp lettered "BC" with a marked re-entry. It should be mentioned that the eight sheets of red stamps printed on Dickinson paper (with silk threads through the paper) on or about 1st May, 1841, were from this plate, and this factor was of very great assistance in enabling many of the stamps originally to be identified.

EXPLANATION

OF THE TABULAR DESCRIPTIONS.

The similar stamps from all the eleven plates are described in batches, according to corner-letters, each lettering being taken in order and followed through the various plates: the heavy letters, placed centrally on the pages, indicate the stamp on the sheet which is being dealt with.

In the first column is the number of the plate, with the necessary foot-note references for "Ray-flaw" and " 'O'-flaw".

Next follows the description of the position, each in its own square, of the two corner-letters—first that on the left, then that on the right.

Finally, further Characteristics, selected as distinguishing between other-wise very similar stamps, are set out in, what is hoped, sufficient detail.

The upper left and right squares are respectively indicated by "N.W." and "N.E."

The illustrations, on the facing pages, will be found of the greatest assistance: they have not been touched-up in any way, and are the most faithful reproductions which could be obtained.

Plate.	*Position of Corner-letter*		*Further distinguishing characteristics.*
	at left.	*at right.*	
		AA	
1a*	central	slightly low, to right	minute dot on margin to left of first "A" square, and another touching left side of N.W. square.
1b*	central	slightly low, to right	similar, but trace of missing ray.
2*	central	central	horizontal guide-line below first "A" square.
3	rather high, to right	central	first "A" with closed top.
4	high, to right	high, central	right line extends beyond bottom.
5	central	low, to left	bottom line extends on right.
6	very low, central	central—slopes up	right line extends slightly beyond bottom.
7†	very low, to left	central	
8†	central	central	dot on margin above "S" of "POSTAGE"; vertical guide-line N.E. square, wide of frame.
9†	very high to right	low, to left	right line extends beyond bottom; vertical guide-line N E. square, wide of frame; bottom line wavy. Without "O"-flaw in second state
10†	central	very low, slightly to left	
11	central	low to left—slopes down	bottom line extends on right.
		AB	
1a*	central	central, to right	dot outside N.E. square, nearly touching side line.
1b*	central	central, to right	similar, but dot farther off side line.
2*	slightly low, central	high, to right	horizontal guide-line below "A" square.
3	central, to right	high, to right	
4	low, central	central, slightly to left	right line extends slightly beyond bottom.
5	central	high, to left	right and bottom lines cross. In second state the frame-lines have been strengthened or recut
6	central, to right	high, central	
7†	central	central	right line extends slightly beyond bottom.
8†	high, to left	central, to right	dot on margin below corner of "B" square.
9†	high, central	central, to left	two vertical guide-lines N.E. square; horizontal guide-line on lower margin and dot above; bottom line slightly wavy. Without "O"-flaw in second state.
10†	high, central	high, central	
11	central—slopes down	low, to left	

**Shows the Ray-flaw.* †*Shows the "O"-flaw.*

1a 1b 2 3 4 5
6 7 8 9 10 11

1a 1b 2 3 4 5
6 7 8 9 10 11

Plate.	Position of Corner-letter		Further distinguishing characteristics.
	at left.	at right.	
		AC	
1a*	central, slightly to right	central	vertical guide-line N.E. square, close to frame.
1b*	central, slightly to right	central	no guide-line.
2*	central, slightly to right	very low, to left	short stroke below "C".
3	very low, to right	central, to left	
4	central, to right	central, to left	left side irregular; dot right side of "A".
5	central, slightly to right	slightly low, to left	right line extends beyond bottom; bottom line extends slightly on left.
6	low, central	central, to left	side line of N.E. square weak.
7†	central	central, to left	
8†	central, to right	central	right line extends slightly beyond bottom.
9†	central, to right	low, slightly to left.	vertical guide-line N.E. square and dot above; bottom line slightly wavy. Without "O"-flaw in second state, and letter "C" faint.
10†	low, central	very low, to left	
11	low, central—slopes down	low, to right.	
		AD	
1a*	central, slightly to right	high, central	
1b*	central, slightly to right	high, central	trace of missing ray.
2*	low, to right	slightly high, central	fine re-entry: each upper square, each letter-square and bottom frame-line.
3	central, to right	low, central	
4	central, to right	central, to left	diagonal blur lower portion of N.E. square.
5	low, central	central, slightly to right	bottom line extends on left; dot in corner of "D" square; foot of "A" long on left.
6	very low, central	high, central	bottom line of "D" square thickened below corner.
7†	central, to right	high, central	foot of "A" long on left.
8†	central, to left	high, to right	dot on margin below "D" square; "A" slightly defective at top.
9†	central	central, far to right	faint vertical guide-line in N.E. square, very close to frame; bottom line slightly wavy. Without "O"-flaw in second state and letter "D" faint.
10†	high, central	high, slightly to left	right line extends slightly beyond bottom.
11	low, to right	slightly high, far to right	each letter slopes down.

**Shows the Ray-flaw.* *†Shows the "O"-flaw.*

1a 1b 2 3 4 5
6 7 8 9 10 11

1a 1b 2 3 4 5
6 7 8 9 10 11

Plate.	Position of Corner-letter		Further distinguishing characteristics.
	at left.	at right.	
		AE	
1a*	central, to right	central, to left	double "E".
1b*	central, to right	central, to left	similar, but trace of missing ray.
2*	low, central	central, to left	line below, "E" thin.
3	low, central	central, far to right	"A" slopes down.
4	central	central, far to right	"A" slopes up.
5	low, central	high, central	trace of guide-line, through "A" square and value; dot below and close to S.E. corner of "E" square.
6	low, to right	high, to left	right side line extends beyond bottom.
7†	very low, central	high, to left	
8†	high, central	high, to left	faint vertical guide-line N.E. square, very close to frame; right side line extends beyond bottom.
9†	high, central	high, to left	vertical guide-line N.E. square, wide of frame, and "E " square close to frame; slight trace of double "E". Without "O"-flaw in second state.
10†	central	low, central	
11	central	central, to right	trace of vertical guide-line in "E" square.
		AF	
1a*	low, to right	central	small dot in N.E. square, nearly touching side line.
1b*	low, to right	central	dot faint; trace of missing ray.
2*	very low, to left	central	
3	high, central	low, central	
4	very low, to left	very high, central	
5	central, to left	low, to left	traces of outer line on left; vertical guide-lines in N.E. square, close to frame, and horizontal one below "A" and "F" squares; left side line extends beyond bottom.
6	high, to right	low, to left	vertical guide-line N.E. square, very close to frame. Spotting around "O" of "ONE" and "A" square.
7†	high, central	central, to left	vertical guide-line N.E. square, wide of frame.
8†	high, to right	low, central	vertical guide-line N.E. square; minute dot at S.E. corner of "F" square; bottom line extends right and left squares.
9†	central, to right	high, to left	left side-line extends beyond bottom; vertical guide-line N.E. square. Without "O"-flaw in second state.
10†	very high, central	low, central	letter "F" slopes down.
11	low, to left	low, central	

**Shows the Ray-flaw.* *†Shows the "O"-flaw.*

1a
1b
2
3
4
5
6
7
8
9
10
11

1a
1b
2
3
4
5
6
7
8
9
10
11

Plate.	Position of Corner-letter		Further distinguishing characteristics.
	at left.	at right.	
		AG	
1a*	high, to right	high, to left	"A" with long foot on left.
1b*	high, to right	high, to left	"A" with long foot on left; short vertical line from "P" of "POSTAGE" into top margin, dot on margin just to right of N.E. square.
2*	central, to right	high, to left	"G" square broken at S.E. corner.
3	central	high, to left	left margin complete; dot above corner of N.E. square.
4	central, to right	high, to left	left side irregular.
5	central	high, central	horizontal guide-line below letter "G"; mark in top right corner of N.E. square.
6	central, to right	central, to left	bottom line extends on right.
7†	central, to right	high, to left	bottom line extends on each side; side line of N.E. square weak.
8†	high, to left	very high, close to left	right side line extends beyond bottom.
9†	central, to left	low, to left	vertical guide-line N.E. square, wide of frame.
10†	central, to right	low, central	scratches on left margin.
11	very high, central	high, slightly to right	
		AH	
1a*	high, to right	central, to left	dot on margin to right of N.E. square.
1b*	high, to right	central, to left	dot on margin to right of N.E. square; top line of N.E. square very thin, long vertical scratch L.H. margin.
2*	very low, to left	high, central	
3	central	low, to right	
4	central	very high, close to left	left foot of "H" defective.
5	central, to left	high, to left	"A" with long foot on left; minute dot in "P" of "POSTAGE".
6	central	central, slightly to left	minute dot to right of "H".
7†	central, to right	high, to left	
8†	high, central	very high to right—slopes slightly up	dot on margin touching bottom of "H" square, near corner.
9†	high, to right	central, to left	vertical guide-line N.E. square, and dot on margin above.
10†	high, to right	low, to left	squat "H".
11	very low, central	central, slightly to right	"A" with long foot on left.

*Shows the Ray-flaw. †Shows the "O"-flaw.

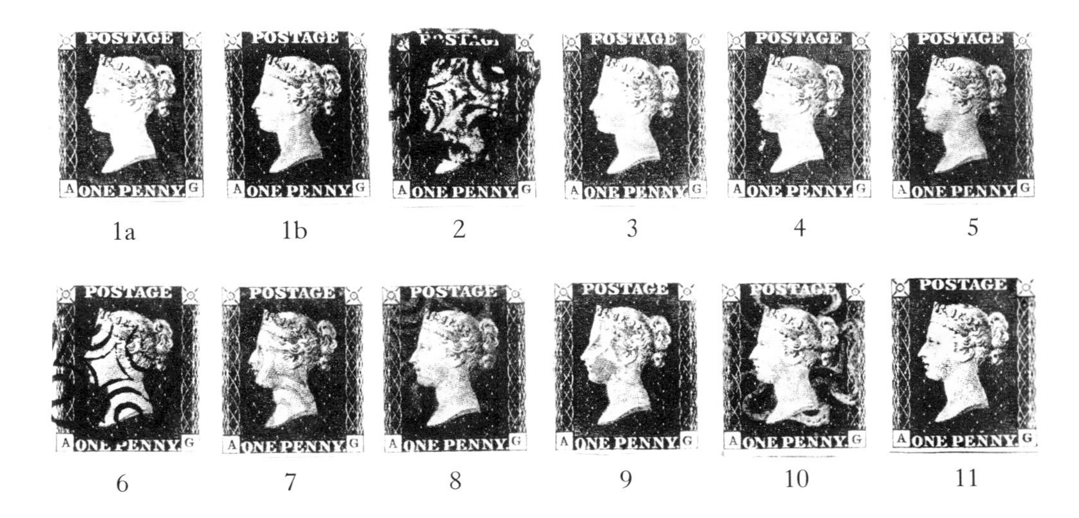
1a
1b
2
3
4
5
6
7
8
9
10
11

1a
1b
2
3
4
5
6
7
8
9
10
11

Plate.	Position of Corner-letter		Further distinguishing characteristics.
	at left.	*at right.*	
		AI	
1a*	central, to right	low, central	vertical guide-line N.E. square, very close to frame.
1b*	central, to right	low, central	no guide-line.
2*	slightly low, to right	high, well to right	
3	low, to right	low, central	dot above corner of N.E. square.
4	central, slightly to right	central, slightly to left	"I" with right side of foot defective.
5	low, to left	central, close to left	vertical guide-line N.E. square, very close to frame.
6	central, slightly to right	high, to left	faint dot to right of "A".
7†	central	central	mark on margin, top left.
8†	central, to left	central, to right	right side line extends beyond bottom.
9†	low, central	central	vertical guide-line N.E. square, and dot on margin above. Without "O"-flaw in second state.
10†	very high, to right	central, well to right	vertical guide-line N.E. square, close to frame; tall "I".
11	central, to right	high, central	tall "I".
		AJ	
1a*	high, to right	high, central	
1b*	high, to right	high, central	left side line strengthened; horizontal guide-line below "A" square.
2*	low, central	very low, central	
3	low, to left	high, to left	top of "J" slopes down.
4	low, central	high, central	
5	central, to right	high, to left	top of "J" slopes down.
6	central	high, to left	dot in front of and after "J".
7†	central, to left	central, slightly to left	vertical guide-line N.E. square, very close to frame.
8†	central, to right	high, to left	faint vertical guide-line N.E. square.
9†	high, central	high, central	vertical guide-line N.E. square, and dot on margin above. Without "O"-flaw in second state.
10†	low, to right	high, to right	square "J".
11	low, to right	high, to right	square "J"; bottom line extends slightly on right.

**Shows the Ray-flaw.* *†Shows the "O"-flaw.*

1a
1b
2
3
4
5
6
7
8
9
10
11

1a
1b
2
3
4
5
6
7
8
9
10
11

Plate.	*Position of Corner-letter*		*Further distinguishing characteristics.*
	at left.	*at right.*	
		AK	
1a*	high, to right	high, central	small dot on right margin, near top.
1b*	high, to right	high, central	small dot on right margin, near top; "A" square broken at corner.
2*	low, central	central	vertical stroke of "K" faint.
3	central	low, to left	left side very irregular.
4	low, central	central	vertical stroke in S.W. corner of "A" square; right foot of "K" defective.
5	central, to left	central, to left	
6	high, to right	central	dot in "O" of "POSTAGE".
7†	central	high, central	vertical guide-line N.E. square, very close to frame.
8†	high, central	high, to left	vertical guide-line N.E. square, wide of frame; dot below corner of "K" square.
9†	high, central	very low, to left	vertical guide-line N.E. square. Without "O"-flaw in second state.
10†	high, central	central, to right	
11	central—slopes down	central	
		AL	
1a*	central, to right	high, to left	dot above corner of N.E. square, diagonal scratch through "L" square, not always visible.
1b*	central, to right	high, to left	similar, but trace of missing ray.
2*	central	central	two vertical guide-lines N.E. square.
3	central, to left	central, to left	bottom line extends on right.
4	low, central	high, to right	
5	central, to right	central	left side very irregular.
6	high, to right	high, to left	two faint dots above "A", and one in "N" of "ONE".
7†	central, to right	low, to left	dot in "L" square near corner touching line.
8†	central	high, to left	vertical guide-line N.E. square; dot on middle of side line of "L" square.
9†	central—slopes down	central, to left	
10†	very low, central	low, to right	dot on right margin, halfway down N.E. square.
11	high, to right	central, far to right	

**Shows the Ray-flaw.*　　*†Shows the "O"-flaw.*

1a
1b
2
3
4
5
6
7
8
9
10
11

1a
1b
2
3
4
5
6
7
8
9
10
11

Plate.	Position of Corner-letter at left.	Position of Corner-letter at right.	Further distinguishing characteristics.
		BA	
1a*	central, to right	central	faint guide-line N.E. square.
1b*	central, to right	central	no guide-line.
2*	slightly high, to right	low, to left	dot on margin at S.E. corner of "A" square.
3	slightly high, to right	central	horizontal stroke below "A" square.
4	high, to right	slightly high, central	faint dot to right of middle of "B"; bottom line extends on right.
5	high, to right	central, to right	recut "B"; left side, line extends beyond bottom. In second state frame-lines strengthened or recut; one or both letters faint.
6	low, to right	low, to right	
7†	high, central	high, central	scratches on left margin and below; also on right margin and N.E. square.
8†	central, to right	high, central	vertical line on margin, parallel with N.W. square.
9†	high, central	high, to left	vertical guide-line N.E. square, wide of frame; horizontal and vertical guide-lines close to frame in "A" square.
10†	high, to right	central	lower part of "B" slightly defective. Without "O"-flaw in second state, and each letter is faint.
11	low, central	high, central	
		BB	
1a*	central	central	vertical guide-line N.E. square, close to frame.
1b*	central	central	slight traces of re-entry N.E. square.
2*	very low, to right	rather high, to right	two dots on margin outside S.E. corner of second "B" square.
3	high, to right	high, to right	
4	high, to right	high, slightly to right	
5	low, central	high, close to left	in the second state the frame-lines are strengthened or recut, and one or both letters faint.
6	low, to right	central	
7†	central, to right	central, rather close to left	top of first "B" slopes up.
8†	central, to right	high, slightly to right	
9†	high, to right	high, central	guide-lines through value and letter squares; also in N.E. square, close to frame. Without "O"-flaw in second state.
10†	central, little to right	high, to left	without "O"-flaw in second state, and first "B" faint.
11	central, to left	low, to left	second "B" double.

**Shows the Ray-flaw.* *†Shows the "O"-flaw.*

1a 1b 2 3 4 5
6 7 8 9 10 11

1a 1b 2 3 4 5
6 7 8 9 10 11

Plate.	Position of Corner-letter at left.	at right.	Further distinguishing characteristics.
		BC	
1a*	low, to right	high, to left	faint vertical guide-line N.E. square, very close to frame.
1b*	low, to right	high, to left	similar, but trace of missing ray.
2*	low, to right	very low, close in to left	bottom line extends on right; vertical guide-line N.E. square, very close to frame; scratches on right side margin.
3	central, to right	high, to left	top line N.E. square thin.
4	low, central	low, central	vertical guide-line N.E. square.
5	low, central	low, to left	in the second state the frame-lines are strengthened or recut; one or both letters faint.
6	central, to right	very low, to left	vertical guide-line N.E. square, wide of frame; right side line rather defective.
7†	very high, to right	central	
8†	central	central, to left	vertical guide-line N.E. square; bottom line extends slightly on right.
9†	very high, central	slightly low, to left	vertical guide-line N.E. square, wide of frame.
10†	very high, to right	high, central	without "O"-flaw in second state, and letter "C" faint.
11	central	low, well to right	very fine re-entry; each upper square and "B" square, etc.
		BD	
1a*	very low, to right	central, to left	
1b*	very low, to right	central, to left	trace of missing ray.
2*	central	central, to left	mark above "D", which is defective. Possible dot above N.E. corner.
3	very low, to right	central	top line of N.E. square thin.
4	high, to right	central	dot above and nearly touching "B".
5	central, to right	central	scratches on margin below stamp.
6	very low, to right	central	
7†	central, slightly to left	central	
8†	central	central, to right	
9†	high, to left	low, to right	vertical guide-line N.E. square.
10†	high, to right	high, central	without "O"-flaw in second state, and letter "D" faint.
11	rather low, slightly to left	low, well to right	

**Shows the Ray-flaw.* *†Shows the "O"-flaw.*

POSTAGE
B ONE PENNY C
1a 1b 2 3 4 5
6 7 8 9 10 11

POSTAGE
B ONE PENNY D
1a 1b 2 3 4 5
6 7 8 9 10 11

Plate.	Position of Corner-letter		Further distinguishing characteristics.
	at left.	at right.	
		BE	
1a*	low, to right	central, to right	
1b*	low, to right	central, to right	trace of missing ray.
2*	central, to left	central	bottom line of "E" square appears double; dot outside corner "E" square.
3	very low, to left	central, well to right	top line of N.E. square thin.
4	very low, to right	central, far to right	left and bottom lines cross.
5	central, slightly to right	central, slightly high	scratches below stamp.
6	central, to right	central, to left	vertical guide-line N.E. square, close to frame.
7†	central, to right	high, central	bottom line extends on right.
8†	central, to right	central	
9†	low, to right	very low, central	vertical guide-line N.E. square; "B" double.
10	very high, to right	very low, central	not found with "O"-flaw.
11	central, to right	central, close to left	
		BF	
1a*	low, to right	high, central	
1b*	low, to right	high, central	distinct trace of missing ray.
2*	central	central	dot at extreme corner of "F" square
3	high, to right	low, to left	trace of line below "B" square, at left side.
4	central	central	
5	high, central	central	vertical scratches in "B" square; trace of guide-line through value; left side line incomplete.
6	central, to right	slightly low, to left	vertical guide-line N.E. square, very close to frame.
7†	central	central, to left	top of "B" slopes upwards; guide-line through "NNY".
8†	central, to right	central	right line N.E. square weak.
9†	high, to right	high, central	vertical guide-line N.E. square, close to frame; faint scratch joins "B" to bottom line; scratches below; also seen with faint line joining "F" to right side line.
10	central, to right	low, central	not found with "O"-flaw.
11	low, to right	central	

**Shows the Ray-flaw.* *†Shows the "O"-flaw.*

1a
1b
2
3
4
5
6
7
8
9
10
11

1a
1b
2
3
4
5
6
7
8
9
10
11

Plate.	Position of Corner-letter at left.	Position of Corner-letter at right.	Further distinguishing characteristics.
		BG	
1a*	central	central	
1b*	central	central	top line of N.E. square very thin.
2*	central, to left	low, to left	
3	very low, to left	high, to left	
4	central, to right	slightly high, to left	small mark on margin opposite top of "G" square.
5	central	high, central	line connects loop of "B" to foot of square; seen with other scratches in "B" square.
6	low, to right	high, to left	"B" very slightly double.
7†	central, to right	high, to left	
8†	high, central	high, central	faint vertical guide-line N.E. square, very close to frame.
9†	high, to left	very low, to left	vertical guide-line N.E. square, close to frame.
10†	central, to right	high, to left	blur outside N.W. square.
11	very low, to left	high, central	
		BH	
1a*	low, to right	central, slightly to left	right line extends beyond bottom.
1b*	low, to right	central, slightly to left	no extension.
2*	central, to left	high, to right	dot on margin at S.E. corner of "H" square.
3	central, to right	high, central	
4	central, to right	high, to left	faint vertical guide-line N.W. square, close to frame, trace through "H" square.
5	high, to left	central	vertical scratches "B" square; trace of guide-line through value and "H" square.
6	central, to right	rather high, central	side line of N.E. square almost absent.
7†	central	high, to left	vertical guide-line N.E. square.
8†	high, slightly to right	high, to right	scratches below "H" square.
9†	high, central	very low, to left	right side and bottom lines cross.
10	low, to right	very low, to left	blur outside N.W. square; "H" short and stumpy. Not found with "O"-flaw.
11	low, central	central, to right	

**Shows the Ray-flaw.* †*Shows the "O"-flaw.*

1a
1b
2
3
4
5
6
7
8
9
10
11

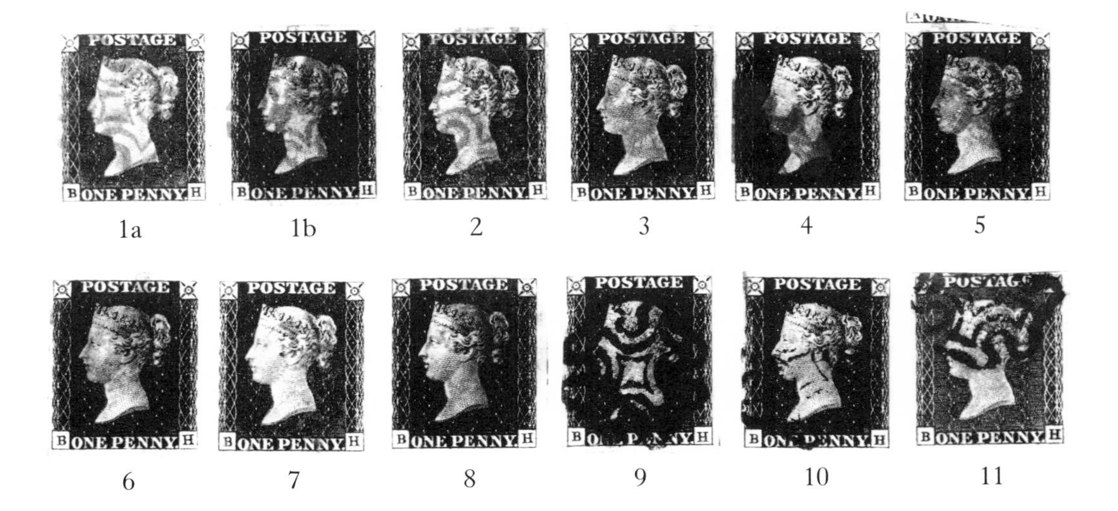
1a
1b
2
3
4
5
6
7
8
9
10
11

Plate.	Position of Corner-letter at left.	Position of Corner-letter at right.	Further distinguishing characteristics.
		BI	
1a*	slightly low, to right	slightly low, to right	
1b*	slightly low, to right	slightly low, to right	"I" slightly thinner.
2*	high, to left	low, central	
3	low, central	high, slightly to left	
4	central, to left	low, central	each letter defective; conspicuous dot in front of foot of "B".
5	central, to left	central, slightly to left	
6	central, to right	central	vertical guide-line N.E. square, close to frame.
7†	central, to right	central, to left	very faint vertical guide-line N.E. square, close to frame.
8†	central, to right	rather high, central	vertical guide-line N.E. square.
9†	very high, to right	low, central	vertical guide-line N.E. square; bottom line extends on right.
10†	low, to right	central, slightly to right	tall "I".
11	central	high, to right	tall "I".
		BJ	
1a*	central, to right	high, to left	
1b*	central, to right	high, to left	left side line strengthened.
2*	central, to left	central	
3	very high, to right	high, to left	
4	slightly low, central	central	
5	rather high, to left	central	very minute dot on bottom of margin between "P" and "E" of "PENNY".
6	central, to right	high, to left	several small dots in "J" square.
7†	slightly low, central	central	vertical guide-line N.E. square, close to frame.
8†	central, to right	high, central	slight extension of bottom line on left.
9†	central, to right	high, to left	blur outside N.W. square.
10†	low, to right	very low, to left	vertical guide-line N.E. square; square "J". Not found with "O"-flaw.
11	low, far to left	high, far to right	square "J".

**Shows the Ray-flaw.* *†Shows the "O"-flaw.*

1a
1b
2
3
4
5
6
7
8
9
10
11

1a
1b
2
3
4
5
6
7
8
9
10
11

Plate.	*Position of Corner-letter*		*Further distinguishing characteristics.*
	at left.	*at right.*	
		BK	
1a*	central, to right	high, to left	
1b*	central, to right	high, to left	top line of N.E. square very thin.
2*	central, to left	central	bottom line extends slightly on right.
3	central, to right	rather high, to left	
4	central	central	vertical guide-line N.E. square.
5	high, to right	central	
6	central, to right	high, to left	small stroke in "B" square near bottom line; vertical guide-line N.E. square, wide of frame.
7†	central	high, to left	
8†	central	central	vertical guide-line N.E. square.
9†	high, to left	low, to left	vertical guide-line N.E. square, close to frame.
10	very high, to right	central, to right	not found with "O"-flaw.
11	high, to right	central	
		BL	
1a*	central, to right	high, to left	
1b*	central, to right	high, to left	top line of N.W. square appears double.
2*	high, to right	very high, to left	
3	central, to right	central, to left	
4	central, to left	central, to right	bottom line extends on right.
5	high, central	central, to left	left side line very irregular.
6	central, to right	central	minute dot corner of "L" square; faint vertical guide-line N.E. square, close to frame.
7†	low, to left	high, to left	left side line irregular; dot in S.E. corner of "L" square.
8†	central	high, central	trace of vertical guide-line N.E. square, wide of frame; marks on margin above "B" square.
9†	high, to left	low, to left	double "B"; dot in S.E. corner of "L" square.
10†	slightly high, to right	central, far to right	vertical guide-line N.E. square and "L" square.
11	central, to left	high, far to right	vertical guide-line N.E. square, close to frame.

**Shows the Ray-flaw.* *†Shows the "O"-flaw.*

POSTAGE
B ONE PENNY. K
1a 1b 2 3 4 5
6 7 8 9 10 11

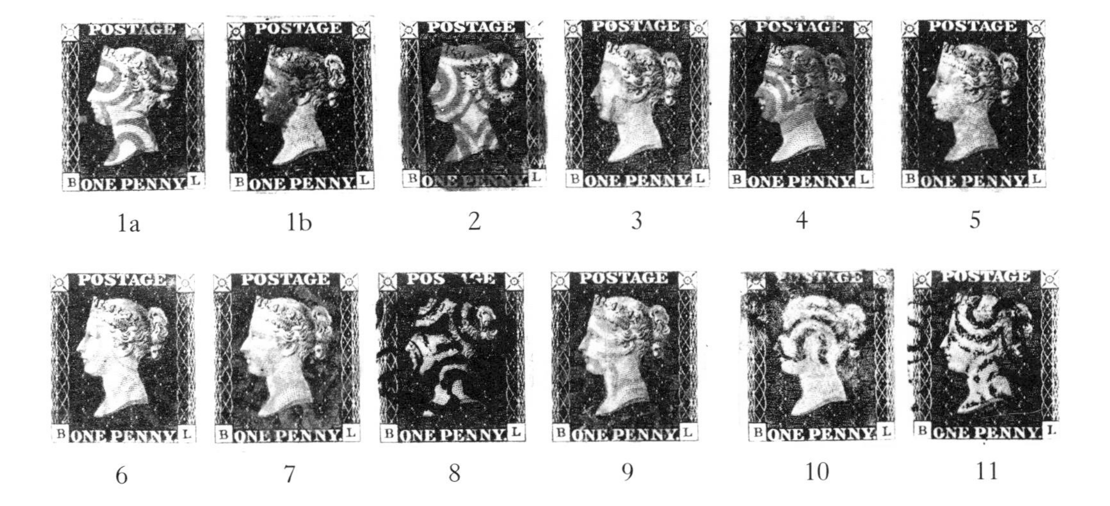

POSTAGE
B ONE PENNY. L
1a 1b 2 3 4 5
6 7 8 9 10 11

Plate.	Position of Corner-letter		Further distinguishing characteristics.
	at left.	at right.	
		CA	
1a*	central, to left	low, to right	faint vertical guide-line N.E. square; bottom line extends on left and right.
1b*	central, to left	low, to right	trace of outer line outside left side; bottom line extends on left and right.
2*	low, central	central	
3	slightly low, central	central	bottom line extends on right.
4	high, to right	central	two minute dots on left arm of "Y" of "PENNY"; line N.E. corner very thin.
5	low, to left	low, central	faint vertical guide-line N.E. square, close to frame. In the second state, the frame-lines are strengthened or recut; one or both letters faint.
6	high, central	low, central	left side extends beyond bottom; vertical guide-line N.E. square, very close to frame; N.W. square weak at right corner.
7†	central, to left	high, central	stroke after "C"— trace of double letter.
8†	central, to left	central, slightly to left	blur outside N.W. square.
9†	low, to left	central	vertical guide-line N.E. square.
10†	low, to left	high, to right	left side extends beyond bottom. Without "O"-flaw in second state.
11	central, slightly to right	very high, to right	
		CB	
1a*	central	central	vertical guide-line N.E. square, very close to frame.
1b*	central	central	no guide-line.
2*	rather high, central	low, to right	
3	central	very high, to right	
4	low, to left	central, to right	right side extends beyond bottom; small dot N.W. corner of "C" square; very faint vertical guide-line N.E. square and "B" square (not on all).
5	low, to left	central	faint vertical guide-line N.E. square, close to frame. In the second state, the frame-lines are strengthened or recut; one or both letters faint.
6	low, central	low, central	
7†	central, well to left	central, to left	blur outside N.W. square.
8†	central	central, to right	
9†	low, central	central, to right	vertical guide-line N.E. square and in "B" square, close to frame.
10†	central	low, to right	without "O"-flaw in second state.
11	low, to left	high, to right	

**Shows the Ray-flaw.* *†Shows the "O"-flaw.*

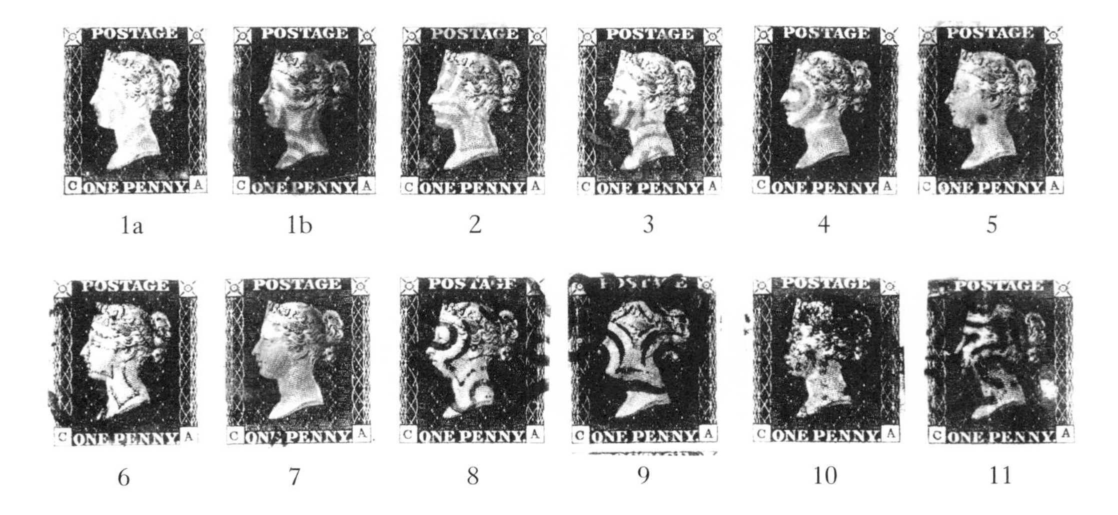
1a
1b
2
3
4
5
6
7
8
9
10
11

1a
1b
2
3
4
5
6
7
8
9
10
11

Plate.	Position of Corner-letter		Further distinguishing characteristics.
	at left.	at right.	
		CC	
1a*	central	central, to left	vertical guide-line in N.E. square and "C" square, very close to frame.
1b*	central	central, to left	vertical guide-line in second "C" square, very close to frame; horizontal scratch through first "C" square.
2*	low, to left	low, to left	right side extends beyond bottom; very faint vertical guide-line N.E. square, very close to frame.
3	high, central	high, central	
4	low, to left	high, to left	minute dot above first "C", and in "E" of "ONE"; vertical guide-line N.E. square.
5	central, to left	central, slightly to left	bottom line extends slightly on right. In the second state, the frame-lines are strengthened or recut; one or both letters faint.
6	central, slightly to left	low, to left	left side very irregular; vertical guide-line N.E. square, close to frame.
7†	high, to left	high, far to left	N.W. square blurred; bottom line extends slightly on right.
8†	central, to right	high, central	vertical guide-line N.E. square; bottom line extends on right.
9†	central, to left	low, slightly to left	
10†	central	low, to left	blur N.W. square. Without "O"-flaw in second state.
11	high, to left	high, well to right	
		CD	
1a*	central, to left	high, central	"D" double.
1b*	central, to left	high, central	similar, but left side line recut.
2*	central	central	
3	high, central	central, to right	
4	central	low, central	dot below "C"; many dots on lower margin; short line on right of "C" square.
5	central	very low, far to right	scratches below "NNY". In the second state the frame-lines are strengthened or recut; one or both letters faint.
6	central, to left	central, slightly to right	horizontal stroke outside stamp below "E" of "ONE"; dot in "S" of "POSTAGE".
7†	central, to left	central	blur outside N.W. square.
8†	high, central	central, to right	left side extends slightly beyond bottom; vertical guide-line N.E. square, close to frame.
9†	very low, to left	central, to right	faint blur N.W. square.
10†	high, central	central, slightly to left	left side extends slightly beyond bottom; blur N.W. square.
11	low, central	high, far to right	vertical guide-line N.E. square.

**Shows the Ray-flaw.* *†Shows the "O"-flaw.*

POSTAGE
C ONE PENNY C
1a
1b
2
3
4
5
6
7
8
9
10
11

POSTAGE
C ONE PENNY D
1a
1b
2
3
4
5
6
7
8
9
10
11

Plate.	Position of Corner-letter at left.	Position of Corner-letter at right.	Further distinguishing characteristics.
		CE	
1a*	high, central	high, slightly to left	
1b*	high, central	high, slightly to left	trace of missing ray.
2*	low, central	slightly low, to left	
3	central	high, to right	
4	slightly low, central	slightly low, far to right	right and bottom lines cross.
5	very low, far to left	central, to left	bottom line extends on right; left side line extends beyond bottom; scratches on right side margin; left side irregular. In second state, the frame-lines have been strengthened or recut.
6	low, central	central, to left	very faint blur N.W. square.
7†	central, to left	low, to left	left side irregular.
8†	high, to right	high, to left	
9†	very low, to left	very low, to left	vertical guide-line N.E. square, close to frame; blur N.W. square.
10†	low, central	very low, to left	N.W. blurred. Without "O"-flaw in second state, and with faint "E".
11	low, to left	high, to right	bottom line extends on right; vertical guide-line N.E. square, wide of frame.
		CF	
1a*	central, to left	high, central	"C" blurred.
1b*	central, to left	high, central	similar, but "NE" of "ONE" nearly joined.
2*	low, slightly to left	central	faint vertical guide-line in "F" square, close to frame.
3	central	central, to left	dot on left of "F".
4	central	low, central	dot in "C" square, nearly touching right side; side line N.E. square thin.
5	low, to left	low, central	trace of horizontal guide-line near top of "F" square.
6	low, to left	central	right side very irregular.
7†	central, to left	high, central	short vertical stroke in "F" square, touching left side.
8†	high, central	high, central	left line extends very slightly beyond bottom.
9†	high, central	central, to left	vertical guide-line N.E. square and "F" square.
10†	high, to left	very low, central	without "O"-flaw in second state.
11	low, to left	central	blur outside N.W. square.

**Shows the Ray-flaw.* *†Shows the "O"-flaw.*

1a
1b
2
3
4
5
6
7
8
9
10
11

1a
1b
2
3
4
5
6
7
8
9
10
11

Plate.	Position of Corner-letter		Further distinguishing characteristics.
	at left.	at right.	
		CG	
la*	central	high, central	
lb*	central	high, central	outer lines of N.E. square thin.
2*	central	high, central	faint line across "C" square.
3	central, to right	central	faint dot above "G".
4	central, to left	high, to left	indistinct dot in middle of "C".
5	low, slightly to left	high, central	side line of N.E. square weak.
6	high, to left	high, to left	
7†	high, to left	high, to left	right side line extends beyond bottom.
8†	very low, slightly to right	high, central	
9†	high, central	low, to left	faint vertical guide-line N.E. square and through value; right and bottom lines cross.
10†	high, to left	central	blur in N.W. square. Without "O"-flaw in second state.
11	low, central	high, to right	blur outside N.W. square.
		CH	
1a*	high, to right	central	left side irregular.
1b*	high, to right	central	left side recut; dot in "P" of "POSTAGE".
2*	central	low, central—slopes up	left line extends slightly beyond bottom.
3	central, slightly low	central—slopes up	"H" square weak at corner.
4	central	high, to left	dot below and after "H".
5	central, far to left	low, to right	trace of guide-line through value and "H" square.
6	low, to left	central	left side irregular.
7†	high, slightly to right	high, central	
8†	low, to left	high, to right	
9†	high, central	high, to left	vertical guide-line N.E. square.
10†	central, to left	very low, to right	blur in N.W. square; squat "H". Without "O"-flaw in second state.
11	high, central	central, to right	

*Shows the Ray-flaw. †Shows the "O"-flaw.

1a
1b
2
3
4
5
6
7
8
9
10
11

1a
1b
2
3
4
5
6
7
8
9
10
11

Plate.	*Position of Corner-letter*		*Further distinguishing characteristics.*
	at left.	*at right.*	
		CI	
1a*	high, to right	low, central	side line N.E. square thick.
1b*	high, to right	low, central	side line N.E. square thin.
2	central, to left	rather low, central	right line extends above.
3	central	central	right side line of "I" square thinner.
4	rather low, central	low, central	right side rather irregular; break in left side line towards top.
5	central, to left	central	
6	very low, central	central, to left	very minute dot above "C"; foot of "I" defective on right.
7†	high, to left	central	bottom line extends on each side.
8†	high, to right	central	vertical guide-line N.E. square.
9†	high, central	low, to right	vertical guide-line N.E. square, close to frame.
10†	low, far to left	central	tall "I"; blur N.W. square.
11	central, to left	high, central	tall "I".
		CJ	
1a*	high, central	high, central	
1b*	high, central	high, central	top line of N.E. square thinner. Trace of horizontal guide-line N.W. square
2	very low, central	central, to left	
3	central	high, slightly to right	
4	central, to left	rather high, to left	minute dot in N.E. square.
5	rather high, central	rather high, central	scratches on margin below and above, and in N.E. square.
6	central, to right	low, to left	vertical guide-line N.E. square, close to frame; dot on margin above "P" of "POSTAGE"; dot under curve of "C".
7†	high, to right	central	very faint vertical guide-line N.E. square, close to frame.
8†	very high, to right	central	bottom line extends on right.
9†	high, central	central	trace of guide-line through value and "J" square; top line of N.E. square thin.
10†	high, central	very high, to right	square "J".
11	very low, central	high, well to right	square "J"; dot in "N" of "ONE".

**Shows the Ray-flaw.* *†Shows the "O"-flaw.*

1a
1b
2
3
4
5
6
7
8
9
10
11

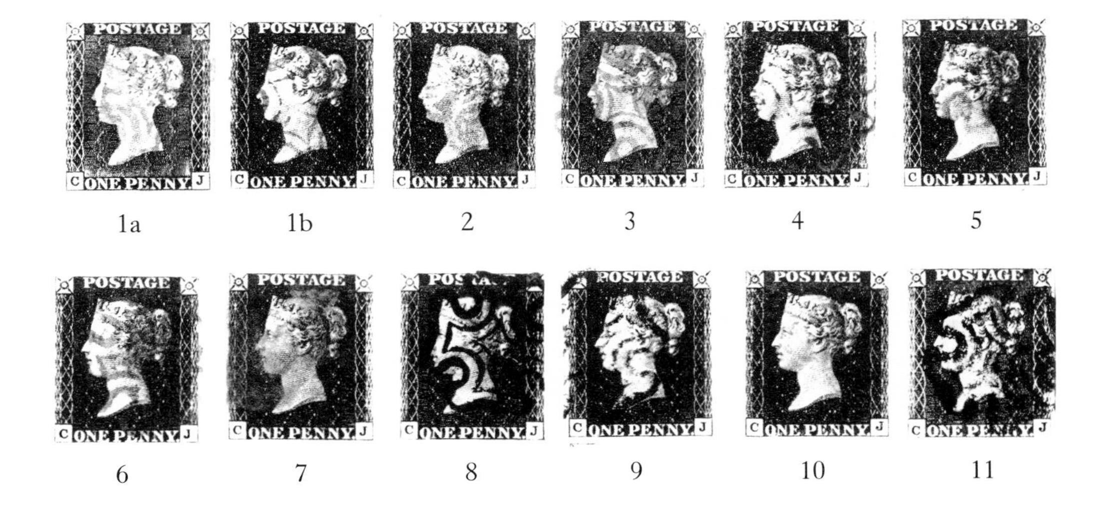

1a
1b
2
3
4
5
6
7
8
9
10
11

Plate.	Position of Corner-letter		Further distinguishing characteristics.
	at left.	at right.	
		CK	
1a*	high, to right	high, central	
1b*	high, to right	high, central	
2	central, to right	central	faint line extending above N.E. square.
3	high, central	high, central	
4	central, to left	central, slightly to left	faint vertical guide-line N.E. square, close to frame; trace of horizontal guide-line through bottom of "K" square; left side irregular.
5	high, to left	low, to left—slopes up	
6	high, central	central, to left	faint dot in N.E. corner of "C" square; top line of N.E. square defective.
7†	central, to left	slightly high, central	vertical guide-line N.E. square, wide of frame; left side irregular.
8†	high, central	central	
9†	high, central	central, to right	double letter "C".
10†	central	central, well to right	left side extends well beyond bottom.
11	low, central	low, to left	vertical guide-line N.E. square, wide of frame.
		CL	
1a	central	high, to left	dot below corner of "L" square.
1b	central	high, to left	dot below corner of "L" square; marks of re-entry N.W. and "L" squares, etc.
2	low, central	central, to left	dot below left corner of "C" square.
3	slightly low, slightly to left	central, slightly to right	
4	low, central	high, central	dot on outside of side line of "L" square, near corner; scratches on margin N.W. square.
5	rather low, central	low, to right	dot in N.W. square, between lower left hand ray and side line.
6	central, to left	central	small dot in S.E. corner of "L" square.
7†	central, to left	central, to left	left side extends beyond bottom; vertical guide-line N.E. square, close to frame.
8†	high, to left	high, to left	left side weak and blurred; vertical guide-line N.E. square.
9†	high, to left	low, central	vertical guide-line N.E. square.
10†	central	low, central	blur in N.W. square.
11	low, to left	high, well to right	

Shows the Ray-flaw. †Shows the "O"-flaw.

1a 1b 2 3 4 5
6 7 8 9 10 11

1a 1b 2 3 4 5
6 7 8 9 10 11

Plate.	*Position of Corner-letter*		*Further distinguishing characteristics.*
	at left.	*at right.*	
		DA	
1a*	central, to right	slightly low, to right	smudge over "A"; mark in left side of "A" square.
1b*	central, to right	slightly low, to right	no smudge; mark below "E" of "ONE".
2	high, central	low, to left	top of "D" rather defective; vertical guide-line N.E. square; distinct guide-line along bottom margin; large "D".
3	high, to right	central, slightly to left	line under "D" faint.
4	central, to right	central	several dots in and outside "A" square; dot in "N" of "ONE"; side line N.E. square weak; "D" slightly double at top.
5	high, to right	low, central	in the second state the frame-lines are strengthened or recut; one or both letters faint.
6	central, to right	low, to left	faint vertical guide-lines N.E. square, close to frame; mark on top margin between "E" and square.
7†	central	rather high, to left	"D" slightly double; bottom and right side lines cross.
8†	central, slightly to right	central	vertical guide-line N.E. square.
9†	low, to right	high, central	vertical guide-line N.E. square; and trace in "A" square, but close to frame.
10†	very low, far to left	high, central	left line extends distinctly beyond bottom; vertical guide-line N.E. square, wide of frame.
11	low, to right	central	weakness at left corner of N.E. square.
		DB	
1a*	central	central	
1b*	central	central	trace of missing ray.
2	central, to right	central, to right	vertical guide-line N.E. square; horizontal guide-line in each letter-square.
3	low, to right	high, to right	dot in "D" square, middle of left side; large "D".
4	central, to right	high, to right	"D" slightly double; distinct dot below top serif of "B".
5	low, central	central, slightly to left	"D" slightly double, faint vertical guide-line N.E. square, close to frame. In the second state the frame-lines are strengthened or recut; one or both letters faint.
6	central, to right	low, to right	faint vertical guide-line N.E. square, close to frame.
7†	low, to left	central, to right	
8†	central, to left	high, central	minute extension at bottom right.
9†	central	central	vertical guide-line N.E. square, wide of frame.
10†	central	low, to right	left and bottom lines cross.
11	low, central	central	

**Shows the Ray-flaw.* *†Shows the "O"-flaw.*

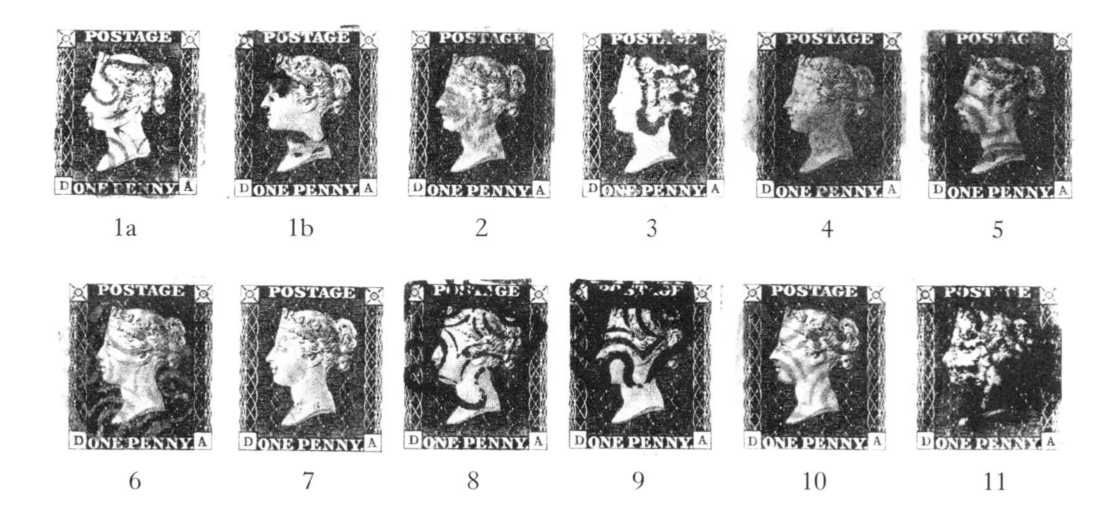
1a 1b 2 3 4 5
6 7 8 9 10 11

1a 1b 2 3 4 5
6 7 8 9 10 11

Plate.	Position of Corner-letter		Further distinguishing characteristics.
	at left.	at right.	
		DC	
1a*	central, to right	central, to left	frame-lines perfect.
1b*	central, to right	central, to left	line of left of "D" square grows weak towards base.
2	high, central	high, central	vertical guide-line N. E. square, and along bottom margin; left side of "C" square extends slightly; large "D".
3	central, to right	low, to left	
4	very low, to right	central, to left	indistinct dot in N.E. and "D" squares; bottom line extends slightly on left and right.
5	low, to right	central, well to left	vertical guide-line in N.E. square, in first state. In the second state the frame-lines are strengthened or recut; one or both letters faint.
6	low, to right	central	side line of N. E. square weak.
7†	very low, central	central, well to left	
8†	central, to right	central, to left	vertical guide-line N.E. square; bottom line extends on right. No "O"-flaw in second state.
9†	central	low, to left	"D" distinctly double; vertical guide-line N.E. square, close to frame.
10†	low, to right	slightly low, close to left	left line extends slightly beyond bottom.
11	low, to right	high, central	trace of vertical guide-line N.E. square; weakness at left corner of N.E. square.
		DD	
1a*	high, to right	high, to left	upper portion of each "D" slightly defective; right line extends beyond bottom.
1b*	high, to right	high, to left	letters not so defective; weak junctions of frame-lines at lower right square; each "D" large.
2	central, to right	high, to left	guide-line along outside of bottom margin.
3	low, to right	high, to right	
4	high, to right	high, central	first "D" distinctly double.
5	low, to right	low, central	right line extends distinctly beyond bottom. In second state the frame-lines are strengthened or recut; one or both letters faint.
6	central, to right	central	vertical scratch in first "D" square.
7†	central, to right	central	faint guide-line through value; scratches on lower margin.
8†	central, to right	high, to right	vertical guide-line N.E. square.
9†	low, central	central, to right	vertical guide-line N.E. square.
10†	very low, to right	very high, to right	faint vertical guide-line N.E. square, wide of frame.
11	central, to right	central, far to right	first "D" slightly double; guide-line N. E. square.

**Shows the Ray-flaw.* *†Shows the "O"-flaw.*

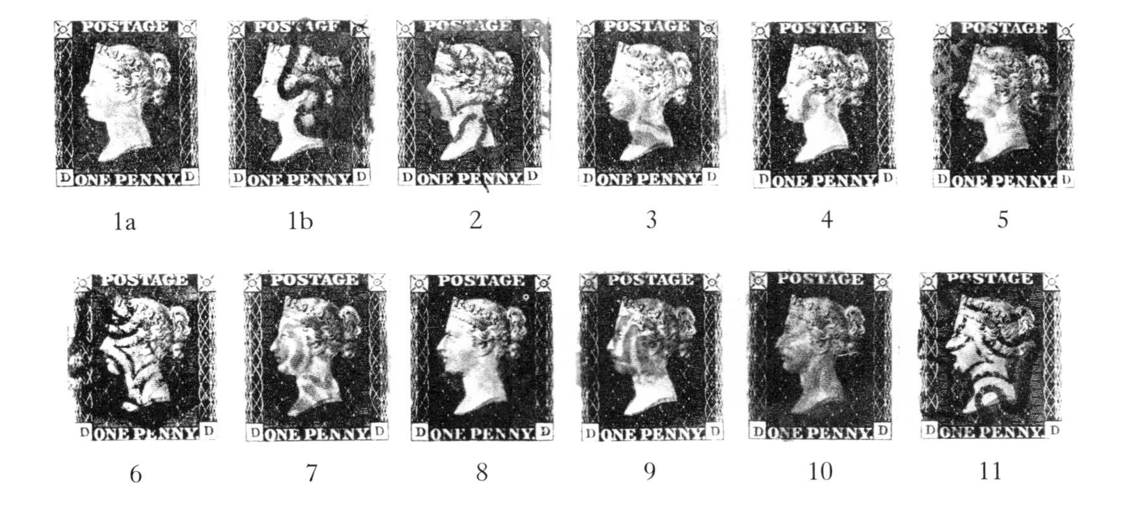

Plate.	*Position of Corner-letter*		*Further distinguishing characteristics.*
	at left.	*at right.*	
		DE	
1a*	high, to right	low, to left	frame-lines perfect.
1b*	high, to right	low, to left	side line of N.E. square weak.
2	high, to right	central	distinct guide-line along outside of bottom margin; large "D".
3	central, to right	high, far to right	side and bottom lines of "D" square slightly thinner.
4	low, to right	high, far to right	tiny dots before and after "D"; short vertical stroke in "E" square.
5	very low, to right	high, slightly to left	scratches on margin below left side margin.
6	low, to right	central, to left	left side irregular.
7†	central, to right	central	
8†	central, to right	high, central	
9†	central	central	vertical guide-line N.E. square, closer to frame in "E" square.
10†	high, to right—slopes down	central, close to left	blur N.W. square.
11	low, to right	high, far to right	
		DF	
1a*	high, to right	central	
1b*	high, to right	central	"NE" of "ONE" nearly joined; bottom of "D" weak.
2	central	central	large "D".
3	low, to right	very low, central	
4	low, central	high, well to left	tiny dot below "D" square, and above N.W. square.
5	high, to right	rather high, central	bottom line extends slightly on right.
6	high, to right	central, to left	side line of N.E. square weak; faint guide-line N.E. square.
7†	central, to right	high, central	faint blur N.W. square.
8†	low, to right	very low, central	
9†	high, to right	low, slightly to left	vertical guide-line N.E. square, and closer to frame in "F" square.
10†	high, to right	central	left side line extends slightly beyond bottom.
11	very low, to right	rather low, central	vertical guide-line N.E. square.

**Shows the Ray-flaw.* †*Shows the "O"-flaw.*

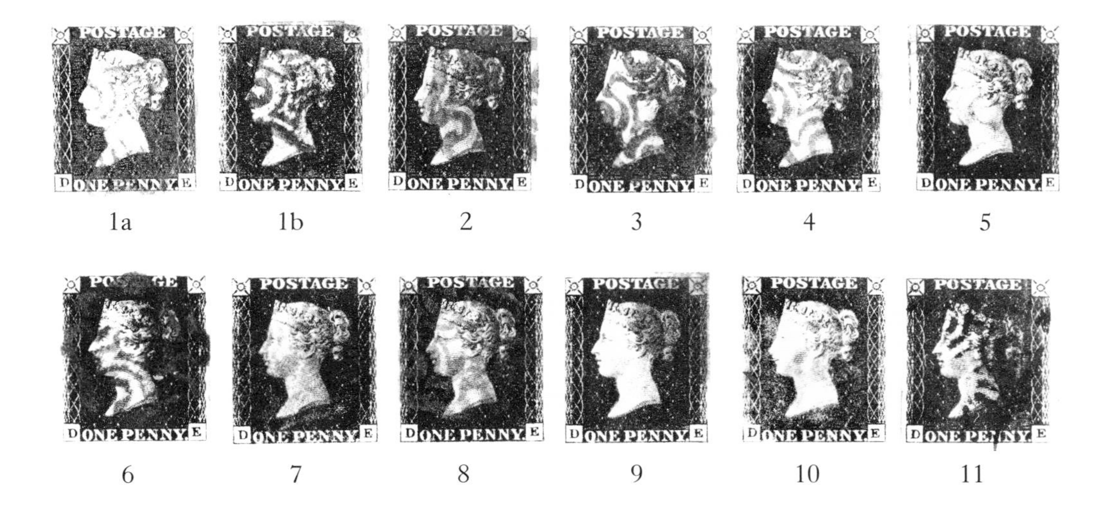
1a
1b
2
3
4
5
6
7
8
9
10
11

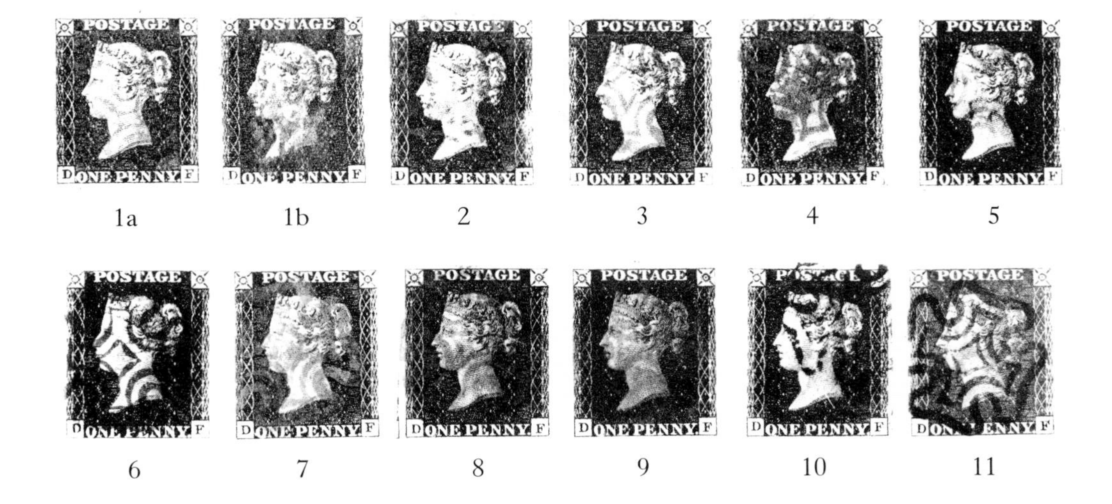
1a
1b
2
3
4
5
6
7
8
9
10
11

Plate.	*Position of Corner-letter*		*Further distinguishing characteristics.*
	at left.	*at right.*	
		DG	
1a*	high, to right	high, to left	
1b*	high, to right	high, to left	thin "G".
2	high, slightly to right	high, central	"D" plainly double; faint vertical guide-line N.E. square.
3	low, central	high, central	
4	low, central	high, to right	vertical guide-line N.E. square, close to frame; left side weak.
5	very high, to right	high, to left	horizontal guide-line or scratch, along outside of bottom margin.
6	high, to right	high, to left	
7†	central	high, central	distinct guide-line through letter-squares and value.
8†	low, to right	high, central	trace of vertical guide-line N.E. square, wide of frame.
9†	high, to right	low, to left	trace of vertical guide-line N.E. square, very close to frame.
10†	very low, to right	central, to left	trace of vertical guide-line N.E. square; blur outside N.W. square.
11	low, to right	very high, to right	
		DH	
1a*	slightly high, to left	low, to left	"D" plainly blurred.
1b*	slightly high, to left	low, to left	"D" not so plainly blurred.
2	high, to right	high, central	large "D".
3	central, to right	high, to left	
4	slightly low, to right	high, to right	
5	high, to right	high, central	faint trace of vertical guide-line N.E. square, very close to frame; faint scratches on lower margin.
6	slightly low, to right	very high, central	tiny dot outside margin, below "Y".
7†	central, to right	high, central	right side very weak.
8†	central, to right	central, to right	bottom line extends on right.
9†	low, to left	central	blur N.W. square.
10†	central, to right	high, central	squat "H".
11	central, far to right	very high, slightly to right	

**Shows the Ray-flaw.* †*Shows the "O"-flaw.*

POSTAGE
D ONE PENNY G
1a
1b
2
3
4
5
6
7
8
9
10
11

POSTAGE
D ONE PENNY H
1a
1b
2
3
4
5
6
7
8
9
10
11

Plate.	Position of Corner-letter		Further distinguishing characteristics.
	at left.	*at right.*	
		DI	
1a*	high, to right	central	vertical guide-line N.E. square, close to frame; bottom line extends on right.
1b*	high, to right	central	guide-line not so distinct; bottom line extends on right; "I" slightly thinner.
2	very high, to right	rather high, central	trace of guide-line on lower margin; large "D".
3	central, to right	central	faint vertical guide-line in "I" square, close to frame.
4	low, to right	central, to left	slight blur outside N.W. square.
5	central, to right	slightly low, central	faint vertical guide-line N.E. square.
6	high, to right	low, to left	faint dot above "D"; defective "I"; faint dots at right and left of "I".
7†	central, slightly to left	central	side line of N.E. square weak.
8†	central, to right	central	vertical guide-line N.E. square, close to frame.
9†	central	high, to right	vertical guide-line N.E. square.
10†	central, to right	central	left side line extends evidently beyond bottom; blur N.W.; tall "I"; very faint vertical guide-line N.E. square.
11	high, to right	central, to right	tall "I".
		DJ	
1a*	high, to right	high, central	faint vertical guide-line N.E. square, close to frame.
1b*	high, to right	high, central	no guide-line; neither letter so thick; ray-flaw not clear.
2	high, to right	rather high, central	vertical guide-line N.E. square, close to frame; large "D".
3	central, to right	high, to left	
4	central, to right	high, central	small smudge above "D".
5	high, to right	high, central	vertical guide-line N.E. square.
6	high, to right	central, to left	dot to right of "J"; dot at corner of "D" square.
7†	Slightly low, to right	central, to left	N.E. square weak at side.
8†	low, to right	low, central	vertical guide-line N.E. square, very close to frame.
9†	slightly low, to right	central, slightly to left	vertical guide-line N.E. square, close to frame.
10†	low, to right	high, central	square "J"; vertical guide-line N.E. square.
11	low, to right	high, to right	tiny dot to right of "J"; square "J".

**Shows the Ray-flaw.* *†Shows the "O"-flaw.*

1a
1b
2
3
4
5
6
7
8
9
10
11

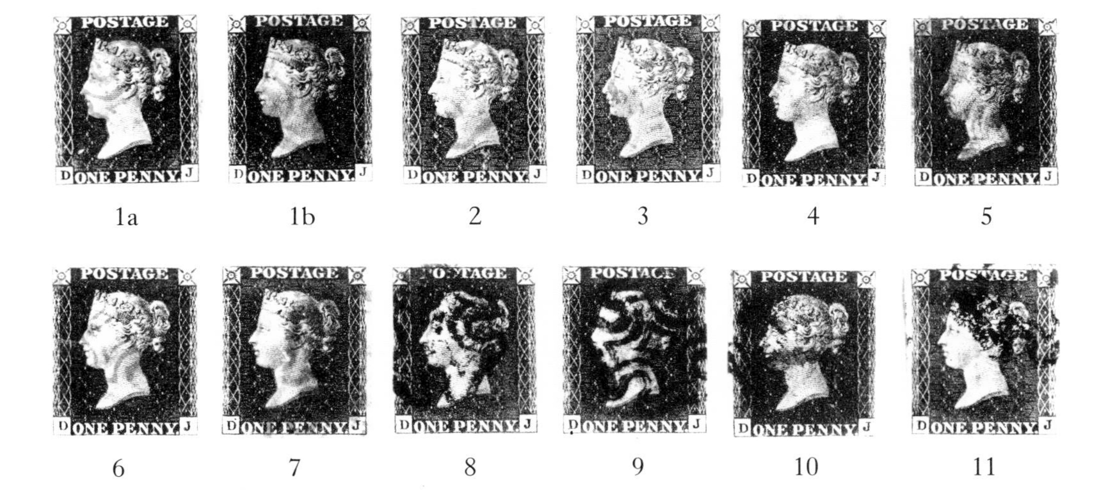
1a
1b
2
3
4
5
6
7
8
9
10
11

Plate.	*Position of Corner-letter*		*Further distinguishing characteristics.*
	at left.	*at right.*	
		DK	
1a*	high, to right	high, central	
1b*	high, to right	high, central	both side lines extend beyond bottom.
2	high, central	low, to left	line below "K" slightly double; large "D".
3	central, to right	central—slopes up	
4	central, slightly to right	central	sometimes scratches on bottom margin.
5	central, to right	central, to left	N.E. square weak at side.
6	high, to right	low, to left	side line of N.E. square absent.
7†	high, to right	central, to left	bottom line extends on left.
8†	central, to right	central, to left—slopes up	trace of vertical guide-line N.E. square. No "O"-flaw in second state.
9†	high, far to left	central, nearly touching left	vertical guide-line N.E. square.
10†	very low, central	low, far to right	without "O"-flaw in second state.
11	low, to right	low, central	scratches below stamp.
		DL	
1a*	high, to right	high, to left	dot below corner of "L" square.
1b*	high, to right	high, to left	dot below corner of "L" square; line below "Y".
2	high, to left	high, slightly to left	line on margin, below "L" square; large "D".
3	central, to right	central	
4	central	high, to right	dot just outside "L" square, near corner.
5	slightly low, to right	central	bottom line extends slightly on left; very faint guide-line inside "L" square, close to frame, vertical guide-line N.E. square.
6	central, to right	central	faint dot below "D", and near side line of "L" square.
7†	slightly high, to right	central	dot in corner of "L" square.
8†	central, to right	slightly high, to left	re-entry in N.E. and "D" squares, and through value.
9†	central, to right	high, to left	indistinct stroke on left side of N.W. square.
10†	central	very low, central	dot in N.W. square, near top. Without "O"-flaw in second state.
11	central, to right	central, to right	vertical guide-line N.E. square.

**Shows the Ray-flaw.* *†Shows the "O"-flaw.*

1a
1b
2
3
4
5
6
7
8
9
10
11

1a
1b
2
3
4
5
6
7
8
9
10
11

Plate.	Position of Corner-letter		Further distinguishing characteristics.
	at left.	at right.	
		EA	
1a*	high, to right	high, to right	vertical guide-line N.E. square, close to frame; "A" blurred.
1b*	high, to right	high, to right	side line of N.E. square thin; "A" not so blurred; guide-lines visible both left and right side lines.
2	central, to left	central, to right	bottom serif of "E" bifurcated; line right side of "E".
3	central, to left	central	bottom line of "A" square thin.
4	central	central	vertical guide-line N.E. square, close to frame.
5	high, to right	central	minute dot to left of "E".
6	high, central	very low, to right	lower portion of "E" faint.
7†	central	central, to right	
8†	high, central	central	vertical guide-line N.E. square.
9†	high, to right	central, to left	very faint vertical guide-line N.E. square.
10†	central	high, central	
11	low, central	very low, central	break at left corner of N.E. square.
		EB	
1a*	central, slightly to right	central, to right	
1b*	central, slightly to right	central, to right	trace of missing ray.
2	low, to left	central	very faint vertical guide-line N.E. square, close to frame.
3	high, to right	high, to right	line below "E" rather thin.
4	high, central	central, to right	tiny dot in N.E. square; horizontal scratch below.
5	high, to left	central	bottom serif of "E" bifurcated.
6	central, slightly to left	very low, central	trace of vertical guide-line N.E. square.
7†	central	central	
8†	central, to left	central, to left	left side weak.
9†	central, to right	central	vertical guide-line N.E. square; "B" slightly double.
10†	very low, central	central, to right	blur outside N.W. square, and on margin.
11	central	very low, central	top serif of "E" faint.

**Shows the Ray-flaw.* *†Shows the "O"-flaw.*

1a
1b
2
3
4
5
6
7
8
9
10
11

1a
1b
2
3
4
5
6
7
8
9
10
11

Plate.	Position of Corner-letter at left.	Position of Corner-letter at right.	Further distinguishing characteristics.
		EC	
la*	low, to right	central	vertical guide-line N.E. square.
lb*	low, to right	central	similar, but trace of missing ray.
2	low, central	central, to left	distinct dot on margin, below left of "C" square.
3	high, central	high, to left	
4	central	low, central	left side weak; line on margin below "NNY".
5	central	low, to left	lower half of vertical stroke of "E" weak.
6	high, central	high, central	vertical guide-line N.E. square, wide of frame.
7†	central, to left	central, to left	
8†	central, to left	low, central	trace of vertical guide-line N.E. square, wide of frame.
9†	very high, to right	high, to left	bottom line extends slightly on right. Without "O"-flaw in second state.
10†	low, central	high, to left	
11	central	central	thin "C".
		ED	
1a*	central	high, central	vertical guide-line N.E. square, very close to frame.
1b*	central	high, central	left side line strengthened.
2	central, to right	central, to right	
3	high, to right	central, to right	bottom line of "E" square thin; scratches on margin below "PENNY".
4	central, to right	central	indistinct dots below "N" of "ONE".
5	central	central, slightly to right	top line of N.W. square thin.
6	slightly high, central	central, to right	horizontal guide-line through "D" square.
7†	rather high, slightly to left	high, central	dot in "E" of "PENNY".
8†	slightly high, to right	high, central	
9†	very high, central	low, to right	vertical guide-line N.E. square, wide of frame.
10†	very low, central	central, to left	trace of vertical guide-line N.E. square.
11	very low, to right	low, to right	faint blur side of N.W. square.

**Shows the Ray-flaw.* †*Shows the "O"-flaw.*

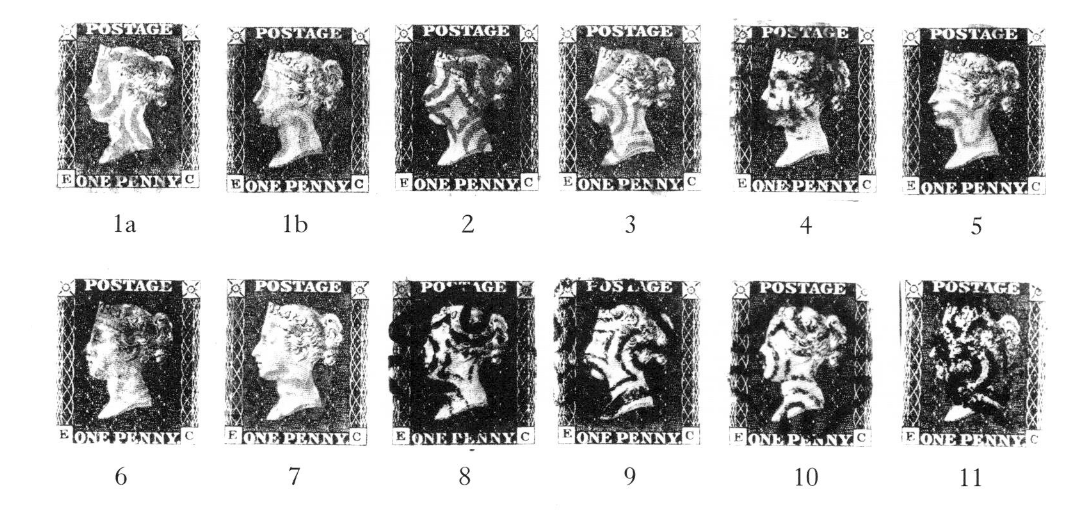
1a
1b
2
3
4
5
6
7
8
9
10
11

1a
1b
2
3
4
5
6
7
8
9
10
11

Plate.	Position of Corner-letter		Further distinguishing characteristics.
	at left.	at right.	
		EE	
1a*	low, to right	high, to right	vertical guide-line N.E. square, very close to frame; white mark on bottom limb of second "E"; left bottom serif of first "E" long.
1b*	low, to right	high, to right	side line of N.E. square weak; left bottom serif of first "E" long.
2	central, to left	central	vertical guide-line N.E. square, close to frame.
3	high, to right	high, central	lines of bottom squares rather thin.
4	central, to right	high, central	distinct dot in front of first "E"; dot below "N" of "ONE".
5	central	central	bottom limb of second "E" faint.
6	central	rather high, central	vertical guide-line N.E. square, close to frame.
7†	low, to left	very low, central	
8†	high, central	high, central	bottom line extends slightly on right; side line of N.E. square thin.
9†	central, to right	central	vertical guide-line N.E. square and, closer to frame, in "E" square.
10†	low, to right	low, central	second "E" slightly double.
11	very high, to right	very high, to right	left side line thin.
		EF	
1a*	low, to left	high, central	vertical guide-line N.E. square, close to frame.
1b*	low, to left	high, central	guide-line not so clear; trace of missing ray.
2	central, to left	central	trace of vertical guide-line N.E. square, close to frame.
3	very high, close to right	very low, to left	
4	central	high, to left	side line of N.E. square somewhat thin.
5	central	central	
6	high, slightly to left	central	trace of vertical guide-line N.E. square, close to frame.
7†	central	high, to left	
8†	central	central	side line of N.E. square weak.
9†	high, central	central, to left	vertical guide-line N.E. square.
10†	low, to right	low, central	vertical guide-line N.E. square.
11	central, to right	high, central	break at left corner of N.E. square.

**Shows the Ray-flaw.* *†Shows the "O"-flaw.*

1a
1b
2
3
4
5
6
7
8
9
10
11

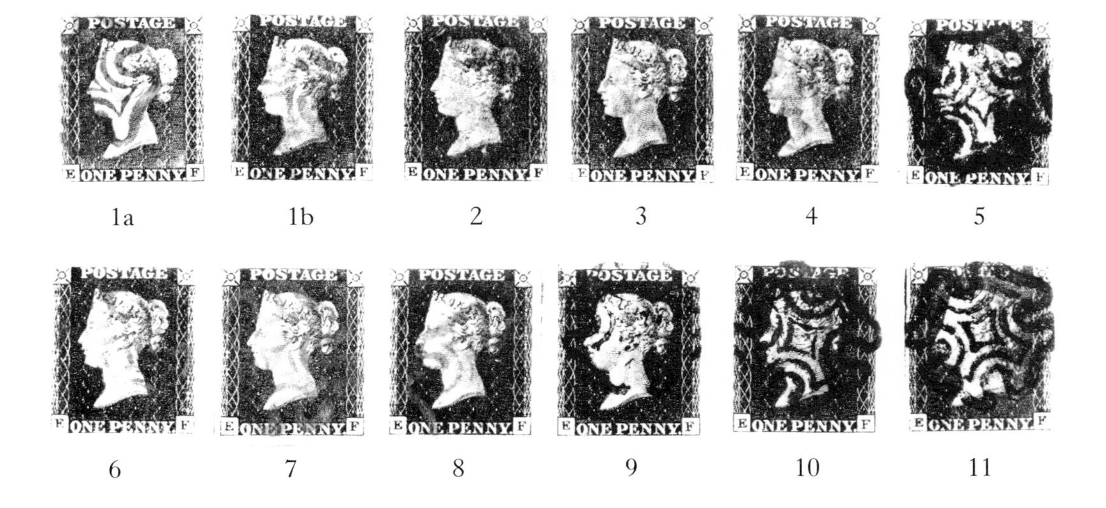
1a
1b
2
3
4
5
6
7
8
9
10
11

Plate.	Position of Corner-letter		Further distinguishing characteristics.
	at left.	at right.	
		EG	
1a*	high, to right	high, to left	dot outside right corner of "G" square; vertical guide-line N.E. square, close to frame.
1b*	high, to right	high, to left	dot missing; bottom line of "E" square thin; guide-line not so distinct.
2	central, to left	slightly low, close to left	
3	high, to right	central, to left	
4	central, slightly to left	central	faint guide-line on margin below "E" square.
5	central, to right	very high, to left	line below "E".
6	central, to left	high, close to left	horizontal and vertical guide-lines in N.E. square.
7†	central	high, central	bottom line extends on left; scratches on lower margin; white dot on bottom serif of "E".
8†	central	high, central	vertical guide-line N.E. square, wide of frame; side line of N.E. square nearly absent.
9†	high, central	central, to left	
10†	low, to right	low, central	vertical guide-line N.E. square.
11	high, to right	high, central	
		EH	
1a*	low, to right	low, to left	left side line thin.
1b*	low, to right	low, to left	slight traces of re-entry in each upper square; thin "H".
2	central	very high, central	
3	very high, to right	central	
4	central, to left	low, to right	trace of vertical guide-line N.E. square.
5	central	very high, central	top line of N.W. square weak.
6	high, to left	central, to right	trace of vertical guide-line N.E. square.
7†	central, close to left	central	bottom line extends on left; scratches on lower margin.
8†	high, to left	high, to right	
9†	high, central	central, to left	re-entry N.E. and "H" squares, etc.
10†	central, to right	very low, central	squat "H"; left line extends beyond bottom.
11	high, central	central—slopes up	

**Shows the Ray-flaw.* *†Shows the "O"-flaw.*

1a
1b
2
3
4
5
6
7
8
9
10
11

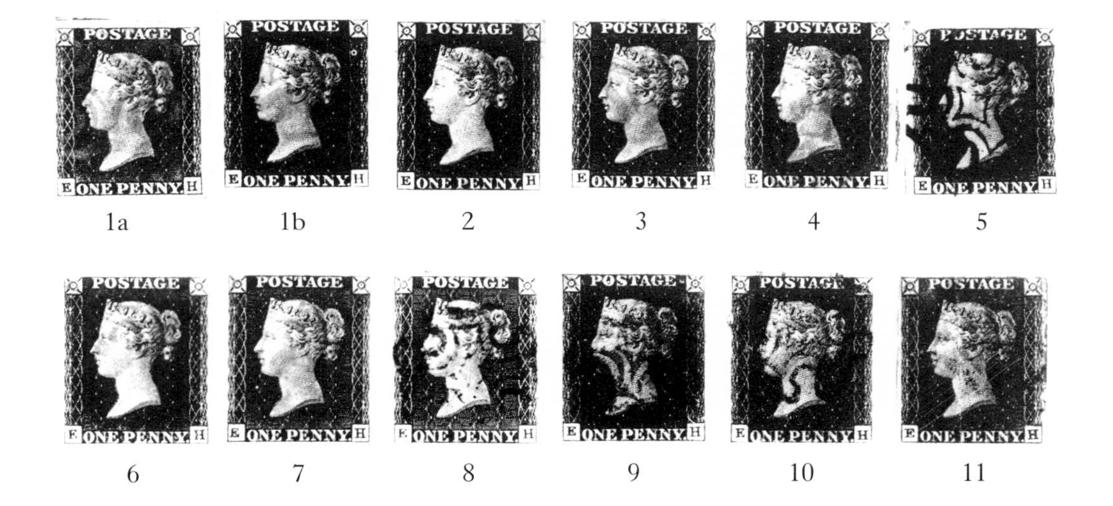
1a
1b
2
3
4
5
6
7
8
9
10
11

Plate.	Position of Corner-letter at left.	Position of Corner-letter at right.	Further distinguishing characteristics.
		EI	
1a*	low, to right	low, central	vertical guide-line N.E. square, close to frame.
1b*	low, to right	low, central	indistinct mark in right of N.W. square; top line of N.W. square thin.
2	central	very low, central	
3	high, to right	central, to left	
4	central	central	trace of vertical scratches outside N.W. square.
5	low, central	central	upper portion of left side weak; vertical guide-line N.E. square, close to frame.
6	high, slightly to left	central, to left	lower portion of right side weak; trace of vertical guide-line N.E. square.
7†	central	low, to right	lower portion of "E" weak.
8†	central	high, central	vertical guide-line N.E. square, wide of frame.
9†	high, central	low, central	vertical guide-line N.E. square, wide of frame; and in "I" square, close to frame.
10†	low, central	high, to right	tall "I"; trace of vertical guide-line in N.E. square, close to frame.
11	high, to right	central	tall "I"; distinct dot in N.W. square.
		EJ	
1a*	central, to right	high, central	letters normal.
1b*	central, to right	high, to right	both letters recut and enlarged; trace of re-entry in each upper square.
2	central, to left	central	lower portion of "E" faint.
3	central	very high, to left	right side line N.E. square thin.
4	low, central	high, to right	vertical guide-line N.E. square.
5	high, to left—slopes down	high, central	top line of N.W. square thin.
6	high, to left	central	vertical guide-line N.E. square.
7†	slightly high, to right	central, to left	top lines of corner-squares thin.
8†	central	high, central	vertical guide-line N.E. square, close to frame.
9†	low, central	high, central	faint vertical guide-line N.E. square, wide of frame.
10†	high, to right	very low, to right	square "J" with stroke after it.
11	low, to right	high, central	square "J".

**Shows the Ray-flaw.*   *†Shows the "O"-flaw.*

1a
1b
2
3
4
5
6
7
8
9
10
11

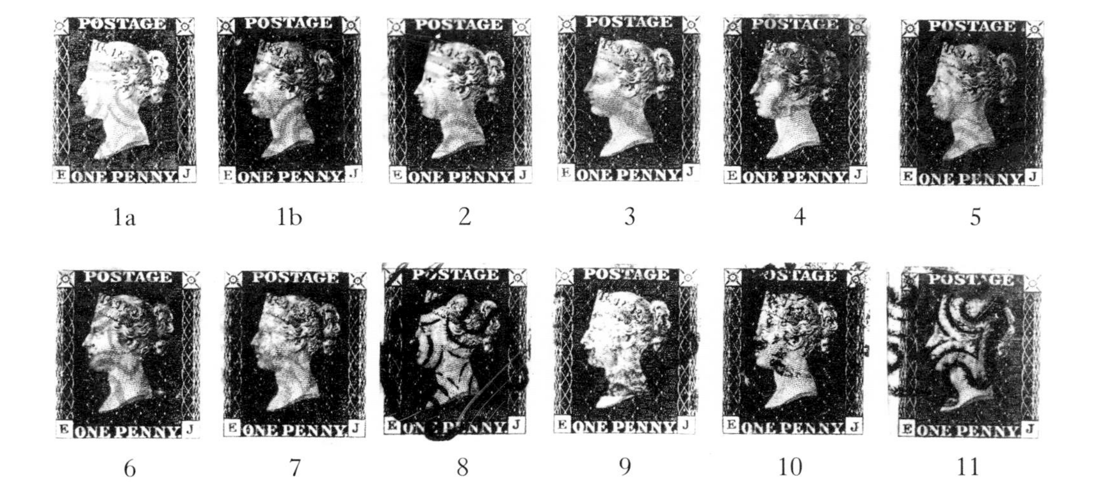
1a
1b
2
3
4
5
6
7
8
9
10
11

Plate.	Position of Corner-letter		Further distinguishing characteristics.
	at left.	at right.	
		EK	
1a*	central, to right	high, central	trace of vertical guide-line N.E. square, very close to frame.
1b*	low, to right	high, to right	both letters recut and enlarged; trace of re-entry through "POSTAGE" and N.E. square.
2	central	central	lower portion of "K" faint.
3	very high, to right	central, to right	scratches on upper and lower margins.
4	low, to left	central, to right	scratches on left margin.
5	central	slightly low, central	top line of N.W. square thin; scratches on margin above N.E. square.
6	high, central	low, to left	dot above "E"; mark in N.E. square; trace of guide-line N.E. square, wide of frame.
7†	central	slightly low, central	bottom line extends slightly on left.
8†	central	central	bottom line extends slightly on right; vertical guide-line N.E. square; side line of N.E. square faint.
9†	very high, to right	central, to left	vertical guide-line N.E. square, wide of frame.
10†	central, to right	central, to right	dot after top of "K".
11	central	slightly low, central	break at left corner of N.E. square.
		EL	
1a*	central, to right	high, slightly to left	right side line extends beyond bottom.
1b*	central, to right	high, slightly to left	right line normal; slight re-entry N.W. square.
2	central, to left	high, to left	two distinct dots below "L" square.
3	central	high, slightly to left	top left ray in N.W. square short; dot outside corner of "L" square.
4	central	central, to right	left and bottom lines cross; indistinct dot outside right of "L" square.
5	central	low, central	slight trace vertical guide-line N.E.; tiny dot below corner of "L" square; left side irregular.
6	central, to left	central	two dots in centre of right star; top line of N.W. square thin.
7†	high, central	low, central	
8†	slightly high, to left	slightly high, to left	tiny dot in corner of "L" square; vertical guide-line N.E. square, wide of frame; horizontal guide-line in "L" square.
9†	high, central	central	
10†	high, to right	central	
11	low, central	high, to right	"L" with short foot; right side extends beyond bottom.

**Shows the Ray-flaw.* *†Shows the "O"-flaw.*

1a
1b
2
3
4
5
6
7
8
9
10
11

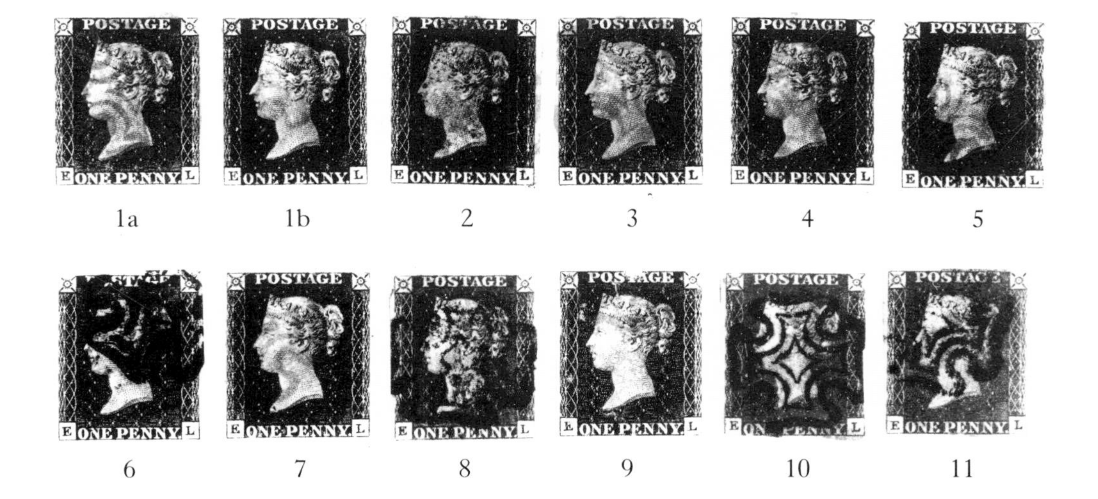
1a
1b
2
3
4
5
6
7
8
9
10
11

Plate.	*Position of Corner-letter*		*Further distinguishing characteristics.*
	at left.	*at right.*	
		FA	
1a*	high, central	low, to right	trace of double "F"; trace of vertical guide-line N.E. square, close to frame.
1b*	high, central	low, to right	trace of double "F"; no guide-line.
2	low, central	central	
3	very low, to left	low, to right	left of bottom serif of "F" long.
4	central, to right	central	distinct dot on top margin between "G" and "E"; guide-line through "NY" of "PENNY", and "A" square; right side of N.E. square thin; vertical guide-line N.E. square.
5	central	low, central	side line of N.E. square almost absent, but normal in second state. In second state the frame-lines have been strengthened or recut; letter "A" faint.
6	central, slightly to left	very low, to right	top line of N.W. square thin; left line extends slightly beyond bottom.
7†	low, central	central, to right	trace of double "F".
8†	central, to left	central	
9†	central	central, to left	bottom line wavy.
10†	low, to right	central	
11	low, to right	central	"A" weak.
		FB	
1a*	high, to right	central, to right	trace of vertical guide-line N.E. square.
1b*	high, to right	central, to right	no guide-line.
2	low, to right	high, to right	
3	central, to left	high, to right	bottom line of "F" square very thin.
4	central, to right	very high, to right	faint vertical guide-line N.E. square, close to frame.
5	low, to left	very low, central	
6	central, to left	central, to right	side line of N.E. square thin; mark in vertical stroke of first "N" of "PENNY".
7†	low, central	low, slightly to left	left of bottom serif of "F" defective.
8†	central, to left	high, central	faint horizontal guide-line in "B" square
9†	very high, to right	high, central	bottom line wavy; vertical guide-line N.E. square; vertical line right side of "B".
10†	central, to right	low, central	vertical guide-line N.E. square.
11	low, to right	central, to right	

**Shows the Ray-flaw.* *†Shows the "O"-flaw.*

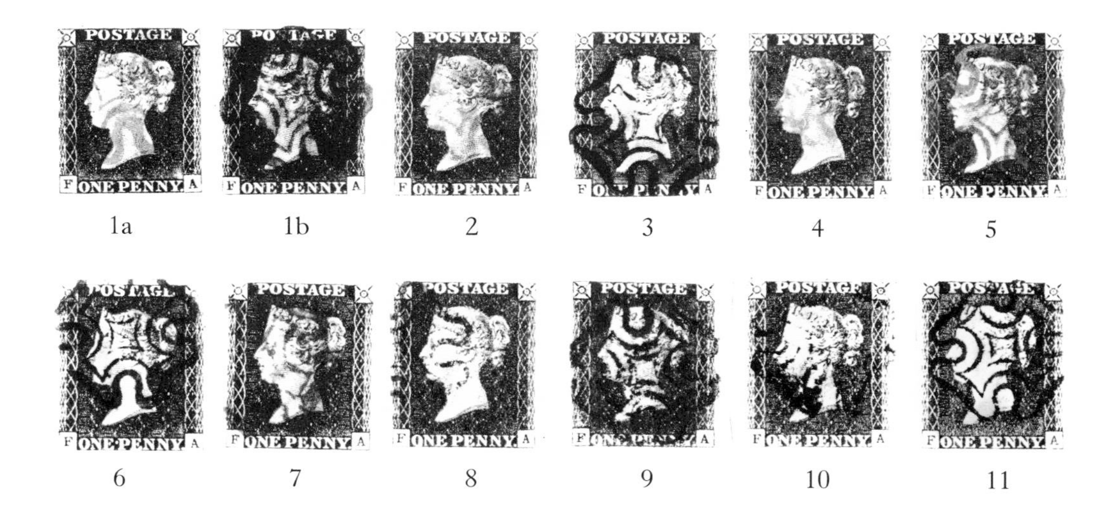
1a
1b
2
3
4
5
6
7
8
9
10
11

1a
1b
2
3
4
5
6
7
8
9
10
11

Plate.	Position of Corner-letter		Further distinguishing characteristics.
	at left.	at right.	
		FC	
1a*	high, central	high, central	
1b*	high, central	high, central	scratches below "F" square and "ONE".
2	low, to left	low, to left	
3	very low, central	central, to left	bottom line of "F" square thin.
4	central, to right	low, to left	dots at left and right of "C".
5	central, to right	high, to left	distinct dot in N.E. square, about middle of left side; faint vertical guide-line N.E. square, wide of frame.
6	central	low, to right	
7†	central	low, to left	
8†	central	high, central	vertical guide-line N.E. square, wide of frame.
9†	central, to left	central, to left	bottom margin wavy; right line extends beyond bottom; vertical guide-line N.E. and "C" squares, very close to frame.
10†	very low, to left	very high, central	horizontal guide-line through "C" square.
11	very high, to right	central, to left	right line extends beyond bottom.
		FD	
1a*	high, central	central, to left	
1b*	high, central	central, to left	"NE" of "ONE" nearly joined; side line of N.E. square weak.
2	high, to right	high, central	right line extends beyond bottom.
3	low, central	central, to right	bottom line of "F" square thin; "F" slightly double.
4	central	high, central	
5	central, to right	high, to right	two vertical guide-lines N.E. square, and horizontal guide-line through "D" square; line below second "N" of "PENNY".
6	central	central	top and left side of N.E. square incomplete.
7†	central, to left	central, to right	faint scratches on margin above. "POS" of "POSTAGE".
8†	central, to right	high, central	faint vertical guide-line N.E. square, wide of frame.
9†	low, central	central, to right	trace of double bottom.
10†	low, central	high, central	left line extends slightly beyond bottom.
11	high, to right	central, to right	

**Shows the Ray-flaw.* *†Shows the "O"-flaw.*

1a
1b
2
3
4
5
6
7
8
9
10
11

1a
1b
2
3
4
5
6
7
8
9
10
11

Plate.	*Position of Corner-letter*		*Further distinguishing characteristics.*
	at left.	*at right.*	
		FE	
1a*	central	central, to right	
1b*	central	central, to right	slight weakness at left corner of N.W. square; scratches at point of "F" square.
2	central, to right	central	
3	low, to right	very high, to right	bottom line of "F" square thin; scratches on lower margin.
4	central, to right	low, central	tiny dot in "E" of "POSTAGE"; slight smudge in N.W. square.
5	central	central, slightly to left	top line of corner-squares thin.
6	central	low, to right	top line of N.W. square thin.
7†	central, to left	low, to left	
8†	high, to right	central	right line of N.E. square thin.
9†	high, to right	high, to right	vertical guide-line N.E. square, close to frame; bottom line wavy. Without "O"-flaw in second state.
10†	low, to right	very low, central	
11	high, to right	high, to right	
		FF	
1a*	central, to left	central	
1b*	central, to left	central	mark in bottom serif of "E" of "PENNY".
2	high, to right	high, central	
3	central, to right	low, to right	top line of N.E. square thin.
4	low, to right	central	right line of N.E. square thin; scratches below "ONE".
5	low, central	central, to right	first "F" with left bottom serif long.
6	central	rather low, central	top and side lines of N.E. square thin.
7†	central, to right	high, to left	faint scratches on lower margin.
8†	central	high, not so far to left	right line of N.E. square thin.
9†	high, central	central	horizontal guide-line in first "F" square; vertical guide-line in N.E. and "F" squares, close to frame; bottom line slightly wavy.
10†	central, to right	high, central	
11	high, to right	very high, central	

**Shows the Ray-flaw.*   *†Shows the "O"-flaw.*

1a
1b
2
3
4
5
6
7
8
9
10
11

1a
1b
2
3
4
5
6
7
8
9
10
11

Plate.	*Position of Corner-letter*		*Further distinguishing characteristics.*
	at left.	*at right.*	
		FG	
1a*	central	high, to left	frame-lines perfect; vertical guide-line N.E. square, very close to frame.
1b*	central	high, to left	"E" of "POSTAGE" nearly runs into top margin; scratches left margin; side line of N.E. square thin.
2	high, central	central	trace of double letter "G".
3	central, to right	very low, to left	left side complete.
4	very low, central	high, central	
5	low, central	very low, to left	faint trace of vertical guide-line N.E. square.
6	low, central	high, to left	
7†	low, to right	high, slightly to left	
8†	high, central	high, central	trace of guide-line through each letter N.E. square.
9†	central	high, close to left	bottom line wavy.
10†	low, central	low, central	trace of vertical guide-line N.E. square.
11	central, to right	very low, to left	upper portion of left side weak; break at left of N.E. square.
		FH	
1a*	central	low, to left	serifs of "H" nearly touch; vertical guide-line N.E. square.
1b*	central	low, to left	serifs of "H" wider apart; no guide-line; right side of N.E. square thin.
2	central	low, central	
3	high, to right	high, slightly to left	
4	central	central, slightly to right	left side extends slightly beyond bottom.
5	low, central	very high, to left	left side weak; top line of N.W. square weak on right; scratch on margin below "ONE".
6	central	high, to left	side line of N.E. square weak.
7†	central	rather high, slightly to right	small mark on left of "H" square.
8†	central	very high, to right	trace of guide-line through "F" square.
9†	high, central	high, to right	trace of guide-line through "F" square.
10†	low, to right	low, to right	squat "H"; right line of N.E. square thin.
11	high, to right	central	

**Shows the Ray-flaw.* *†Shows the "O"-flaw.*

1a
1b
2
3
4
5
6
7
8
9
10
11

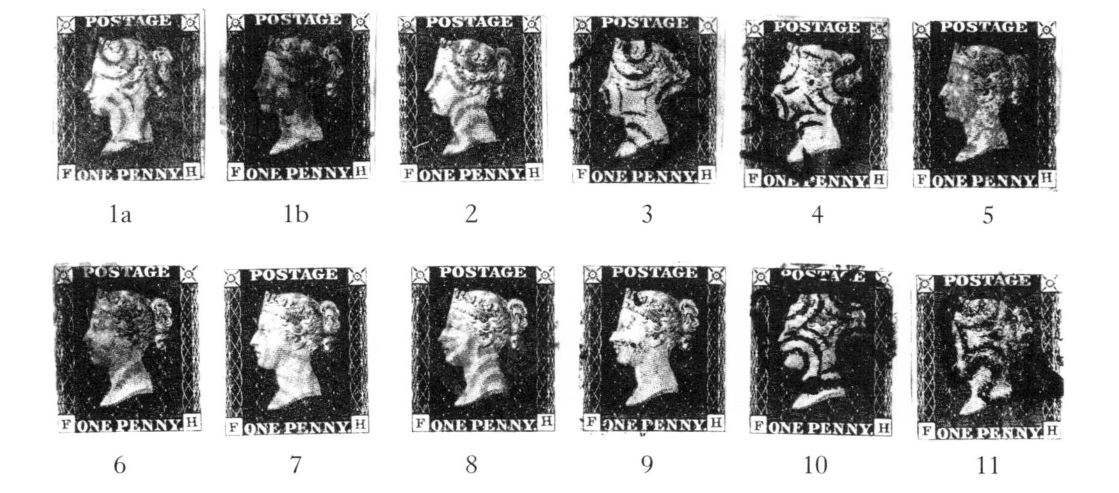
1a
1b
2
3
4
5
6
7
8
9
10
11

Plate.	*Position of Corner-letter*		*Further distinguishing characteristics.*
	at left.	*at right.*	
		FI	
1a*	high, to right	low, central	"F" distinctly double; vertical guide-line N.E. square.
1b*	high, to right	low, central	similar, but trace of missing ray.
2	central, to right	central, to left	tiny dot below corner of "I" square.
3	high, to right	central, to left	bottom line of "I" square thin.
4	central	central	right line of N.E. square weak.
5	central	low, to left	faint vertical guide-line N.E. square; scratch below "ONE".
6	central, to left	low, to left	left corner of N.E. square weak. In second state the frame-lines have been strengthened or recut.
7†	central, to right	central	thin stroke runs from foot of "I" to side line; top serif of "I" is weak on left.
8†	high, to right	high, central	bottom line extends slightly on right; vertical guide-line N.E. square, very close to frame.
9†	high, to left	high, central	trace of guide-line through upper portion of value.
10†	low, central	high, to right	tall "I".
11	very high, to right	low, to right	tall "I"; bottom line extends on right.
		FJ	
1a*	slightly low, to right	central, to left	trace of guide-line N.E. square, close to frame. Top line extends on left.
1b*	slightly low, to right	central, to left	top line extends on left.
2	high, to right	high, central	
3	very high, to right	very high, central	dot below "O" of "ONE".
4	central, to right	high, central	colour extends slightly below frame-line between "O" of "ONE" and letter-square.
5	central, to right	central, to left	top line of N.W. square thin; vertical guide-line N.E. square, wide of frame.
6	central, to left	high, to left	mark at base of "E" of "ONE".
7†	central, to left	high, to left	faint horizontal line through "F" square extending to "O" of "ONE".
8†	high, to right	low, to left	
9†	very high, to right	very high, to left	faint vertical guide-line N.E. square, close to frame.
10†	low to left	high, to right	square "J"; faint vertical guide-line N.E. square, close to frame.
11	high, to right	high, to right	square "J"; dot outside top line of N.W. square.

**Shows the Ray-flaw.* †*Shows the "O"-flaw.*

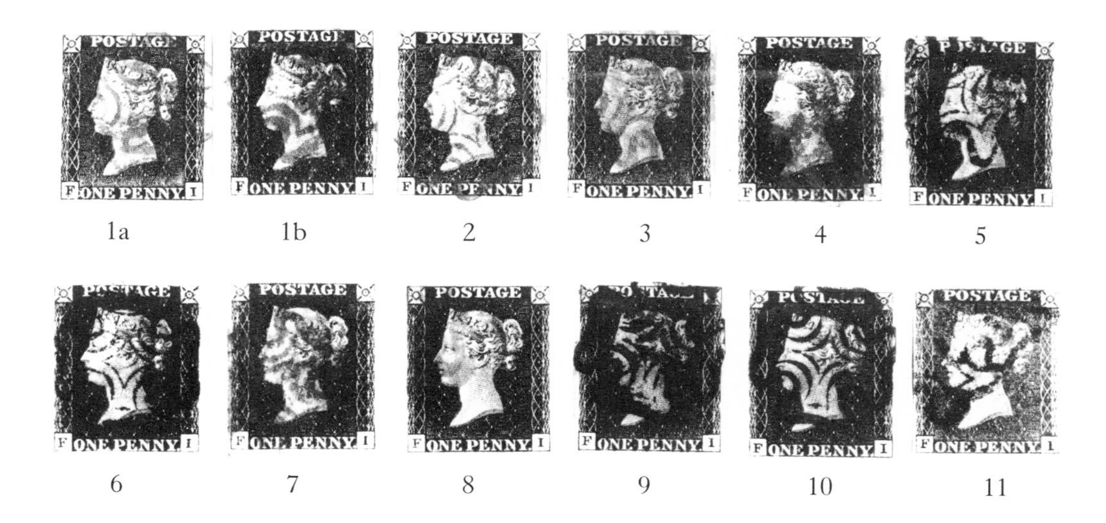
1a
1b
2
3
4
5
6
7
8
9
10
11

1a
1b
2
3
4
5
6
7
8
9
10
11

Plate.	*Position of Corner-letter*		*Further distinguishing characteristics.*
	at left.	*at right.*	
		FK	
1a*	central	central, to left	very faint guide-line N.E. square.
1b*	central	central, to left	"E" of "POSTAGE" nearly into top margin; very faint vertical guide-line N.E. square.
2	high, central	low, to right	bottom line slightly wavy.
3	low, to right	central—touches left	dot on margin between "O" and "N" of "ONE".
4	central, to right	central	lower portion of left side weak.
5	central, to right	high, central	top line of N.W. square thin.
6	central, to left	low, central	top serif of "K" double; distinct dot in N.E. square.
7†	very low, to right	central	
8†	central, to right	central	
9†	high, central	low, to left	vertical guide-line N.E. square, wide of frame.
10†	high, to right	high, to right	vertical guide-line N.E. square.
11	central	high, central	
		FL	
1a*	central	high, central	very faint vertical guide-line N.E. square; faint dot below "L".
1b*	central	high, central	faint dot below "L".
2	high, central	high, to left	bottom line slightly wavy.
3	central, to right	central, slightly to left	
4	high, to right	high, central	dot in left side of "F" square.
5	high, to right	low, to left	two short scratches through bottom line of "L" square; also through "F" square, and in margin below "ONE".
6	central, slightly to left	central, slightly to left	top line of N.W. square almost absent; scratches on bottom margin.
7†	central, slightly to right	low, to left	scratches above stamp.
8†	high, to right	central, to left	trace of dot in corner of "L" square; right side line extends slightly beyond bottom.
9†	very high, central	low, to left	bottom line slightly wavy.
10†	low, to right	rather high, far to right	left side line extends slightly beyond bottom; faint vertical guide-line in "L" square, close to frame; and in N.E. square, wide of frame.
11	low, central	central, far to right	dot above N.W. square.

Shows the Ray-flaw.　　†Shows the "O"-flaw.

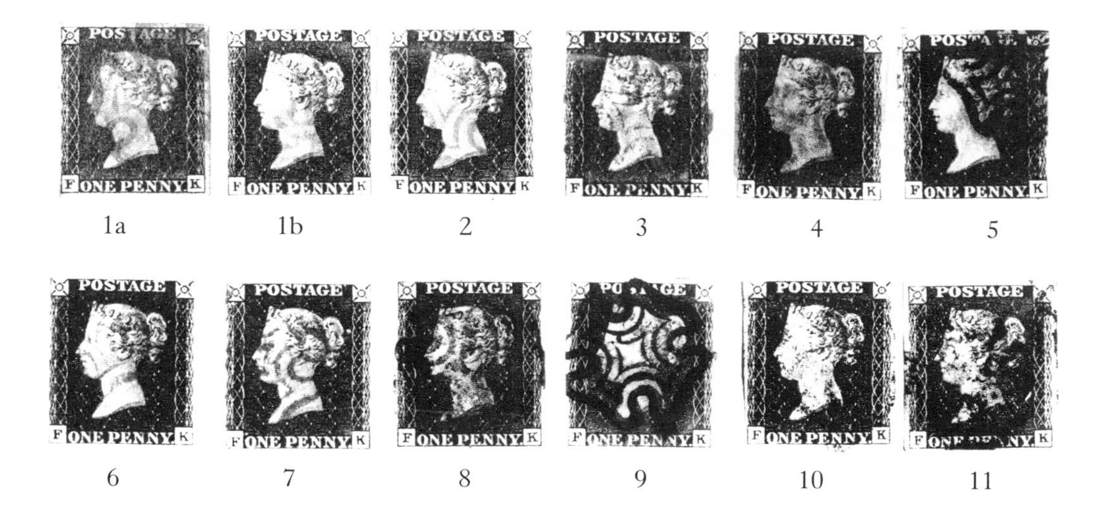
1a
1b
2
3
4
5
6
7
8
9
10
11

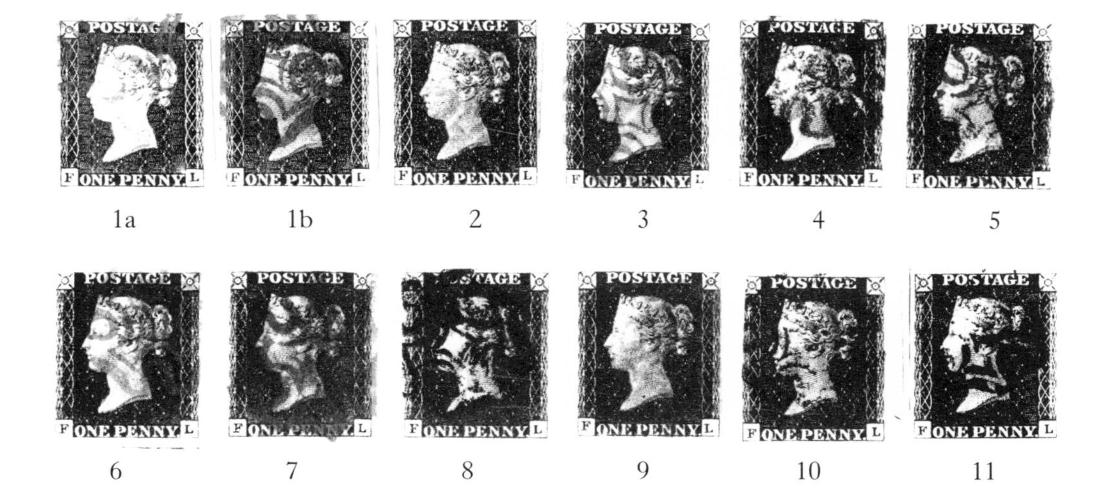
1a
1b
2
3
4
5
6
7
8
9
10
11

Plate.	Position of Corner-letter at left.	Position of Corner-letter at right.	Further distinguishing characteristics.
		GA	
1a*	central	central	
1b*	central	central	slight re-entry "E" of "POSTAGE" and N.E. square; scratches on top and left margins.
2	high, central	central, to left	
3	central	central—slopes down	
4	central	low, to left	minute dot above "A"; side line of N.E. and N.W. squares weak.
5	low, to left	low, central	right side extends slightly beyond bottom.
6	high, to left	central, to right	"G" partly faint; vertical guide-line N.E. square, close to frame; left side extends slightly beyond bottom.
7†	high, to left	central, to left	diagonal blur or stroke joined to foot of "G".
8†	high, to left	central, to left	faint vertical guide-line N.E. square wide of frame.
9†	high, to right	high, to left	vertical guide-line N.E. square, close to frame, and "A" square, wide of frame; bottom line slightly wavy.
10†	central	central	vertical guide-line N.E. square, wide of frame.
11	high, to right	low, slightly to right	bottom line extends on right.
		GB	
1a*	high, central	central, to right	left side line weak.
1b*	high, central	central, to right	left side line recut; curved line through "N" of "ONE".
2	low, to left	high, to right—slopes down	
3	low, central	high, to right	left side line complete.
4	high, central	slightly low, to left	trace of horizontal guide-line below "B" square.
5	central, to left	central	bottom line wavy.
6	high, to left	central, to right	top line of N.E. square weak.
7†	slightly high, to left	central	scratches on bottom margin.
8†	high, to left	central, to left	
9†	low, to left	central	
10†	central	high, central	faint vertical guide-line N.E. square.
11	low, central	central	

**Shows the Ray-flaw.* *†Shows the "O"-flaw.*

1a
1b
2
3
4
5
6
7
8
9
10
11

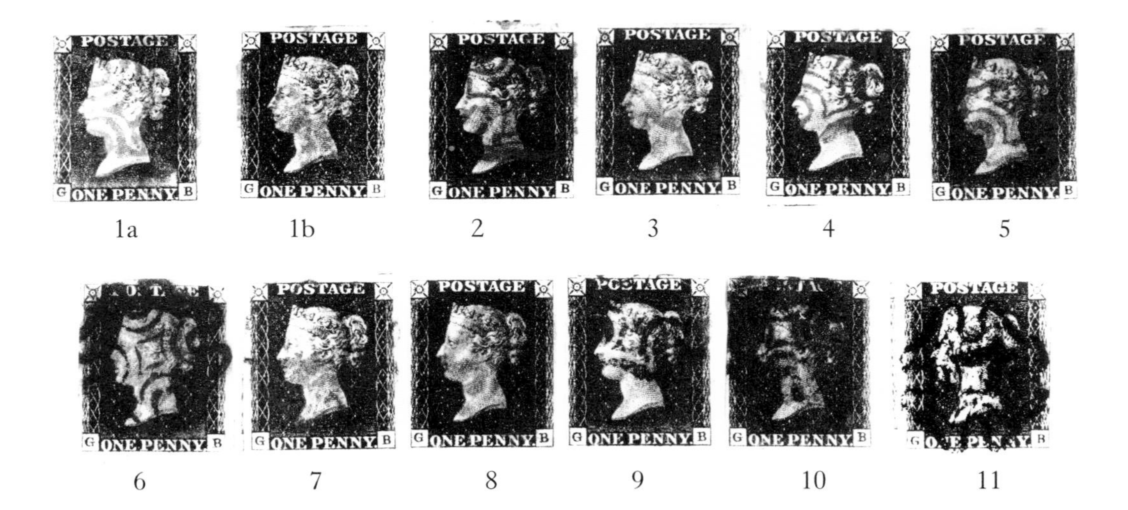
1a
1b
2
3
4
5
6
7
8
9
10
11

Plate.	Position of Corner-letter at left.	Position of Corner-letter at right.	Further distinguishing characteristics.
		GC	
1a*	high, to left	high, to left	corner-letters normal.
1b*	high, to left	central, to left	"C" in a different position; top line of N.W. square faint; "ONE PENNY" thinner.
2	central	central, to left	bottom line wavy.
3	low, central	high, to left	bottom line of "G" square thin.
4	high, to right	central, to left	two minute indistinct dots on margin, outside top of "C" square; very faint guide-line N.E. square, close to frame.
5	central, to left	low, to left	top lines of upper squares thin.
6	high, to left	central, slightly to left	vertical guide-lines N.E. and N.W. squares.
7†	high, to left	very high, to left	right side prolonged slightly into margin below N.E. square.
8†	high, to left	central	
9†	low, to right	high, to left	vertical guide-line N.E. and "C" squares.
10†	central	slightly high, to left	
11	slightly low, central	slightly high, to left	
		GD	
1a*	low, to left	high, central	right side line perfect.
1b*	low, to left	high, central	trace of horizontal guide-line through "G" square; right side weak near top.
2	high, to left	central	
3	low, central	central, to right	
4	slightly high, to left	central, far to right	right and bottom side lines cross; dot in top margin above "A".
5	central	very high, to right	trace of two vertical guide-lines N.E. square.
6	high, to left	very low, central	top line of upper corner-squares thin.
7†	central, to left	central	scratches on margin below "NNY".
8†	slightly high, to left	low, central	blur on upper left side margin.
9†	central, to left	high, to right	vertical guide-line N.E. square.
10†	central, to right	high, to right	dot in N.E. square near top.
11	very low, central	very low, slightly to left	

**Shows the Ray-flaw.* *†Shows the "O"-flaw.*

1a
1b
2
3
4
5
6
7
8
9
10
11

1a
1b
2
3
4
5
6
7
8
9
10
11

Plate.	Position of Corner-letter		Further distinguishing characteristics.
	at left.	at right.	
		GE	
1a*	high, to left	low, well to right	right side line perfect.
1b*	high, to left	low, well to right	side line of N.E. square weak; faint horizontal guide-line through "G" square.
2	central, to left	high, central	stamps seen have appearance of thumbprint on lower right in margin.
3	central	high, central	left side line extends beyond bottom; bottom line of "G" square thin.
4	high, to right	high, slightly to left	side line of N.E. square defective; dot in second "N" of "PENNY".
5	low, central	central, to left	faint vertical guide-line N.E. square.
6	high, to left	high, to left	indistinct diagonal line joins "G" to top of square; slight weakness in lower curve of "G".
7†	high, to left	low, central	
8†	high, to left	high, central	without "O"-flaw in second state.
9†	low, central	very low, to left	vertical guide-line, N.E. square, very close to frame.
10†	low, central	central, to right	
11	central, to right	high, to right	
		GF	
1a*	low, to left	central	faint guide-line on margin below value and "F" square.
1b*	low, to left	central	minute dot above "G"; left side line re-cut for greater part of its length.
2	high, to left	central	dot on margin between "E" and "P".
3	central, to left	central, to right	
4	high, slightly to left	central	bottom line extends slightly beyond right.
5	low, to left	slightly low, to right	vertical guide-line N.E. square, wide of frame; left side line extends beyond bottom; scratches below "G" square.
6	high, to left	low, slightly to left	margin of N.W. blurred; vertical guide line N.E. square, close to frame.
7†	high, to right	high, to left—slopes down	long horizontal stroke to "G".
8†	high, well to left	central	side line of N.E. square slightly weak.
9†	central	central, to left	vertical guide-line N.E. square, very close to frame; right side line extends slightly beyond bottom.
10†	low, central	central, to left	vertical guide-line N.E. square.
11	central, to right	high, to right	

**Shows the Ray-flaw.* *†Shows the "O"-flaw.*

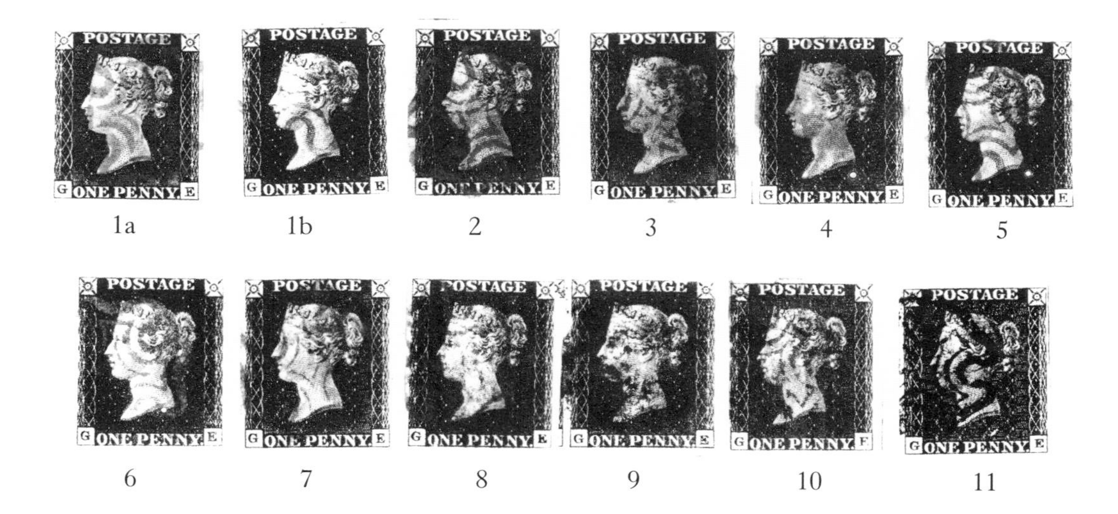
1a 1b 2 3 4 5
6 7 8 9 10 11

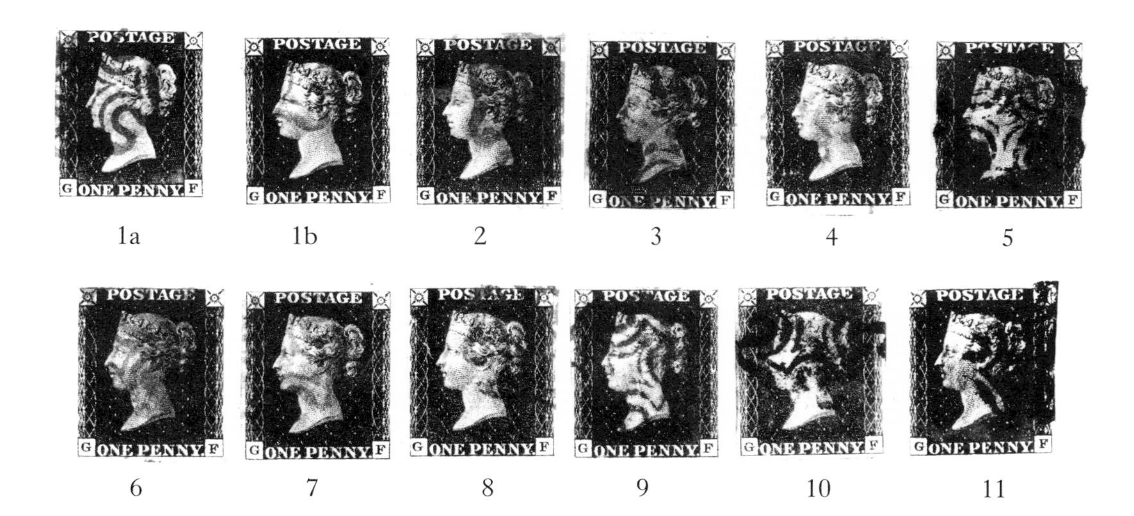
1a 1b 2 3 4 5
6 7 8 9 10 11

Plate.	Position of Corner-letter		Further distinguishing characteristics.
	at left.	at right.	
		GG	
1a*	low, to right	high, to left	
1b*	low, to right	high, to left	"E" of "PENNY" runs nearly into bottom margin.
2	central	high, to left	
3	low, central	central, to right	bottom line of first "G" square thin; also left side line of N.W. square.
4	high, to right	high, central	vertical guide-line N.E. square faint; stroke or blur above first "G"; side line of N.E. square thin.
5	central, to left	low, to left	top line of N.W. square thin; very faint vertical guide-line N.E. square, close to frame; left side line irregular.
6	high, central	low, to left	top line of N.E. square defective.
7†	central	high, to left	
8†	high, central	high, central	
9†	central	central, to right	vertical guide-line N.E. square; and through second "G" square, but wider.
10†	central	low, to left	
11	central	central	
		GH	
1a*	low, to left	low, slightly to left	
1b*	low, to left	low, slightly to left	letter "H" thin.
2	slightly high, to right	rather high, to right	dot on lower part of right side margin.
3	central, to left	rather high, central	
4	high, to right	rather low, central	very faint vertical guide-line N.E. square, very close to frame; faint line on margin below "P" of "PENNY".
5	low, central	central, to left	top line of N.W. square thin.
6	very high, to left	high, to right	
7†	high, to left	high, central	
8†	high, to left	high, to right	trace of vertical guide-line N.E. square, very close to frame.
9†	central, to right	central, to right	blur on margin outside N.W. square.
10†	low, central	slightly high, to right	very faint vertical guide-line N.E. square; squat "H".
11	central	low, central	

*Shows the Ray-flaw. †Shows the "O"-flaw.

1a
1b
2
3
4
5
6
7
8
9
10
11

1a
1b
2
3
4
5
6
7
8
9
10
11

Plate.	Position of Corner-letter at left.	Position of Corner-letter at right.	Further distinguishing characteristics.
		GI	
1a*	low, central	low, central	double "I".
1b*	low, central	low, central	double "I"; foot of "I" not so complete; top line of N.W. square thin.
2	high, to left	central, slightly to left	minute dot left side of lower ray in N.W. square.
3	central	central, to left	bottom line of "G" square thin.
4	central, to right	central, to left	bottom line of "G" square thick.
5	high, to right	low, to left	bottom line extends on right.
6	high, to left	low, to left	small but distinct dot below "G"; minute dot to right of "I".
7†	very high, central	central, far to right	
8†	high, to left	central, slightly to left	side line of N.E. square thin; bottom line extends slightly on right.
9†	central, to right	low, central	
10†	high, central	central, to right	tall "I"; very faint vertical guide-line N.E. square, close to frame.
11	high, to right	central, to right	tall "I".
		GJ	
1a*	high, central	high, to left	distinct scratch or guide-line below on right
1b*	high, central	high, to left	faint scratches on lower margin.
2	high, central	central, to left	
3	high, to left	central	
4	low, to right	high, slightly to left	left side line almost absent, but extends beyond bottom.
5	low, to left	central, to left	right side line of "J" square appears to be recut, and extends beyond bottom; scratches in N.E. square.
6	high, to left	low, to left	tiny dot in "G" square, near centre of right side.
7†	high, slightly to left	high, to left	
8†	high, to left	very high, central	
9†	high, to left	very low, to left	vertical guide-line N.E. square, close to frame.
10†	central	high, central	square "J", its serif slightly double.
11	central	high, to right	square "J".

**Shows the Ray-flaw.* *†Shows the "O"-flaw.*

1a
1b
2
3
4
5
6
7
8
9
10
11

1a
1b
2
3
4
5
6
7
8
9
10
11

Plate.	*Position of Corner-letter*		*Further distinguishing characteristics.*
	at left.	*at right.*	
		GK	
1a*	central, to left	high, to left	
1b*	low, central	central, to right	each letter shifted; re-entry N.W. square, etc.
2	low, to left	slightly low, central	dot below corner of "K" square; vertical stroke of "K" slightly defective.
3	high, to left	central, to left	
4	central, to right	central, to right	side line of N.E. square defective; left foot of "K" defective.
5	central, to right	low, to left	right side very weak; top line of N.W. square thin.
6	high, to left	central, very close to left	scratches below, on right.
7†	high, to right	central	both side lines extend beyond bottom, that on the right side sometimes interrupted, but connecting with stamp below.
8†	high, to left	central, close to left	left side line extends beyond bottom.
9†	very low, central	central	very faint vertical guide-line N.E. square, very close to frame.
10†	high, central	central, to right	
11	central	low, central	
		GL	
1a*	high, central	high, to left	right side line extends beyond bottom.
1b*	high, central	high, to left	re-entry N.W. square and each letter square.
2	central, slightly to right	slightly high, to left	tiny dot in "L" square, about middle of right side.
3	high, to left	central	
4	high, to left	high, central	blurred line below "NY" of "PENNY"; scratch down right side.
5	central	low, to left	left side very irregular.
6	high, to left	central	several dots in "G" and "L" squares.
7†	high, to right	low, to left	dot in "L" square touching bottom line.
8†	high, to left	central, to left	
9†	central, to left	central	
10†	very low, central	very low, central	vertical guide-line N.E. square, wide of frame.
11	central, to right	high, to right	

**Shows the Ray-flaw.* *†Shows the "O"-flaw.*

1a
1b
2
3
4
5
6
7
8
9
10
11

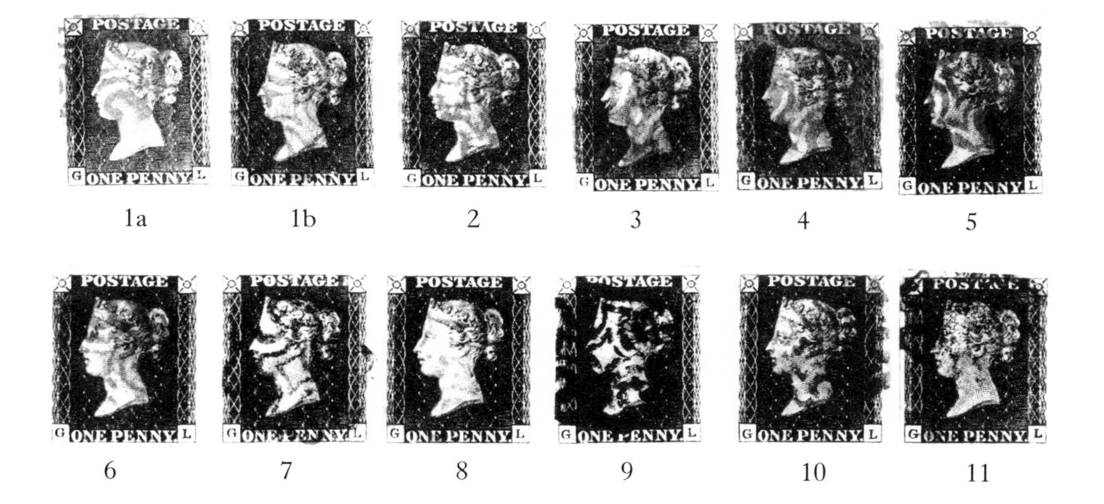
1a
1b
2
3
4
5
6
7
8
9
10
11

Plate.	Position of Corner-letter at left.	Position of Corner-letter at right.	Further distinguishing characteristics.
		HA	
1a*	low, to left	central, to right	distinct scratch or guide-line on lower margin; small dot in upper part of "H".
1b*	low, to left	central, to right	faint scratches left side margin; small dot in upper part of "H".
2	central, to right	central	small dot in "A" square; and larger dot below; "H" defective or faint.
3	very high, to right	central	trace of double "H"; left line extends beyond bottom.
4	high, slightly to right	rather high, central	bottom line extends slightly on right.
5	high, to left	rather low, central	dot in corner of "A" square; faint vertical guide-line N.E. square, close to frame.
6	high, to right	high, to right	guide-line through "E" of "ONE" and partly through "PENNY".
7†	very high, to left	central	"O" of "ONE" cuts nearly into lower margin.
8†	high, to left	low, central	"A" blurred on left; faint vertical guide-line N.E. square, very close to frame.
9†	central	rather high, central	vertical guide-line N.E. and "A" squares, very close to frame; and through "H" square and "ON" of "ONE".
10†	central, to right	low, slightly to right	trace of double "H"; vertical guide-line N.E. square, close to frame.
11	low, central	high, to right	"H" defective on left; faint guide-line through "H" square.
		HB	
1a*	low, to left	rather low, to right	fine re-entry each upper square, and through "H" and "ONE PENNY"; left side line thin.
1b*	low, to left	rather low, to right	fine re-entry, as before; lower part of right side line double.
2	central, to right	central, slightly to right	
3	low, to left	high, to right	bottom line of letter-squares thin.
4	high, nearly touching right	central, to left	horizontal line above N.W. square; dot below "B" square; side line of N.E. square thin.
5	high, to left	central, to right	"H" slightly double.
6	rather high, to right	central, slightly to right	dot under "H".
7†	high, to left	central	faint scratches top and bottom margins.
8†	very high, to left	central, to right	
9†	very low, central	central, to right	trace of double "H".
10†	rather high, to right	low, central	both side lines extend slightly beyond bottom.
11	low, central	very high, far to right	letter "B" small; top line of N.E. square thin with vertical guide-line, wide of frame.

**Shows the Ray-flaw.* *†Shows the "O"-flaw.*

1a 1b 2 3 4 5
6 7 8 9 10 11

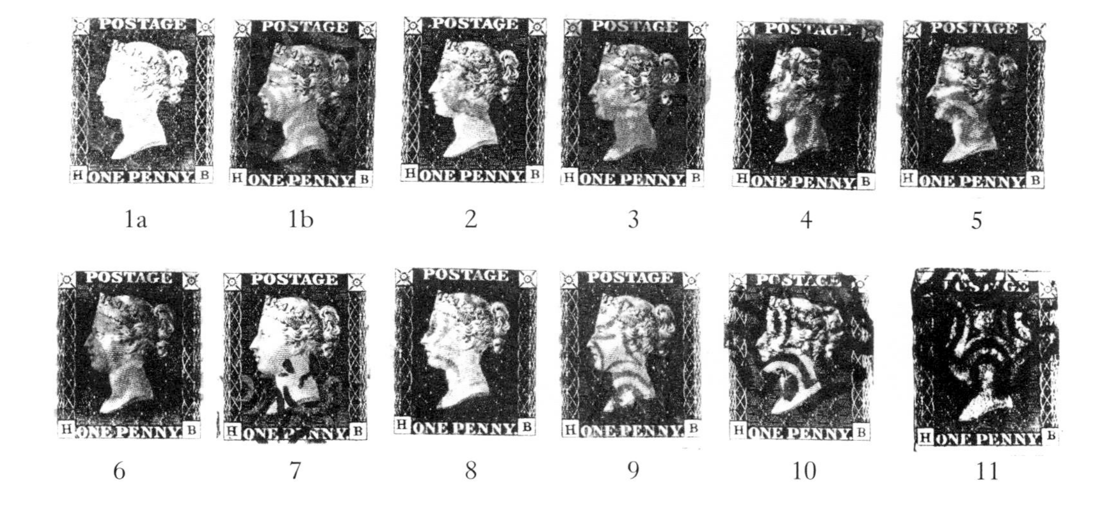
1a 1b 2 3 4 5
6 7 8 9 10 11

Plate.	*Position of Corner-letter*		*Further distinguishing characteristics.*
	at left.	*at right.*	
		HC	
1a*	low, to left	central, to left	left side line thin.
1b*	low, to left	central, to left	left side line strengthened.
2	central, to right	very low, to left	bottom line extends on right.
3	low, to right	high, to left	faint scratches on left margin.
4	low, to right	central, to left	bottom line extends slightly on right.
5	very high, to left	rather low, to left	vertical guide-line N.E. square, wide of frame.
6	central, to right	very low, to left	vertical guide-line N.E.; also through "C" square, but closer to frame.
7†	high, to left	high, to left	
8†	slightly high, slightly to left	low, slightly to left	vertical guide-line N.E. square; scratches on left margin.
9†	central, slightly low	high, to left	horizontal guide-line "H" square.
10†	high, to right	very high, central	trace of vertical guide-line N.E. square, close to frame; "H" defective on right.
11	low, to left	central, to left.	
		HD	
1a*	rather low, to left	high, central	fine re-entry each upper square, and through value; left side line thin.
1b*	rather low, to left	high, central	similar, but left side line strengthened
2	low, to right	rather low, slightly to right	tiny dot below "D" square; also seen with faint guide-line through top of "PENNY".
3	central, to right	central, to right	N.E. square weak at left corner.
4	very low, to right	central	right line extends beyond bottom.
5	high, to left	high, slightly to right	trace of vertical guide-line N.E. square, close to frame; scratches on right side margin.
6	high, to right—slopes up	high, to right	
7†	central, to left	central	scratches below stamp.
8†	high, slightly to left	central, to left	
9†	central, to right	low, far to right	
10†	high, to right	very high, to right	vertical guide-line N.E. square, wide of frame.
11	central, to right	central, to right	horizontal guide-line through value.

**Shows the Ray-flaw.* *†Shows the "O"-flaw.*

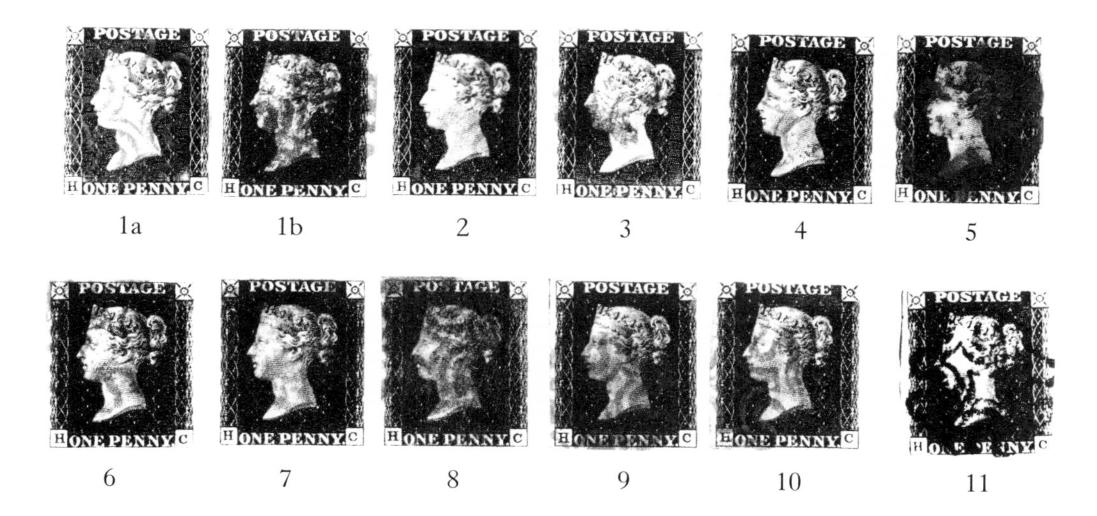
1a
1b
2
3
4
5
6
7
8
9
10
11

1a
1b
2
3
4
5
6
7
8
9
10
11

Plate.	Position of Corner-letter at left.	Position of Corner-letter at right.	Further distinguishing characteristics.
		HE	
1a*	central, to left	low, to right	
1b*	central, to left	low, to right	shows trace of missing ray.
2	central, to right	very high, to right	lower part of "E" faint; dot below "E" square.
3	high, to right	high, to right	
4	high, to right	central, to left	tiny dot above "E"; dot in "Y"; dots on lower margin below "PE" of "PENNY".
5	high, to left	high, central	"H" distinctly double.
6	central, to right	central	left side irregular; horizontal stroke below "H" square.
7†	high, central	rather high, central	
8†	high, to right	central	bottom line extends on right. No flaw in second state.
9†	low, central	low, to left	vertical guide-line N.E. and "E" squares, close to frame; horizontal guide-line through "H" square and value, very close to frame.
10†	central	low, central	right side line of N.E. square defective.
11	low, to right	central	
		HF	
1a*	low, to left	central, to left	
1b*	low, to left	central, to left	left side line thicker than on plate 1a; shows trace of missing ray.
2	high, to right	central, slightly to left	
3	low, to right	low, central	plate dot left margin opposite lower lip.
4	very low, to right	central	dot after "H"; bottom line extends on right.
5	high, to left	very high, to right	dot below second "N" of "PENNY".
6	central, to right	low, to left	bottom line extends towards left, but not constant.
7†	very high, to left	central	very faint scratches on right side margin.
8†	high, slightly to right	central	bottom line extends on right.
9†	high, to left	low, to left	right line extends slightly beyond bottom; very faint scratches top right margin.
10†	central, to right	rather high, central	faint trace of guide-line on left of N.W. square.
11	low, to right	high, to left	

**Shows the Ray-flaw.* *†Shows the "O"-flaw.*

1a
1b
2
3
4
5
6
7
8
9
10
11

1a
1b
2
3
4
5
6
7
8
9
10
11

Plate.	Position of Corner-letter at left.	Position of Corner-letter at right.	Further distinguishing characteristics.
		HG	
1a*	low, to left	high, to left	distinct scratch or guide-line on lower margin, close to frame.
1b*	low, to left	high, to left	left side line strengthened.
2	central	central	
3	central, to right	low, to left	faint mark at base of "Y" of "PENNY".
4	central, to right	central, to left	
5	central, slightly to left	high, to left	trace of vertical guide-line N.E. square; scratches on lower margin.
6	rather high, to right	slightly high, central	right side line extends slightly beyond bottom.
7†	rather high, to left	rather high, to left	
8†	high, to left	high, to left	vertical guide-line N.E. square, close to frame.
9†	high, to right	central, to left	
10†	central, to right	low, to left—slopes down	faint vertical guide-line N.E. square, very close to frame.
11	low, to left	high, to left	
		HH	
1a*	low, to left	low, to left	
1b*	low, to left	low, to left	faint mark above left side of second "H".
2	low, to right	high, to right—slopes up	
3	high, to right	high, slightly to right	mark at base of "Y"; seen with scratches in left margin
4	central, to right	high, central	mark on margin above corner of N.E. square; bottom line extends slightly on right.
5	central	high, to left	horizontal stroke below first "H" square.
6	central, to right	central, to right	horizontal and vertical guide-lines N.E. square; tiny dot in corner of second "H" square.
7†	high, central	slightly high, central	
8†	high, central	high, central—slopes up	vertical guide-line N.E. square, close to frame.
9†	central	rather high, central	horizontal guide-line through first "H" square.
10†	central, to right	low, central	
11	high, central	high, to left	second "H" defective on left; guide-line through first "H" square.

**Shows the Ray-flaw.* *†Shows the "O"-flaw.*

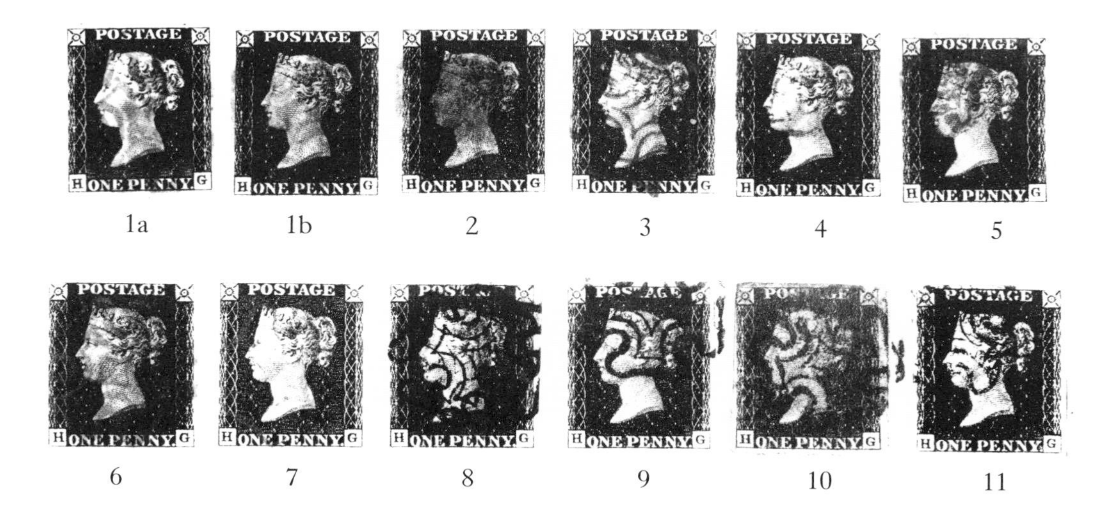
1a 1b 2 3 4 5
6 7 8 9 10 11

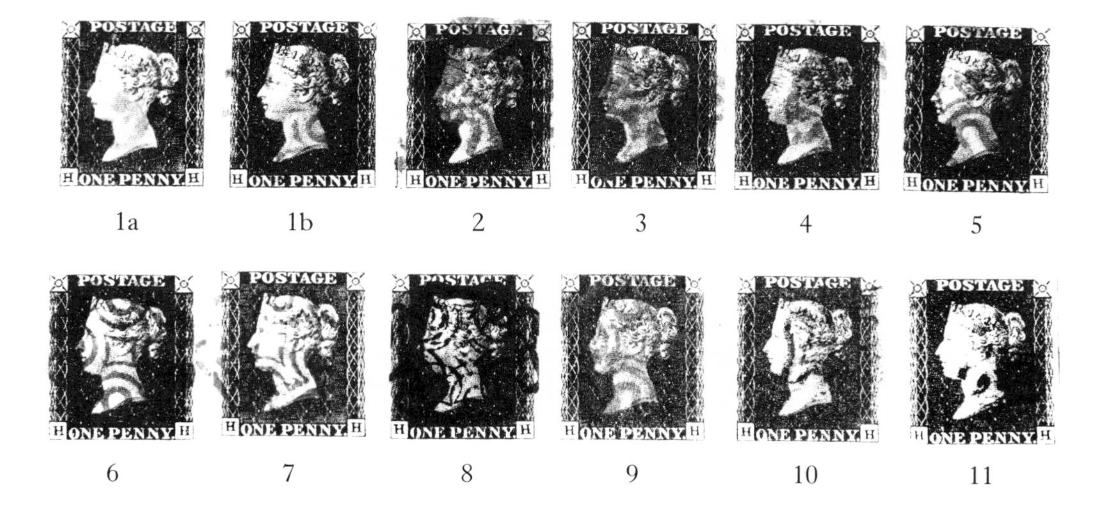
1a 1b 2 3 4 5
6 7 8 9 10 11

Plate.	Position of Corner-letter at left.	Position of Corner-letter at right.	Further distinguishing characteristics.
		HI	
1a*	low, to left	low, central	
1b*	low, to left	low, central	side line of N.E. square thin.
2	rather low, central	central	
3	low, to right	central, to left	
4	high, to right	central, to left	top line of N.E. square weak.
5	high, central	very low, close to left	"H" partly double.
6	very high, to right	central, to left	tiny dot below "H".
7†	high, central	low, slightly to left	
8†	high, to left	high, central	vertical guide-line N.E. square.
9†	very low, to left	low, slightly to left	
10†	central, to right	low, to right	tall "I".
11	central	central, to right	tall "I"; very faint guide-line from "H" square to "I" square, very close to bottom line.
		HJ	
1a*	rather low, to left	central, to left	
1b*	rather low, to left	central, to left	right side line thinner than on plate 1a; scratches on top margin.
2	central, to left	central	left side line complete.
3	central, to right	high, to left	
4	low, to right	rather high, central	right line extends faintly above.
5	central, slightly to left	central	left side irregular; side line of N.E. square weak.
6	high, central	rather high, to left	several tiny dots in "H" square; also faint guide-line close to side line.
7†	rather high, central	central	bottom line extends on left.
8†	high, central	central, to left	
9†	central, to left	very high, to left	"J" nearly square; side line of N.E. square weak.
10†	low, to right	central, to left	square "J".
11	very low, to left	high, central	square "J".

**Shows the Ray-flaw.* *†Shows the "O"-flaw.*

POSTAGE
H ONE PENNY I
1a
1b
2
3
4
5
6
7
8
9
10
11

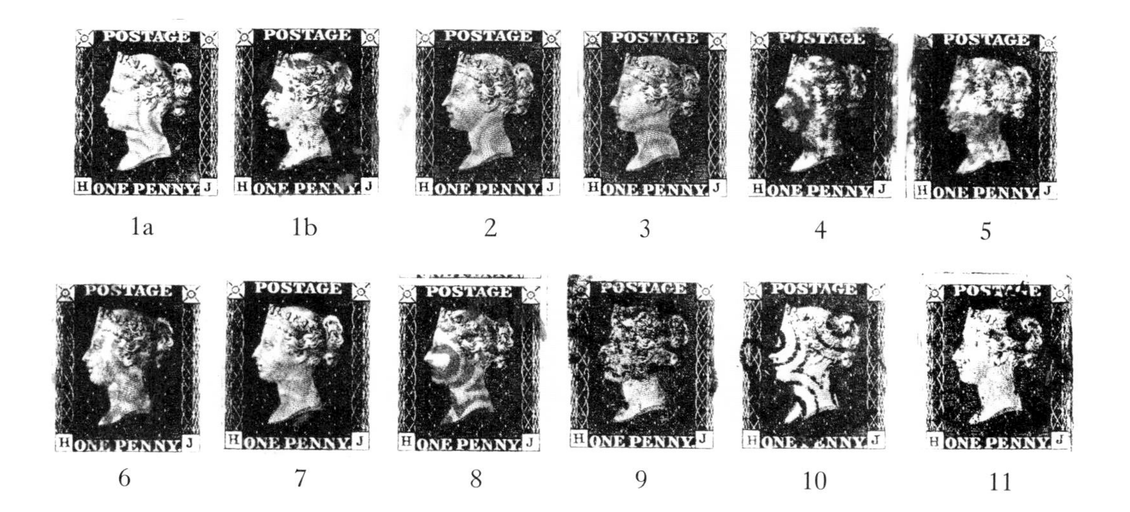
POSTAGE
H ONE PENNY J
1a
1b
2
3
4
5
6
7
8
9
10
11

Plate.	Position of Corner-letter at left.	Position of Corner-letter at right.	Further distinguishing characteristics.
		HK	
1a*	low, to left	very low, close to left	
1b*	low, to left	very low, close to left	fine re-entry each upper square; guide-line left side of "H"; dots left side of "K".
2	central	central	trace of guide-line below "H" square.
3	high, central	high, to left	frame-lines of lower left square do not quite join.
4	low, slightly to right	central	bottom line extends on right; left line extends slightly beyond bottom.
5	high, central	rather low, to left	trace of horizontal guide-line through value.
6	rather high, to right	central, well to left	left side irregular; tiny dot opposite foot of "K".
7†	rather high, to right	central, slightly to left	right line, extends upwards, joining to stamp above.
8†	high, slightly to left	central, to left	right line extends above; scratches on right margin.
9†	central, to left	low, to left	vertical guide-line N.E. and "K" squares; trace of horizontal guide-line through value and "K" square.
10†	rather high, to right	high, to right	
11	high, to right	central, to right	
		HL	
1a*	low, to left	high, central	tiny dot below corner of "L" square.
1b*	low, to left	high, central	"H" square distinctly broken at corner; value running nearly into margin.
2	low, central	high, to left	fine re-entry each upper square and value; loop at top of "H"; dot below "H".
3	very high, to right	central	
4	very low, to right	low, central	faint vertical guide-line in "L" square.
5	high, to left	central, to left	
6	central	central	tiny dot above "H", and below "L"; faint vertical guide-line N.E. square.
7†	high, to right	central, to left	scratches on lower margin; also on right side margin.
8†	central	central, to left	dot in corner of "L" square; two dots on margin touching line, above "H" square.
9†	low, far to left	rather high, central	
10†	high, to right	very low, well to right	faint vertical guide-line N.E. square, very close to frame.
11	central	very high, far to right	

**Shows the Ray-flaw.* *†Shows the "O"-flaw.*

1a 1b 2 3 4 5
6 7 8 9 10 11

1a 1b 2 3 4 5
6 7 8 9 10 11

Plate.	Position of Corner-letter		Further distinguishing characteristics.
	at left.	at right.	
		IA	
1a*	low, to right	central, slightly to right	dot in corner of "A" square; dot at point outside "I" square.
1b*	low, to right	central, slightly to right	dot in S.E. corner of "A" square; line at right letter-square weak; vertical stroke through lower part of N.E. square.
2	central	slightly low, to right	vertical guide-line N.E. square, close to frame; dot in "A" square different position from plate 1.
3	central, to left	central, to left	right line extends beyond bottom.
4	slightly low, central	slightly high, central	three small dots after "A"; left line extends slightly beyond bottom.
5	low, central	very low, central	top line of N.W. square weak; vertical guide-line N.E. square, close to frame; minute dots before "I" and after "A".
6	central, slightly to left	central, to right	dot on vertical stroke of "P" of "POSTAGE".
7	central	central	
8†	central	slightly high, central	bottom line extends slightly on right; faint vertical guide-line N.E. square, very close to frame.
9†	central	central	minute dot above "I"; horizontal guide-line partly through lower half of "I" square.
10†	high, to right	high, to right	right side line extends beyond bottom; tall "I".
11	low, central	high, to right	tall "I".
		IB	
1a*	low, central	slightly low, to right	
1b*	low, central	slightly low, to right	re-entry each upper square; marks in "P" of "POSTAGE" and "O" of "ONE".
2	low, central	central, to right	thin vertical stroke connected to top of "I"; vertical guide-line N.E. square, close to frame.
3	central	high, to right	
4	low, to left	slightly high, to left	minute dot in front of "B", and two dots after it; side line of N.E. square thin.
5	central	slightly low, to left	vertical guide-line N.E. square, wide of frame; top line of N.W. square, and side of N.E. square thin.
6	central, very slightly to left	central, slightly to right	vertical and horizontal guide-lines N.E. square; dot in corner of "I" square.
7	central, slightly to left	central, rather more to right than 6	vertical guide-line N.E. square; dot joined to line below "B" square.
8†	slightly high, slightly to left	central	faint vertical guide-line N.E. square.
9†	high, slightly to right	slightly low, to right	faint vertical guide-line N.W. square.
10†	low, central	low, to right	tall "I".
11	high, to right	high, slightly to right	top of N.W. square weak; tall "I".

**Shows the Ray-flaw.* *†Shows the "O"-flaw.*

1a 1b 2 3 4 5
6 7 8 9 10 11

1a 1b 2 3 4 5
6 7 8 9 10 11

Plate.	Position of Corner-letter at left.	Position of Corner-letter at right.	Further distinguishing characteristics.
		IC	
1a*	low, slightly to right	slightly high, central	line under "C" square thick.
1b*	low, slightly to right	slightly high, central	minute dot in front of top part of "I"; vertical line through ray in N.E. square; bottom line of "C" square thin.
2	high, slightly to right	high, to left	vertical guide-line N.E. square.
3	central, to right	central, to left	right line extends slightly beyond bottom; very faint horizontal guide-line through bottom of "C" square.
4	slightly low, to right	very low, to left	two dots in front of "I", and several in "C" square; top line of N.E. square defective.
5	slightly low, central	central, to left	
6	slightly low, to left	central, slightly to left	faint guide-line left side of "C"; top line of N.E. square thin.
7	central, slightly to left	central, rather close to left	very faint guide-lines N.W. and N.E. squares.
8†	rather high, slightly to left	central	
9†	central, slightly to left	high, to left	
10†	slightly low, to right	very high, slightly to left	tall "I".
11	slightly low, to right	central, to left	tall "I".
		ID	
1a*	low, to right	high, to left	
1b*	low, to right	high, to left	fine, re-entry each upper corner, and through value.
2	central	central, slightly to right	mark in right side of "O" of "ONE".
3	central, to left	high, to right	
4	slightly low, to left	central, to right	several dots in each letter-square; right side line extends beyond bottom.
5	low, central	high, to right	foot of "I" defective on right; right side line extends beyond bottom.
6	low, to left	central	
7	central, to left	slightly low, to right	
8†	slightly low, slightly to right	central, slightly to right	faint scratches on top right margin.
9†	high, to right	high, central	trace of guide-line on right of "I" square.
10†	very low, central	high, to right	trace of vertical guide-line N.W. square; tall "I".
11	central, to right	very high, to right	bottom line extends on right; tall "I".

**Shows the Ray-flaw.* *†Shows the "O"-flaw.*

1a
1b
2
3
4
5
6
7
8
9
10
11

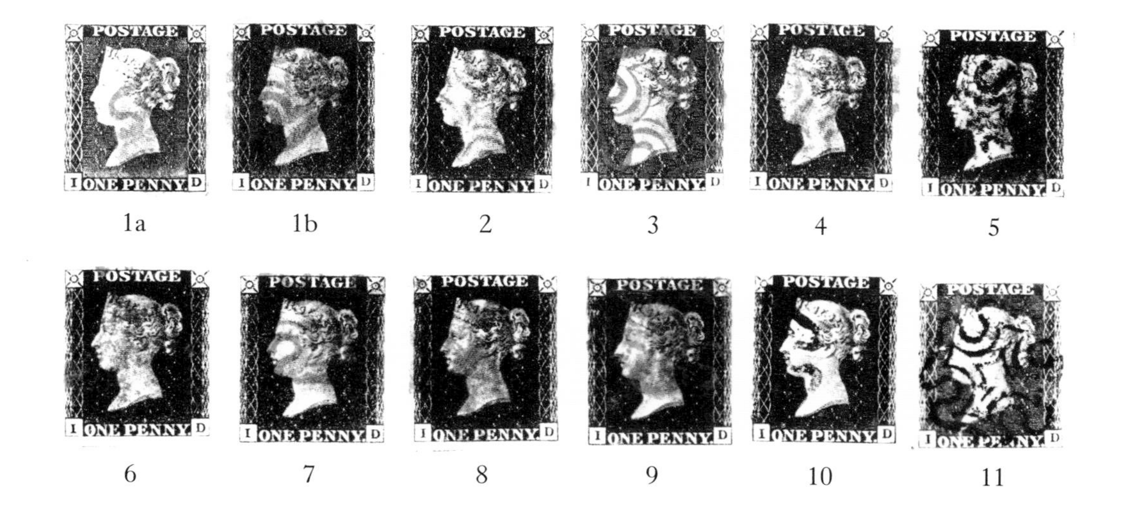
1a
1b
2
3
4
5
6
7
8
9
10
11

Plate.	Position of Corner-letter		Further distinguishing characteristics.
	at left.	at right.	
		IE	
1a*	low, central	low, to right	
1b*	low, central	low, to right	trace of scratch above "POSTAGE"; horizontal stroke through lower part of N.E. square.
2	low, to left	low, to left	bottom line extends on right.
3	very low, to left	very high, slightly to left	mark close to line at left of "E" square.
4	low, central	very high, to right	"I" square recut, above and below.
5	low, to right	high, slightly to right	"E" of "PENNY" runs nearly into bottom.
6	central, to left	very low, central	left side very weak; trace of vertical guide-line in lower part of N.E. square, very close to frame.
7	central	high, close to left	bottom line extends very slightly on right.
8†	high, central	central, to left	diagonal blur through "E"; very faint vertical guide-line N.E. square, very close to frame.
9†	low, central	high, to left	
10†	high, to right	low, central	side line of N.E. square weak; tall "I".
11	central, to right	high, to right	left side weak; dot joined to outside line of "I" square; tall "I".
		IF	
1a*	low, central	high, to left	
1b*	low, central	high, to left	horizontal and vertical strokes through lower part of N.E. square.
2	central, to right	slightly high, to left	trace of double serif at top of "I".
3	high, to left	low, to left	top line of N.W. and N.E. squares thick.
4	central	central	left corner of N.E. square very weak; dot below "E" of "ONE".
5	central, to right	slightly low, central	top line of N.W. square thin.
6	high, to left	low, to left	both sides weak, especially towards top.
7	central, to left	slightly high, to left	bottom line extends on right.
8†	central	rather high, central	
9†	low, central	high, slightly to left	
10†	low, to left	central	tall "I"; faint scratches N.W. square.
11	high, to right	high, to right	tall "I"; lines of N.W. square weak; side line N.E. square weak; horizontal guide-line through value and "F" square.

**Shows the Ray-flaw.* *†Shows the "O"-flaw.*

1a
1b
2
3
4
5
6
7
8
9
10
11

1a
1b
2
3
4
5
6
7
8
9
10
11

Plate.	Position of Corner-letter		Further distinguishing characteristics.
	at left.	at right.	
		IG	
1a*	low, to right	very high, to left	left side line weak.
1b*	low, to right	very high, to left	horizontal guide-line through "G" square; left side line strengthened.
2	low, central	high, to left	
3	very low, slightly to left	central, slightly to left	
4	central	high, to right	scratches right of top margin.
5	low, central	high, to left	left side weak; blur in N.W. square; horizontal guide-line through "I" square.
6	high, central	high, to left	side line of N.E. square weak.
7	central	high, to left	
8†	low, to right	high, to left	frame-line on right appears double.
9†	low, to right	slightly low, to left	
10†	low, slightly to left	high, central	tall "I"; top line of N.W. square thin; right side line extends slightly beyond bottom.
11	low, central	central	tall "I".
		IH	
1a*	low, central	low, to left	left side line weak.
1b*	low, central	low, to left	left line recut; lower half of side-line of N.E. square missing.
2	low, to left	very high, central	
3	high, central	high, slightly to left	trace of horizontal guide-line through "H" square.
4	low, central	high, slightly to left	top line of N.E. square thin.
5	low, central	central, to left	
6	central	high, to left	distinct dot in lower half of "H".
7	central	high, close to left	left stroke of "H" weak.
8†	high, central	high, to right	blur on top left margin.
9†	low, to left	high, to left	scratches on right side margin.
10†	low, central	very low, to right	tall "I"; squat "H".
11	high, to left	low, central	tall "I"; horizontal guide-line through "H" square.

**Shows the Ray-flaw.* *†Shows the "O"-flaw.*

1a
1b
2
3
4
5
6
7
8
9
10
11

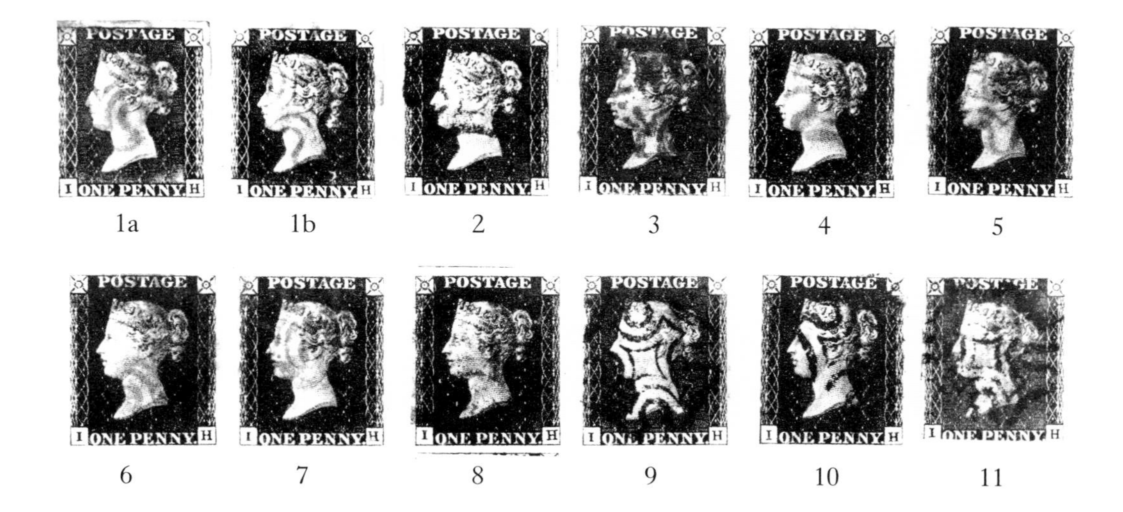
1a
1b
2
3
4
5
6
7
8
9
10
11

Plate.	Position of Corner-letter		Further distinguishing characteristics.
	at left.	at right.	
		II	
1a*	low, central	low, to right	left side line weak.
1b*	low, central	low, to right	left side recut; upper portion of right side weak; horizontal and vertical strokes through lower part of N.E. square.
2	high, central	slightly low, to left	
3	high, central	high, to right	
4	very low, slightly to left	slightly low, to left	left line extends beyond bottom.
5	low, to right	very high, to left	faint marks or scratches below "ONE".
6	slightly low, central	slightly low, central	minute dot N.E. corner of second "I" square; guide-line N.E. square close to frame.
7	central	slightly low, central	side line of N.E. square not quite so thick; faint scratches top margin.
8†	high, to right	slightly high, central	mark at right side of N.E. square.
9†	slightly low, to left	low, to left	
10†	high, to right	low, to left	each "I" tall.
11	low, central	very high, to right	horizontal guide-line through letter-squares and value; each "I" tall.
		IJ	
1a*	low, central	high, central	left side line weak.
1b*	low, central	high, central	left side line re-cut.
2	central	low, central	
3	slightly low, to left	high, to left	
4	slightly low, to left	high, to left	dot top right of "I" square.
5	low, central	very high, central	trace of horizontal guide-line in "I" square, very close to frame; faint scratches below "E" of "PENNY".
6	central	high, central	tiny dots below "I", and to right of "J"; also near top of N.E. square; seen with scratches under "ONE".
7	high, to left	very low, to left	right side extends beyond bottom.
8†	central, slightly to right	high, to left	
9†	very low, to left	very low, to left	
10†	slightly low, to right	very low, central	tall "I" and square "J"; mark side of "J".
11	slightly low, to right	slightly high, central	tall "I" and square "J".

**Shows the Ray-flaw.* *†Shows the "O"-flaw.*

1a
1b
2
3
4
5
6
7
8
9
10
11

1a
1b
2
3
4
5
6
7
8
9
10
11

Plate.	Position of Corner-letter		Further distinguishing characteristics.
	at left.	at right.	
		IK	
1a*	low, central	high, central	frame-lines perfect.
1b*	low, central	high, central	side line of N.E. square almost absent.
2	high, to left	central	"K" somewhat faint.
3	high, to right	central, to left	very faint guide-line through value.
4	slightly low, central	central, to right	bottom line very thick.
5	central, to left	high, slightly to left	bottom line extends on left.
6	high, to left	low, slightly to left	mark below "E" and "P".
7	central, slightly to left	central	scratches top margin; vertical guide-line in upper part of right side margin.
8†	central, to right	central, to left	
9†	low, central	low, central	vertical guide-line N.E. square, very close to frame; scratches top margin.
10†	high, to right	very low, to right	tall "I"; scratches on bottom margin.
11	central, to right	central	tall "I".
		IL	
1a*	low, central	high, central	
1b*	low, to left	central	both letters recut, and much enlarged; two dots below "L" square; slight re-entry each upper square.
2	high, to right	high, central	distinct dot after top part of "L".
3	low, to right	high, to left	dot in lower corner of "L" square; top serif of "I" slopes slightly downwards.
4	low, central	central, to right	tiny dot below corner of "L" square; top line of N.E. square weak at left.
5	low, to left	slightly high, to left	right side line irregular.
6	central	central	several tiny dots in "L" square; dot outside top of N.E. square.
7	central	central, to left	
8†	high, central	high, to left	
9†	very low, central	central	
10†	central	low, central	tall "I".
11	central, to right	central, to right	tall "I".

*Shows the Ray-flaw. †Shows the "O"-flaw.

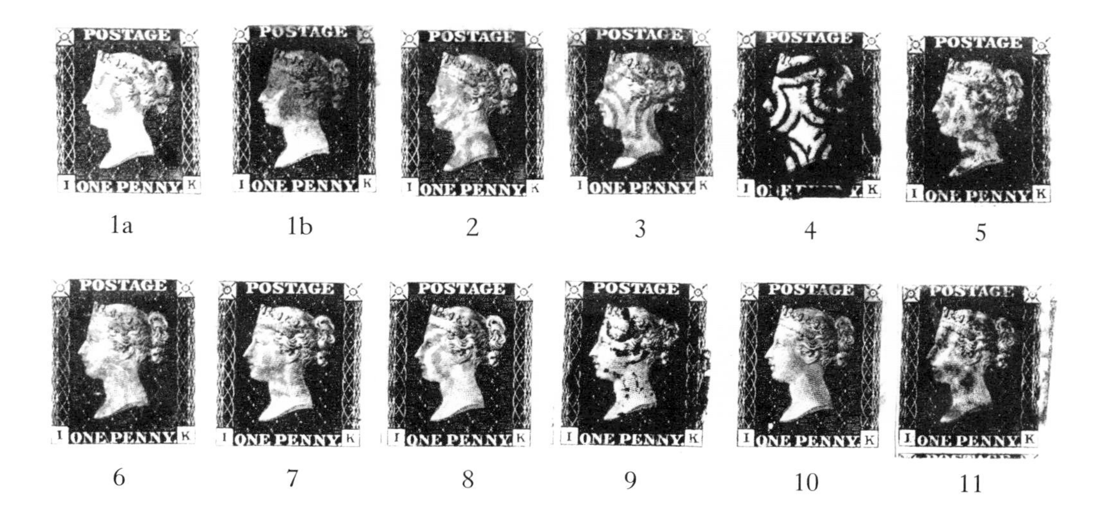
1a
1b
2
3
4
5
6
7
8
9
10
11

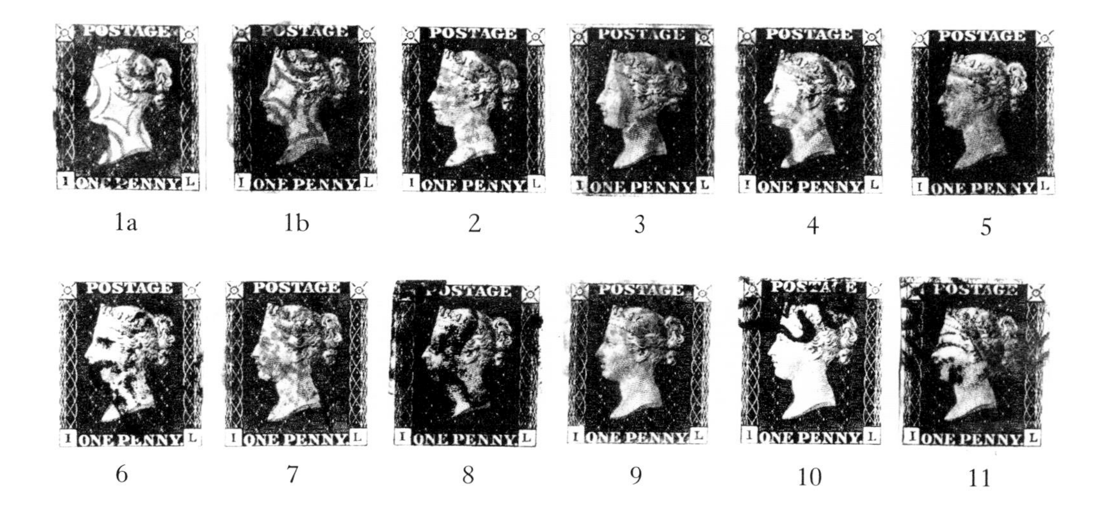
1a
1b
2
3
4
5
6
7
8
9
10
11

Plate.	Position of Corner-letter at left.	Position of Corner-letter at right.	Further distinguishing characteristics.
		JA	
1a*	low, to left	low, to right	blurred "A".
1b*	low, to left	low, to right	vertical stroke through centre of N.E. star; trace of extra outer line on left; horizontal guide-line through N.E. square.
2	high, central	low, central	bottom line of letter-squares double, and extends on left.
3	very high, central	central	faint horizontal guide-line in "A" square.
4	high, central	low, to right	tiny dot in right of N.W. square; dots under "E" and "P" (lower).
5	central, to left	low, to right	tiny dot on margin below "Y" scratches on margin below and scratch outside N.E. square.
6	slightly low, to left	central, to right	vertical guide-line N.E. square, close to frame; dot after "J".
7	central—slopes down	central	
8†	high, central	central, to left	
9†	central, to left	high, central	"J" nearly square.
10†	high, to right	high, central—slopes down	square "J"; trace of guide-line through value.
11	high, to right	high, central	square "J"; bottom line extends on right.
		JB	
1a*	central	slightly low, slightly to right	
1b*	central	slightly low, slightly to right	vertical stroke through N.E. star; horizontal guide-line through top portion of "J" square.
2	high, central	high, to right	bottom line extends on left.
3	high, central	central, to right	bottom line of "J" square thin.
4	central, to left	slightly high, central	several tiny dots on bottom margin.
5	very low, central	central, to right	side line of N.E. square weak; right side line extends beyond bottom; left side line absent.
6	central	low, central	
7	high, to left	central, to right	very faint scratch in middle of right side margin.
8†	high, to right	central	
9†	low, to left	high, central	"J" nearly square.
10†	high, central	very low, to right	square "J".
11	high, to right	central, to right	square "J".

**Shows the Ray-flaw.* *†Shows the "O"-flaw.*

1a
1b
2
3
4
5
6
7
8
9
10
11

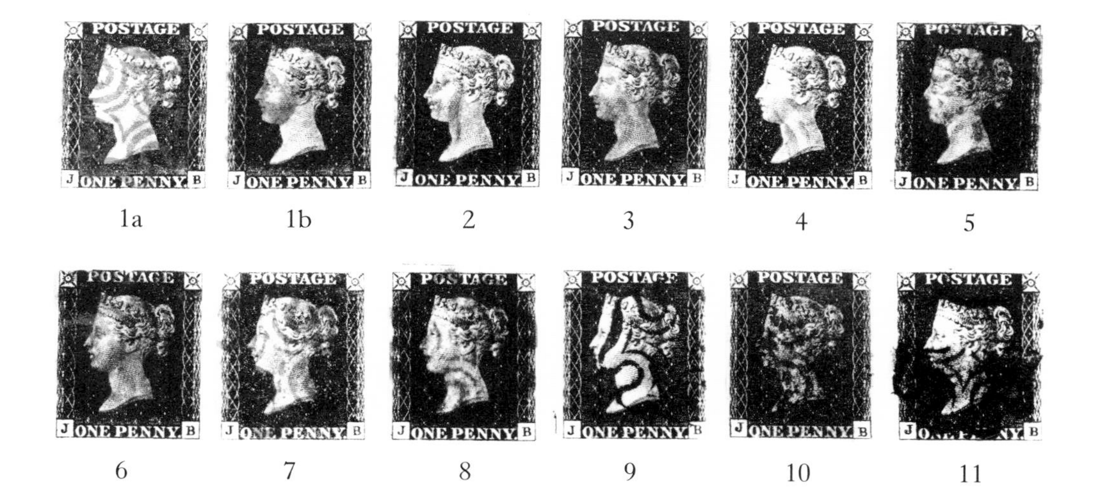
1a
1b
2
3
4
5
6
7
8
9
10
11

Plate.	Position of Corner-letter		Further distinguishing characteristics.
	at left.	at right.	
		JC	
1a*	high, central	low, to left	
1b*	central	high, central	both letters recut and shifted; traces of re-entry N.W. square.
2	very high, central	very high, to left	bottom lines of letter-squares appear double; dot in corner of "C" square.
3	high, to left	very high, to left	side line of N.E. square not quite so thick.
4	central	very low, to left	tiny dot in left of N.W. square; several tiny dots above and below.
5	low, to left	low, to left	
6	high, to left	high, central	upper part of left side line irregular.
7	high, to left	central, to left	
8†	high, to right	high, central	
9†	very high, central	very high, to left	"J" nearly square.
10†	high, to right	central	square "J".
11	high, to right	central—slopes down	square "J".
		JD	
1a*	high, central	high, central	
1b*	high, central	high, central	vertical guide-line through centre of N.E. star; very faint vertical guide-line at side of "J".
2	central, to right	high, to left	"E" of "PENNY" runs nearly into bottom margin; top curve of "D" faint.
3	very high, to right	central	horizontal guide-line partly through value.
4	central, to left	central	dot in "Y" and above "D", also above "T" of "POSTAGE".
5	very low, to left	high, to right	side line of N.E. square thinner.
6	high, to left	high, to right	
7	high, central	very low, central	
8†	high, slightly to left	high, central	mark N.W. square.
9†	central	high, central	horizontal guide-line through value, and faint vertical guide-line N.E. square close to frame; "J" nearly square.
10†	low, central	high, to left	square "J".
11	high, to right	slightly low, to right	square "J".

**Shows the Ray-flaw.* *†Shows the "O"-flaw.*

1a
1b
2
3
4
5
6
7
8
9
10
11

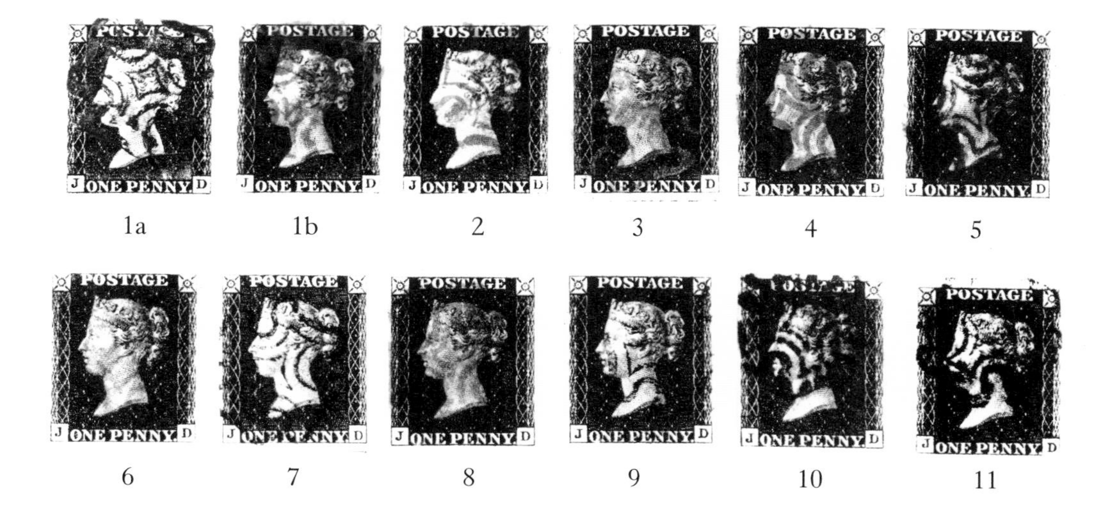
1a
1b
2
3
4
5
6
7
8
9
10
11

Plate.	Position of Corner-letter		Further distinguishing characteristics.
	at left.	at right.	
		JE	
1a*	high, central	low, to right	
1b*	high, central	low, to right	horizontal guide-line through "J" square; trace of re-entry N.E. square.
2	high, central	central, slightly to left	right line extends beyond bottom.
3	low, to left	very high, to right	
4	high, central	low, close to left	two distinct dots in "J" square; side line of N.E. square thin.
5	very low, central	low, to left	scratch outside left of N.W. square.
6	high, central	slightly high, slightly to left	left side weak.
7	high, slightly to right	high, to left	left line complete.
8†	high, to right	high, close to left	faint vertical guide-line N.E. square, very close to frame.
9†	central	central	"J" nearly square.
10†	low, central	low, to left	square "J".
11	high, to right	central, to right	"J" square and double.
		JF	
1a*	central, to right	central	
1b*	central, to right	central—looks lower	horizontal guide-line near top of "J" square; scratches in "J" square.
2	high, central	high, central	slight trace of re-entry lower portion of N.W. square.
3	high, to left	very low, central	faint trace of horizontal guide-line through "J" square.
4	high, to left	low, to left	distinct dot below and close to corner of "F" square.
5	high, central	central	left side of "J" square blurred.
6	central, to left	central, close to left	distinct dot some distance below corner of "F" square.
7	high, central	low, to left	
8†	central, to left	central	bottom line extends slightly on right.
9†	high, central	high, central	"J" nearly square.
10†	central	high, to left	square "J", with stroke after it.
11	very high, to right	very high, to right	square "J".

**Shows the Ray-flaw.* *†Shows the "O"-flaw.*

1a
1b
2
3
4
5
6
7
8
9
10
11

1a
1b
2
3
4
5
6
7
8
9
10
11

Plate.	Position of Corner-letter at left.	Position of Corner-letter at right.	Further distinguishing characteristics.
		JG	
1a*	high, to left	central, to left	
1b*	high, to left	central, to left	left top ray in N.W. square shorter; trace of horizontal guide-lines through N.E. square and letter-squares.
2	high, to right	high, to left	
3	high, to left	low, to left	
4	high, to left	very high, close to left	right line extends slightly beyond bottom.
5	high, central	central, close to left	horizontal guide-line through value; distinct scratches below stamp.
6	central, to left	high, to left	
7	high, to left	high, central	
8†	high, central	high, to left	
9†	low, central	low, to right	trace of guide-line through value; "J" nearly square.
10†	very low, central	very low, slightly to left	square "J"; trace of vertical guide-line N.W. square.
11	very high, to right	very low, slightly to left	square "J".
		JH	
1a*	high, to left	low, to left	tiny dot below corner of "H" square.
1b*	high, to left	low, to left	dot not so distinct; vertical scratch left side of N.W. square; serifs of "H" wider apart.
2	slightly high, central	high, slightly to left	
3	very high, central	high, central	
4	central, to right	high, to left	indistinct blur in N.W. square.
5	high, central	high, to right	upper portion of left side irregular.
6	high, central	high, central	lower portion of right side line very irregular.
7	high, central	very high, close to left	
8†	high, central	high, to right	
9†	central, to right	high, central	"J" nearly square.
10†	very high, to right	very low, to right	square "J" with stroke after it; squat "H".
11	high, to right	high, central	square "J".

**Shows the Ray-flaw.*   *†Shows the "O"-flaw.*

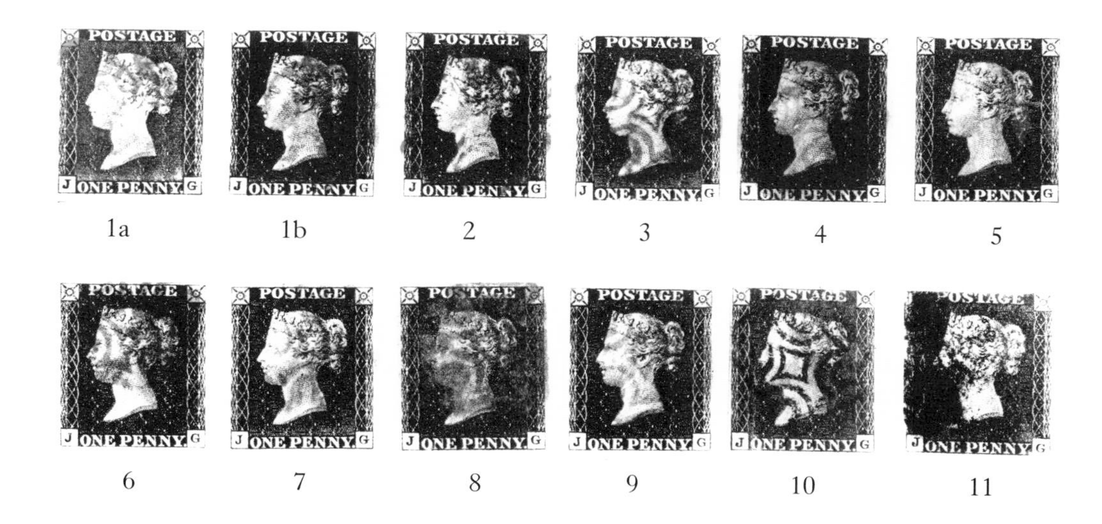
1a
1b
2
3
4
5
6
7
8
9
10
11

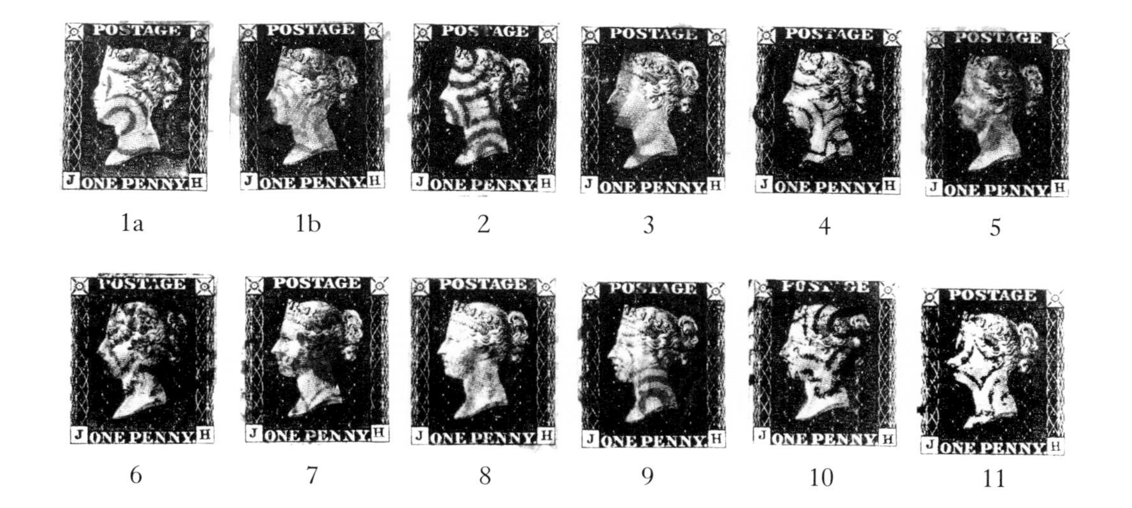
1a
1b
2
3
4
5
6
7
8
9
10
11

Plate.	Position of Corner-letter at left.	Position of Corner-letter at right.	Further distinguishing characteristics.
		JI	
1a*	high, to right	low, central	
1b*	high, to right	low, central	distinct re-entry in each upper square.
2	high, to right	low, central	
3	high, central	high, to left	
4	central	slightly low, central	left side line irregular; scratches on right side margin.
5	central	central, to left	bottom line extends slightly on right; scratch on lower margin on right.
6	slightly high, central	low, to left	side line of N.E. square weak, and distinct dot above the square.
7	high, central	low, slightly to left	
8†	high, to left	central, to left	
9†	central, to right	low, to left	"J" nearly square.
10†	central	central, to right	square "J" with stroke after it; tall "I".
11	very high, to right	central, to right	square "J"; tall "I".
		JJ	
1a*	high, central	very high, central	
1b*	high, central	very high, central	horizontal guide-lines each upper square, and first "J" square; letters recut.
2	central	low, central	
3	central	central	
4	central, to left	central, to left	
5	high, to right	high, central	trace of horizontal guide-line through second "J" square.
6	high, to right	high, to left	tiny dot above each letter; dots on margin below first "J" square.
7	high, not so much to right	high, not so much to left	
8†	high, central	very high, to right	
9†	low, central	high, central	"J" nearly square.
10†	high, central	central, to right	first "J" with faint mark after it; each "J" square.
11	very high, to right	very high, to right	each "J" square.

**Shows the Ray-flaw.* *†Shows the "O"-flaw.*

1a 1b 2 3 4 5
6 7 8 9 10 11

1a 1b 2 3 4 5
6 7 8 9 10 11

Plate.	Position of Corner-letter at left.	Position of Corner-letter at right.	Further distinguishing characteristics.
		JK	
1a*	central	high, central	
1b*	central	high, central	re-entry N.E. square; distinct guide-lines through N.E. and "J" squares.
2	very high, central	high, central	bottom of "E" and "N" of "PENNY" splayed.
3	high, central	high, to right	
4	high, central	central, to left—slopes up	
5	high, central	low, to left	scratches on lower margin.
6	low, to left	central	several dots in N.E. and "K" squares; faint guide-line through value and letter-squares.
7	high, central	central, to right	
8†	high, to left	central	
9†	low, central	central	"J" nearly square; right line N.E. square thin.
10†	high, to right	low, central	square "J"; two distinct dots below second "N" of "PENNY" to "K", connected by guide-line; trace of guide-line through "ONE".
11	high, to right	low, to right	square "J".
		JL	
1a*	high, central	high, central	
1b*	high, central	high, central	left corner of N.W. square very weak; horizontal guide-line through "J" square.
2	slightly high, central	central	indistinct dot outside corner of N.E. square; dot on margin below "L" square.
3	very high, central	high, slightly to left	dot below corner of "L" square.
4	central	central, to left	dot on margin at side of N.W. square.
5	central	central	scratch or line on lower margin below "NE PE" of "ONE PENNY".
6	central	central, to right	N.E. square weak at left corner; bottom line extends slightly on right; mark in "O" of "ONE"; bottom line of "J" square thin at right.
7	high, central	central, to left	faint trace of guide-line through value.
8†	high, central	low, to left	
9†	high, central	low, central	top serif of "L" double; "J" nearly square.
10†	central	high, far to right	square "J"; distinct dot some distance below "L" square.
11	high, to right	high, to right	square "J".

**Shows the Ray-flaw.* *†Shows the "O"-flaw.*

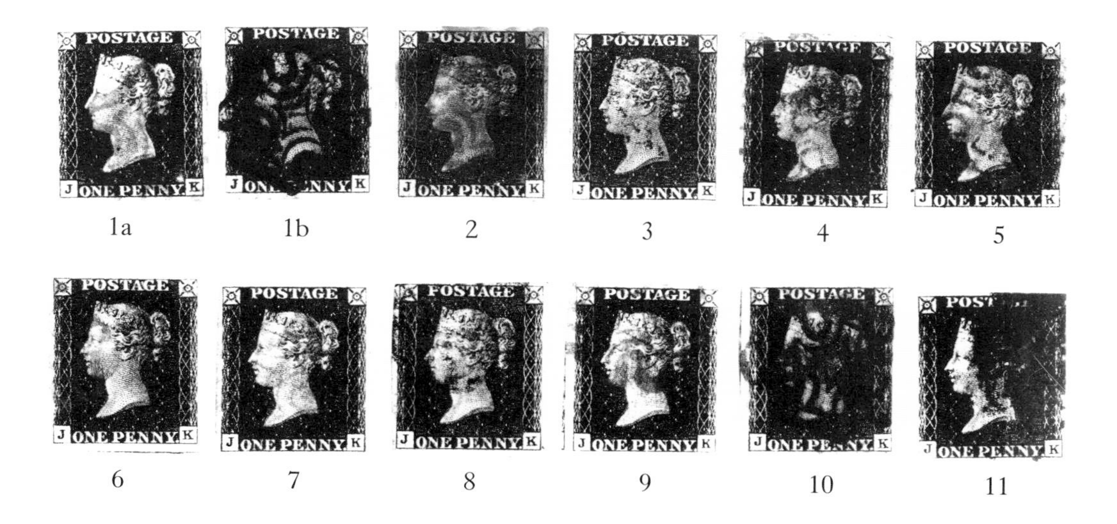
1a
1b
2
3
4
5
6
7
8
9
10
11

1a
1b
2
3
4
5
6
7
8
9
10
11

Plate.	Position of Corner-letter at left.	Position of Corner-letter at right.	Further distinguishing characteristics.
		KA	
1a*	slightly high, to right	central	
1b*	slightly high, to right	central	horizontal guide-line through "A" square.
2*	central, slightly to right	slightly high, slightly to right	two minute dots below serif of upper diagonal stroke of "K".
3	central, slightly to right	central, slightly to right	
4	slightly high, central	central	minute dots in each upper square, and "O" of "ONE"; also two dots below "P" of "PENNY", and between "N" and "Y".
5	high, central	central	trace of guide-line through value and "A" square.
6	central	slightly high, central	vertical guide-line N.E. square, close to frame; top line of N.W. square defective.
7	central, slightly to left	slightly low, central	
8†	central, to right	central, to left	
9†	low, to left	high, central	guide-line through "K" square, and partly through value; vertical guide-line N.E. square and "A" square; close to frame.
10†	high, central	low, central	vertical guide-line N.E. square, close to frame; trace of guide-line through value.
11	low, slightly to right	central, slightly to right	left foot of "A" double.
		KB	
1a*	central	central	
1b*	central	central	horizontal guide-line joining top of "B" to right line of square.
2*	slightly low, central	slightly low, central	
3	central	high, to right	
4	low, central	very high, to right	minute dots in each letter-square and on margin.
5	central	slightly low, central	minute dot in foot of "E" of "PENNY".
6	central	central	vertical guide-line N.E. square, close to frame; right side line extends slightly beyond bottom.
7	central, slightly to left	low, central	mark on margin joining line above "K" square.
8†	central	central, slightly to right	
9†	central	central	guide-line through "K" square, and partly through value; right side line extends slightly beyond bottom.
10	very low, to right	high, central	no flaw; "B" faint; left side line extends beyond bottom.
11	central	very high, to right—slopes down	

**Shows the Ray-flaw.* *†Shows the "O"-flaw.*

1a
1b
2
3
4
5
6
7
8
9
10
11

1a
1b
2
3
4
5
6
7
8
9
10
11

Plate.	Position of Corner-letter at left.	Position of Corner-letter at right.	Further distinguishing characteristics.
		KC	
1a*	central, to left	central, to left	lines of upper squares perfect.
1b*	central, to left	central, to left	vertical guide-line above. "K"; horizontal line through "C" square; line of each upper square weak.
2*	central	low, central	bottom line extends slightly on each side.
3	low, to right	central, slightly to left	left foot of "K" double.
4	central	slightly low, to left	trace of guide-line through "K" square and partly through value; many dots in each lower square, and on top and lower margins.
5	very low, central	slightly low, to left	traces of line below "K"; left side line weak.
6	high, to left	slightly low, to left	vertical guide-line N.E. square, close to frame; trace of guide-line right side of "K" and near right side line of "C" square.
7	central, slightly to left	slightly high, slightly to left	trace of guide-line through "K" square and value.
8†	central, slightly to left	slightly low, central	
9†	central	slightly high, slightly to left	vertical guide-line N.E. square and "C" square, close to frame; guide-line through each letter-square and value.
10†	very low, to right	slightly high, to left	side line of N.E. square thinner.
11	very low, to left	high, central	trace of guide-line through value, and below "K"; dot below "C" square.
		KD	
1a*	high, central	high, central	
1b*	high, central	high, central	horizontal guide-line through each letter square; "D" slightly double.
2*	central	very low, central	mark on lower margin, joining "O" of "ONE".
3	central, slightly to right	low, to right	
4	central, to right	high, to right	minute dots in "K" square; also on upper and lower margins.
5	low, central	high, slightly to right	left side line irregular and extending beyond bottom.
6	central	slightly high, slightly to right	left side line extends slightly beyond bottom; scratches left side margin.
7	central, slightly to right	slightly low, central	
8†	central, slightly to right	central	
9†	central	high, central	horizontal guide-line each letter-square and value.
10†	low, central	high, slightly to left	
11	slightly low, to right	very high, to right	

**Shows the Ray-flaw.* *†Shows the "O"-flaw.*

1a
1b
2
3
4
5
6
7
8
9
10
11

1a
1b
2
3
4
5
6
7
8
9
10
11

Plate.	Position of Corner-letter		Further distinguishing characteristics.
	at left.	at right.	
		KE	
1a*	high, central	central, to right	
1b*	high, central	central, to right	trace of missing ray.
2*	central, slightly to right	central, slightly to right	letter "E" double; flaw on left frame towards top square.
3	low, central	high, slightly to left	
4	central	central, far to right	scratches on left and top margins.
5	central	central, slightly to left	letter "E" double; left side line, extends slightly beyond bottom.
6	central, slightly to right	low, to left	vertical guide-line N.E. and "E" squares. In second state, the frame-lines have been strengthened or recut.
7	central, slightly to left	high, to left	scratches on lower margin.
8†	central	central, slightly to left	
9†	low, to left	very low, central	horizontal guide-line through "K" square and "O" of "ONE"; vertical guide-line "E" square.
10†	slightly low, to left	slightly high, central	
11	central, to right	slightly low, to right	
		KF	
1a*	high, central	high, slightly to left	
1b*	high, central	high, slightly to left	left side line strengthened; horizontal guide-line through "K" square; "F" slightly double.
2*	central, to right	central, far to right	
3	central	low, to left	dot in upper part of N.E. square.
4	central	central, to left	side line of "F" square thin; dot touching lower diagonal stroke of "K".
5	central	low, central	
6	central	central, far to left	in the second state the frame-lines are strengthened or recut.
7	central	central, to left	
8†	slightly high, central	central	
9†	central, to left	very high, to right	horizontal guide-line through "K" square and value; vertical guide-line in "F" square, very close to frame.
10†	very low, central	very low, slightly to right	vertical guide-line N.E. square.
11	central	very high, slightly to right	guide-line N.E. square, close to frame.

**Shows the Ray-flaw.* *†Shows the "O"-flaw.*

1a 1b 2 3 4 5
6 7 8 9 10 11

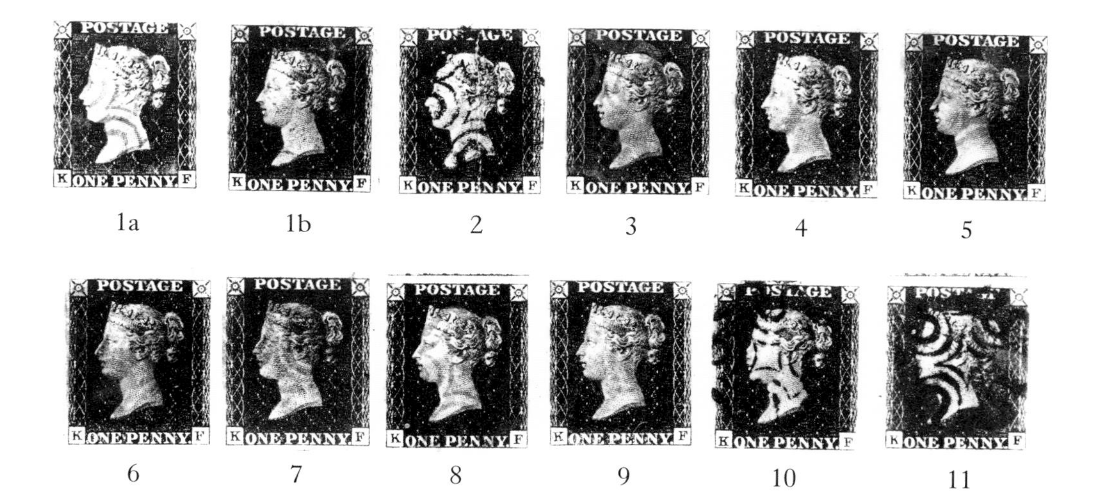
1a 1b 2 3 4 5
6 7 8 9 10 11

Plate.	*Position of Corner-letter*		*Further distinguishing characteristics.*
	at left.	*at right.*	
		KG	
1a*	high, to right	high, slightly to left	left side line extends beyond bottom.
1b*	high, to right	high, slightly to left	extension more evident; side line of N.E. square weak.
2*	very low, central	slightly low, to left	
3	slightly high, central	low, to left	
4	slightly high, to right	high, central	trace of guide-line through "K" square and value; bottom line extends slightly on right.
5	low, central	slightly high, slightly to left	horizontal guide-line through value; horizontal and vertical guide-lines in "G" square; vertical guide-line N.E. square, very close to frame.
6	central	high, to left	guide-line N.E. square, very close to frame.
7	central	high, central	vertical scratch to left, N.W. square.
8†	slightly low, to right	high, central	
9†	low, central	slightly high, slightly to right	strong horizontal guide-line through letter-squares and value; vertical guide-line N.E. square, very close to frame; vertical guide-line "G" square, wide of frame.
10†	slightly low, to left	central, to left	trace of guide-line through value and letter-squares; faint guide-line N.E. square.
11	central	very high, to right	
		KH	
1a*	central	low, central	
1b*	central	low, central	thin "H".
2*	high, to right	central	
3	high, to left	low, central	
4	central	high, to left	dot attached to bottom line below "E" of "ONE"; right side line of "H" square thin.
5	slightly low, slightly to right	very high, to left	horizontal line below "K" square.
6	slightly high, to right	high, to left	minute dot some distance above N.E. square.
7	high, central	very high, to left	mark above N.W. square.
8†	high, to right	central	
9†	very low, to left	low, to left	horizontal guide-line through "K" square and "ON" of "ONE".
10†	very low, to left	low, central	squat "H".
11	low, to left	central, slightly to left	horizontal guide-line through each letter-square.

**Shows the Ray-flaw.* *†Shows the "O"-flaw.*

POSTAGE
K ONE PENNY G
1a
1b
2
3
4
5
6
7
8
9
10
11

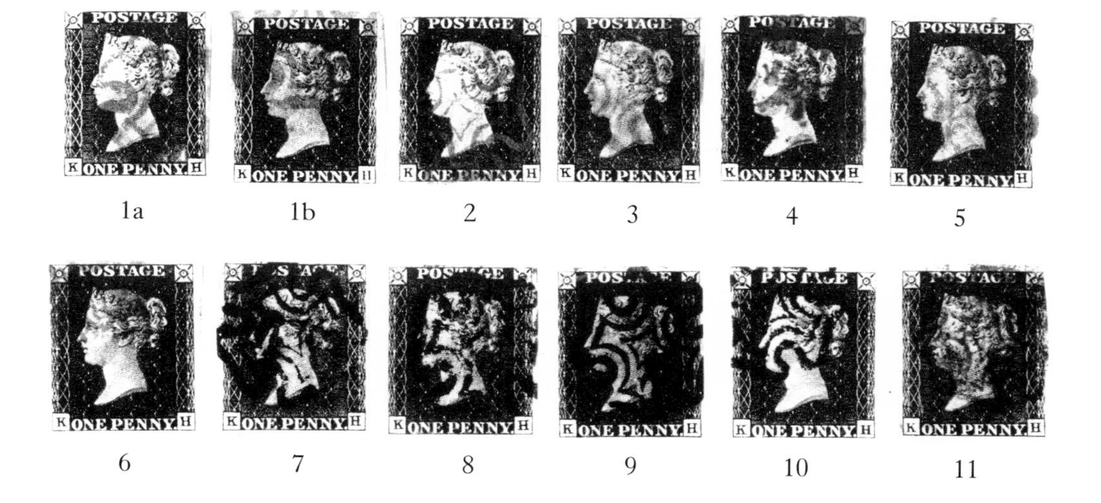
POSTAGE
K ONE PENNY H
1a
1b
2
3
4
5
6
7
8
9
10
11

Plate.	Position of Corner-letter		Further distinguishing characteristics.
	at left.	*at right.*	
		KI	
1a*	high, central	slightly low, far to right	
1b*	high, central	slightly low, far to right	top line of N.E. square thin.
2*	high, slightly to right	central, slightly to right	"E" of "PENNY" runs nearly into bottom margin.
3	slightly low, central	rather high, to left	
4	central	low, central	trace of horizontal guide-line through "K" square and value; left side line irregular.
5	central, slightly to left	very low, to left	left side line practically missing.
6	central	central, to left	minute dots in "K" square; dot outside left of N.W. square; vertical guide-lines N.E. square.
7	central, to left	slightly low, slightly to left	
8†	central	high, slightly to left	diagonal stroke across top right corner of "K" square.
9†	very low, to left	low, slightly to left	bottom line extends on left; guide-line through "K" square; right side line extends slightly beyond bottom.
10†	central, to left	low, slightly to right	trace of double horizontal guide-line through value; vertical guide-line N.E. square, very close to frame; tall "I".
11	central, slightly to right	low, slightly to right	tall "I".
		KJ	
1a*	high, central	high, central	
1b*	high, central	high, central	top line of N.E. square weak.
2*	high, to right	high, to left	"E" of "PENNY" runs nearly into bottom margin.
3	central, to left	very high, to left	
4	slightly high, to right	central, slightly to left	trace of horizontal guide-line through "K" square and value.
5	central, far to left	central	similar guide-line, but more evident and showing through "J" square; right side line extends slightly beyond bottom.
6	central, to right	central	vertical scratches on left margin towards bottom.
7	central	central, slightly to left	trace of horizontal guide-line through "K" square and value.
8†	central, to right	slightly high, central	
9†	low, slightly to right	central	strong horizontal guide-line through "K" square, "ONE" and "PE".
10†	very low, to left	central, to left	square "J"; faint vertical guide-line N.E. square, close to frame; vertical line in front of "J".
11	low, to left	very high, slightly to right.	square "J".

**Shows the Ray-flaw.* *†Shows the "O"-flaw.*

1a 1b 2 3 4 5
6 7 8 9 10 11

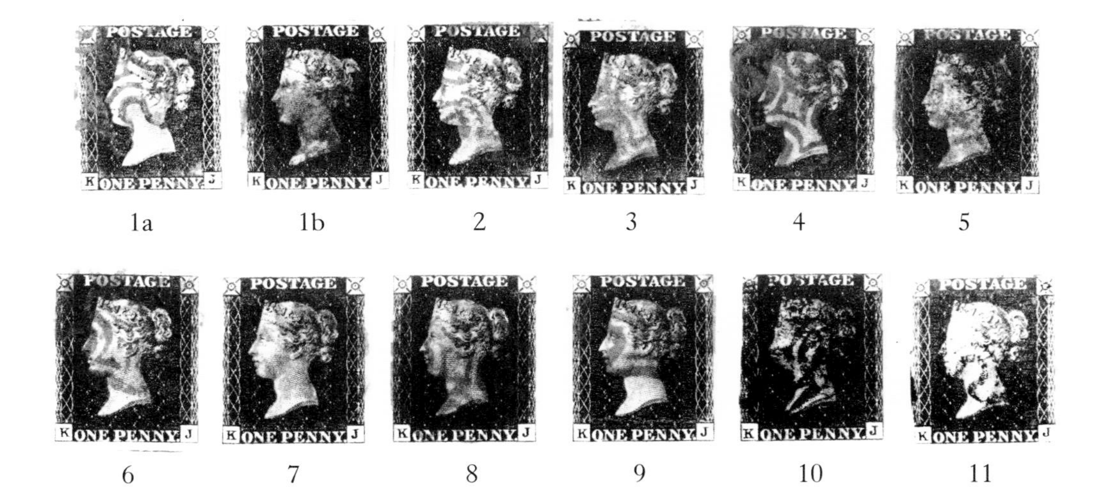
1a 1b 2 3 4 5
6 7 8 9 10 11

Plate.	Position of Corner-letter		Further distinguishing characteristics.
	at left.	at right.	
		KK	
1a*	high, central	high, central	
1b*	high, central	high, central	each letter slightly enlarged.
2*	central	central	part of value runs nearly into bottom margin.
3	high, central	very high, central	faint diagonal stroke to right of second "K", cutting through frame-line.
4	central	low, central	trace of horizontal guide-line through "ONE" and "PE".
5	low, to left	low, to left	
6	low, slightly to left	central, to left	tiny dot above first "K".
7	central, to right	central, to left	re-entry through N.E. square, each letter-square and lower margin.
8†	low, central	central	
9†	central, to right	central	horizontal guide-line through first "K" square and portion of value; vertical guide-line N.E. square, close to frame, and through each letter-square.
10†	high, to right	low, to right	vertical guide-line N.E. square.
11	high, to right	high, central	trace of horizontal guide-line through each letter-square.
		KL	
1a*	high, to right	high, to left	distinct dot some distance above N.E. square.
1b*	high, to right	high, to left	distinct dot some distance above N.E. square; bottom line extends on right; scratches on lower margin; vertical guide-line N.E. square.
2*	high, to right	high, slightly to left	bottom line extends on left; value inclines to run into bottom margin; scratches on right side margin.
3	central, to left	central	short horizontal stroke, from middle of left side of "K" square, and traces through value.
4	central, to left	central	horizontal guide-line through "K" square.
5	low, to right	high, central	left side weak; dot below corner of "L" square.
6	low, central	central	tiny dot before "L".
7	central, to right	central, to left	
8†	high, to right	high, to left	
9†	low, to right	high, to left	horizontal guide-line through "K" square and value.
10†	central, to right	central, to left	short vertical stroke attached to upper serif of "L".
11	central, to right	high, to right	

**Shows the Ray-flaw.* *†Shows the "O"-flaw.*

1a
1b
2
3
4
5
6
7
8
9
10
11

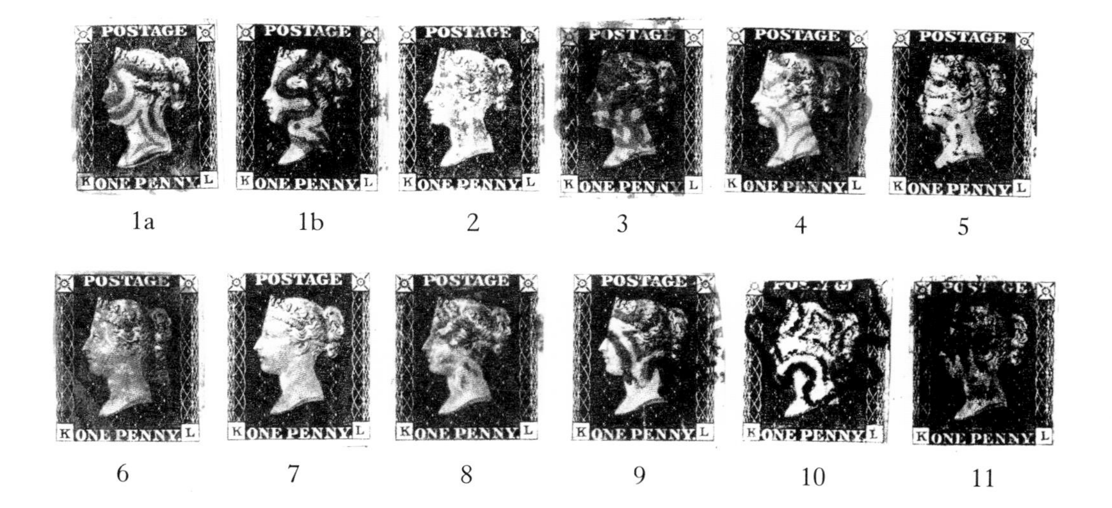
1a
1b
2
3
4
5
6
7
8
9
10
11

Plate.	Position of Corner-letter at left.	Position of Corner-letter at right.	Further distinguishing characteristics.
		LA	
1a*	central, slightly to left	slightly low, central	left side line extends slightly beyond bottom.
1b*	central, slightly to left	slightly low, central	left side line extends slightly beyond bottom; scratches left side margin.
2*	central	central	thin line extending below corner of "A" square; scratches top right margin.
3	central, slightly to left	central, to right	
4	low, to right—slopes up	central	several dots in each letter-square and below; left side of "L" square strongly blurred.
5	low, to left	central	dot touching line right side of N.E. square.
6	slightly low, to left	central, far to right	left side line extends beyond bottom; trace of vertical guide-line in "A" square, close to frame; vertical guide-line N.E. square.
7	central, to right	rather low, little to left	distinct dot in S.E. corner of "L" square.
8†	central	central	
9†	high, central	high, central	
10†	high, to right	slightly high, central	
11	high, to right	high, central	bottom line extends faintly on right.
		LB	
1a*	central	high, to right	
1b*	central	high, to right	lower portion of line on right of N.E. square weak.
2*	high, central	high, to right	horizontal guide-line through each upper square.
3	low, central	slightly high, to right	bottom line below value thick.
4	central, to left—slopes up	central	dot in each letter-square; several dots below "P" of "PENNY"; horizontal guide-line partly through value.
5	low, slightly to left	central	letters of "POSTAGE" run nearly into top margin.
6	central, slightly to left	low, central	"L" with double serif.
7	central	very low, central	"L" without foot on left.
8†	high, to left	central, to left	guide-line N.E. square, close to frame.
9†	central	high, to right	letter "B" double.
10†	low, to right	high, to right	
11	very low, to right	high, central—slopes down	

**Shows the Ray-flaw.* *†Shows the "O"-flaw.*

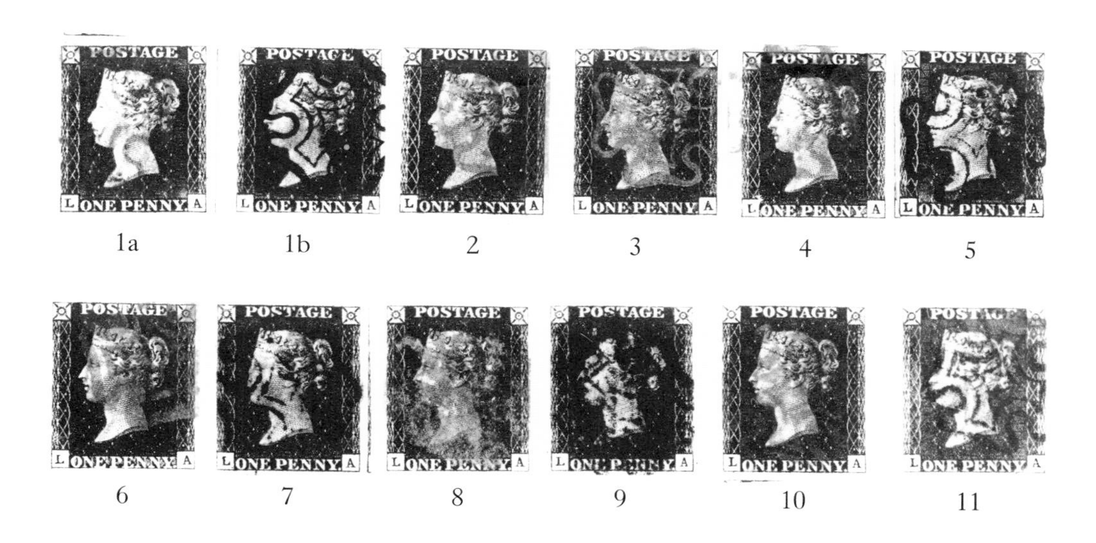
1a 1b 2 3 4 5
6 7 8 9 10 11

1a 1b 2 3 4 5
6 7 8 9 10 11

Plate.	Position of Corner-letter		Further distinguishing characteristics.
	at left.	*at right.*	
		LC	
1a*	high, to right	low, to left	
1b*	high, to right	low, to left	corner of "L" square and top side line of N.W. square weak.
2*	high, central	high, to left	"E" of "PENNY" runs nearly into bottom margin; scratch on each side at top.
3	central	high, to left	bottom line of "L" square thin.
4	low, central—slopes up	low, to left	several dots in each letter-square.
5	central, to left	central	faint mark below "L" square.
6	central	high, to right	bottom line extends slightly on left.
7	central, slightly to left	central, to left	
8†	slightly low, slightly to left	high, central	very thin line running up from N.E. square.
9†	high, central	central	side line of N.E. square appears double.
10†	very low, to right	very high, to left	
11	very low, central	slightly low, central	trace of horizontal guide-line through value and "C" square.
		LD	
1a*	central	high, central	
1b*	central	high, central	corner of "L" square weak.
2*	slightly high, central	central, to right	
3	central, to right	slightly high, to right	
4	central—slopes up	central	distinct dot in middle of "D"; several dots in "L" square and "O" of "ONE"; scratches on left margin.
5	central, to left	high, to right	lines of N.E. square thin; scratches below "ONE".
6	central, slightly to left	central	
7	central	central	"L" with little or no foot on left.
8†	high, to left	central	vertical guide-line N.E. square.
9†	central	central, to right	
10†	low, to right	high, central	
11	low, to right	central, to right	

**Shows the Ray-flaw.* *†Shows the "O"-flaw.*

POSTAGE
L ONE PENNY C
1a
1b
2
3
4
5
6
7
8
9
10
11

POSTAGE
L ONE PENNY D
1a
1b
2
3
4
5
6
7
8
9
10
11

Plate.	*Position of Corner-letter*		*Further distinguishing characteristics.*
	at left.	*at right.*	
		LE	
1a*	central	low, to right	
1b*	central	low, to right	left side line strengthened.
2*	central	central, to right	faint horizontal guide-line through N.E. square; marks in "NY" of "PENNY".
3	central	very high, well to right	bottom line of "L" square thin.
4	central—slopes up	central	several dots in "L" square; left side line irregular.
5	low, central	low, to left	top line of N.E. square thin.
6	high, central	high, central	
7	central, to left	high, to right	"L" with little or no foot on left.
8†	central, to right	high, central	
9†	high, to left	central	trace of vertical guide-line in "E" square.
10†	low, to right	low, to left	
11	very low, central	high, to right	
		LF	
1a*	high, central	high, central	vertical guide-line N.E. square, wide of frame.
1b*	high, central	high, central	guide-line nearly absent.
2*	high, central	slightly low, central	marks in "NY" of "PENNY"; thin line extends from right side line above, with another line parallel to it on margin.
3	central, to right	slightly low, central	bottom line of "L" square thin.
4	central, to right—slopes up	central, to left	
5	high, central	central, to right	faint dot on margin below "Y" of "PENNY".
6	central, to left	low, to left	
7	central	central, to left	
8†	central, to left	very high, central	vertical guide-line N.E. square, left margin has smudge.
9†	high, to right	high, central	vertical guide-line N.E. and "F" squares; scratches in left margin.
10†	low, to right	low, central	
11	very low, central	very high, to right	

**Shows the Ray-flaw.* *†Shows the "O"-flaw.*

1a
1b
2
3
4
5
6
7
8
9
10
11

1a
1b
2
3
4
5
6
7
8
9
10
11

Plate.	Position of Corner-letter		Further distinguishing characteristics.
	at left.	*at right.*	
		LG	
1a*	high, central	high, to left	faint vertical guide-line N.E. square, close to frame.
1b*	high, central	high, to left	dot below left corner of "G" square.
2*	central	high, slightly to left	trace of marks in "NNY" of "PENNY".
3	low, central	high, central	bottom line of "L" square thin.
4	central	high, central	mark in N.E. square; mark on margin, between "E" and "P"; horizontal guide-line through value and "G" square.
5	high, to right	low, to left	horizontal guide-line through "L" square; side line of N.E. square thin.
6	central	high, central	
7	high, slightly to left	slightly low, to left	
8†	high, to left	high, central	
9†	low, central	slightly low, to right	
10†	central, to right	low, slightly to right—slopes down	vertical guide-line N.W. square.
11	central, to right	high, central—slopes down	horizontal guide-line in "G" square, close to frame.
		LH	
1a*	central	slightly low, to left	
1b*	central	slightly low, to left	diagonal scratches through N.W. square—? a re-entry
2*	high, central	low, to right	
3	central	low, to left	
4	central—slopes up	very high, to left	left side line extends beyond bottom.
5	high, central	high, to left	top line of N.E. square thin; horizontal scratch on lower margin.
6	central	central	distinct dot before "H".
7	central	high, to left	right side line extends beyond bottom; "L" without foot on left.
8†	central, to left	central	
9†	high, central	high, to left	trace of vertical guide-line through "H" square.
10†	very low, to right	low, central	squat "H".
11	low, to right	high, central	horizontal guide-line through "H" square.

**Shows the Ray-flaw.* †*Shows the "O"-flaw.*

1a
1b
2
3
4
5
6
7
8
9
10
11

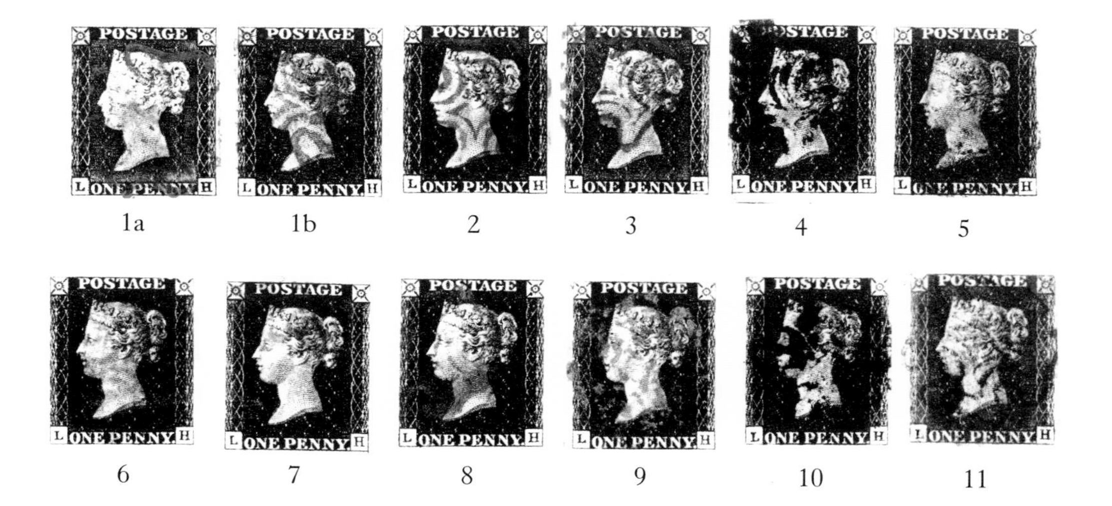
1a
1b
2
3
4
5
6
7
8
9
10
11

Plate.	Position of Corner-letter at left.	Position of Corner-letter at right.	Further distinguishing characteristics.
		LI	
1a*	central	low, to right	
1b*	central	low, to right	"L" square broken at corner.
2*	high, central	very high, central	dot in N.W. square high up; value inclines to run into bottom margin.
3	central	high, to left	
4	central, to left—slopes up	slightly low, central	right side line extends beyond bottom; minute dot on margin between "P" and "E" of "PENNY".
5	high, central	central, slightly to left	right line of N.E. square very weak; trace of horizontal guide-line through "L" square; scratches below stamp.
6	low, to left	slightly low, to left	vertical stroke of "I" extends slightly beyond foot.
7	central, to left	slightly low, central	trace of guide-line through upper part of "E" of "POSTAGE".
8†	high, to left	central	horizontal guide-line through "I" square and value.
9†	high, to right	low, to right	faint line extending from corner of N.W. square.
10†	high, to right	central, to right	trace of horizontal guide-line through value; tall "I".
11	central, to right	high, to right	vertical guide-line, N.E. square; tall "I".
		LJ	
1a*	high, central	high, central	
1b*	high, central	high, central	letter "J" appears to be slightly enlarged.
2*	high, to right	low, to left	
3	low, central	very high, central	bottom line of "L" square thin.
4	central—slopes up	high, central	
5	high, central	central	top line of N.W. square weak.
6	high, central	low, to left	tiny dot in "L" square near N.E. corner; dots below "EN" of "PENNY".
7	central	central, to left	horizontal scratches on bottom margin; "L" with little or no foot on left.
8†	central	central	
9†	high, to right	high, central	
10†	low, to right	very low, to left	square "J".
11	central, to right	very high, central	square "J".

**Shows the Ray-flaw.* *†Shows the "O"-flaw.*

1a
1b
2
3
4
5
6
7
8
9
10
11

1a
1b
2
3
4
5
6
7
8
9
10
11

Plate.	Position of Corner-letter		Further distinguishing characteristics.
	at left.	at right.	
		LK	
1a*	central, to left	low, central	trace of horizontal guide-line through "L" square.
1b*	central, to left	low, central	
2*	high, central	central	serif of upper diagonal stroke of "K" appears double.
3	central, to left	low, central	
4	central—slopes up	high, central—slopes up	
5	high, to right	central	
6	low, central	low, to right	faint dot in "K" square, before letter. In second state frame-lines strengthened.
7	central, to right	central	top line of N.W. square weak, and top right ray incomplete.
8†	high, central	high, central	
9†	central, to right	very low, central	left line extends beyond bottom; guide-line N.E. square, close to frame, and slight trace in "K" square.
10†	central, to right	high, to right	dot below "K", nearly touching letter.
11	central, to right	high, central—slopes up	dot in "T" of "POSTAGE".
		LL	
1a*	central	high, central	dot outside corner of second "L" square.
1b*	central	high, central	corner of first "L" square broken and left side recut; dot outside corner of second "L" square faint.
2*	high, central	high, central	corner of N.E. square extended.
3	central, to left	high, slightly to left	
4	high, to left	slightly high, to right	
5	high, to right	low, central	marks in "O" of "ONE".
6	central	central, to left	minute dot bottom right corner of first "L" square; right side line extends slightly beyond bottom.
7	central	central, to left—slopes down	
8†	high, to left	high, to left	long foot on left of first "L".
9†	low, central	high, central	top of first "L" slightly double; guide-line through value and letter-squares.
10†	low, to right	low, slightly to right	
11	high, to right	high, to right	dot on margin, below left serif of "P".

**Shows the Ray-flaw.* *†Shows the "O"-flaw.*

1a
1b
2
3
4
5
6
7
8
9
10
11

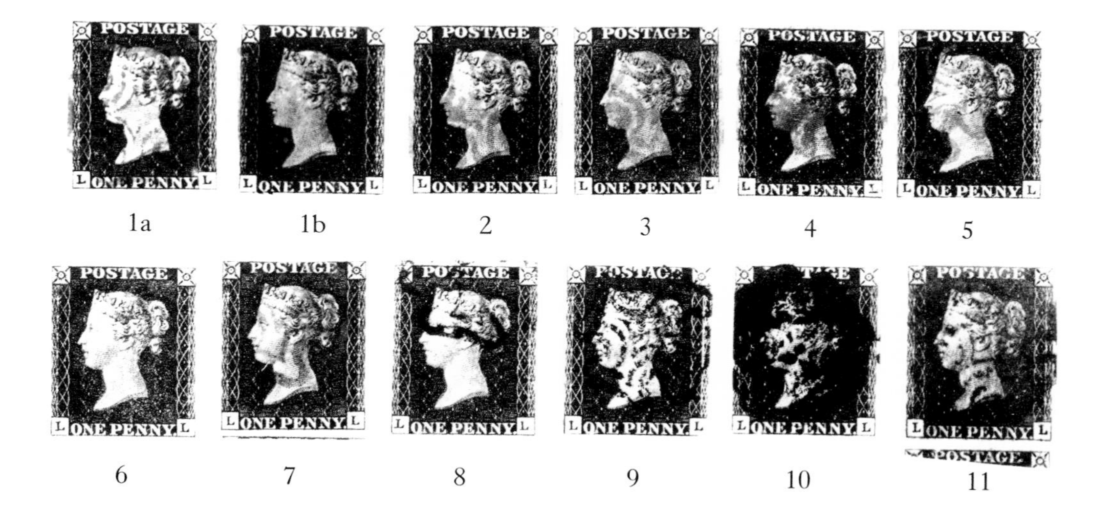
1a
1b
2
3
4
5
6
7
8
9
10
11

Plate.	*Position of Corner-letter*		*Further distinguishing characteristics.*
	at left.	*at right.*	
		MA	
1a*	high, to right	slightly high, to right	
1b*	high, to right	slightly high, to right	corner of "M" square defective; left side strengthened.
2*	high, central—slopes up	high, central	vertical guide-line close to frame on right margin, from top of square to middle of stamp.
3	central—slopes up	central	
4	high, to right—slopes up	very low, central	short vertical stroke in "M" square; several dots above and to side of N.E. square; vertical guide-line N.E. square, close to frame.
5	central—slopes up	low, central	top line of N.W. square thin; mark on lower margin below "Y".
6	low, to right—slopes up	central	vertical guide-line N.E. square, close to frame.
7	high, central—slopes up	high, central	
8†	high, central	central	bottom line extends on right; vertical guide-line N.E. square, close to frame.
9†	low, to right	high, to left	"M" double; vertical guide-line N.E. square.
10†	low, to right	high, central	right stroke of "M" defective; vertical guide-line N.E. square.
11	central, to right	central	
		MB	
1a*	high, central	central	
1b*	high, central	central	faint vertical line outside "M" square.
2*	central	high, slightly to right	trace of double line top N.W. square.
3	central	very high, to right	top line of N.W. square thin.
4	central, to right	central, to right	dot on top margin to left of N.E. square; very faint horizontal guide-line through "PENNY" and "B" square.
5	central	central	top line of N.W. square thin.
6	low, central	central	trace of horizontal guide-line through value, and "B" square; faint vertical guide-line N.E. and "B" square.
7	central, to right	high, to right	faint guide-line N.E. square, wide of frame.
8†	high, central	central	
9†	central, to left	high, to right	trace of vertical guide-line N.E. square, wide of frame.
10†	central	high, central	
11	low, to right	high, to right	

**Shows the Ray-flaw.*　　*†Shows the "O"-flaw.*

1a
1b
2
3
4
5
6
7
8
9
10
11

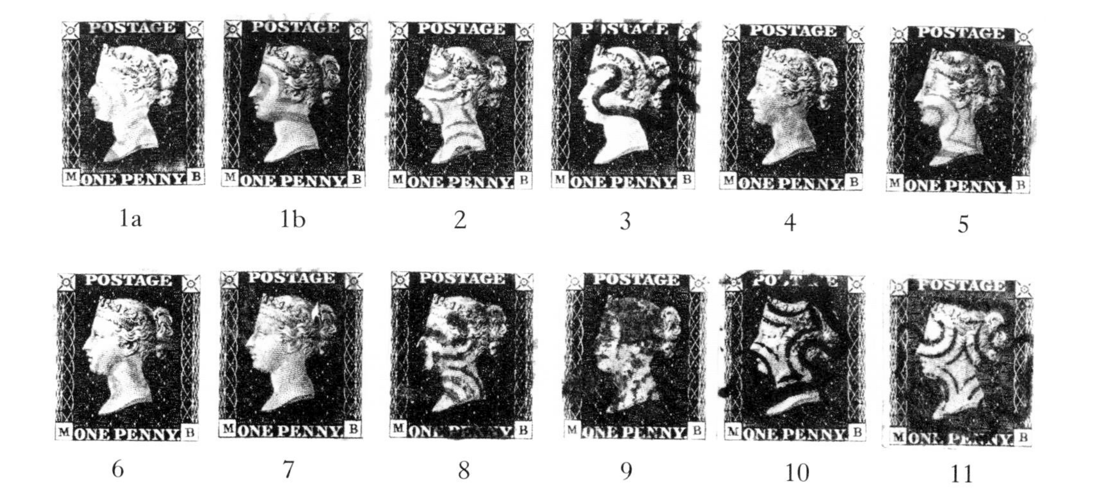
1a
1b
2
3
4
5
6
7
8
9
10
11

Plate.	Position of Corner-letter at left.	Position of Corner-letter at right.	Further distinguishing characteristics.
		MC	
1a*	high, central	central, to left	
1b*	high, central	central, to left	trace of double line on left side; side line of N.E. square thin.
2*	high, central—slopes up	low, to left	
3	high, to right	central, to left	trace of horizontal guide-line, each upper square and "POSTAGE".
4	high, central	central, to left	several dots in each letter-square, and in N.E. square.
5	high, central	high, to left	scratches on top, lower and left margins; vertical guide-line N.E. square, close to frame.
6	low, to right	high, to right	trace of horizontal guide-line through "C" square.
7	high, to right	high, to left	
8†	central, to right	central, to left	blur at side of N.W. square.
9†	low, central	very high, central	vertical guide-line N.E. square, wide of frame; vertical guide-line in "C" square, close to frame.
10†	central, to right	high, central	
11	high, to right	high, central	trace of vertical guide-line N.E. square, very close to frame.
		MD	
1a*	central	high, central	trace of vertical guide-line N.E. square, and above very close to frame.
1b*	central	high, central	right side recut.
2*	central—slopes up	central, to right	top line extends on right; horizontal guide-line above N.W. square.
3	high, to right	central	small blurred "M" with long serifs.
4	central, to left	slightly high, central	several dots in each letter-square and on margin.
5	central	high, to right	tiny dot above "M"; top squares with thin upper lines.
6	central, to right—slopes up	central	vertical guide-line N.E. square. In second state, the frame-line has been strengthened or recut.
7	central, foot touches right	central	short vertical stroke left side of "D" square.
8†	high, slightly to left	central, to right	mark in "O" of "ONE".
9†	very high, to right	very high, to right	
10†	high, to right	high, central	indistinct vertical stroke through "M" square.
11	very low, to right	high, to right	

**Shows the Ray-flaw.* *†Shows the "O"-flaw.*

1a
1b
2
3
4
5
6
7
8
9
10
11

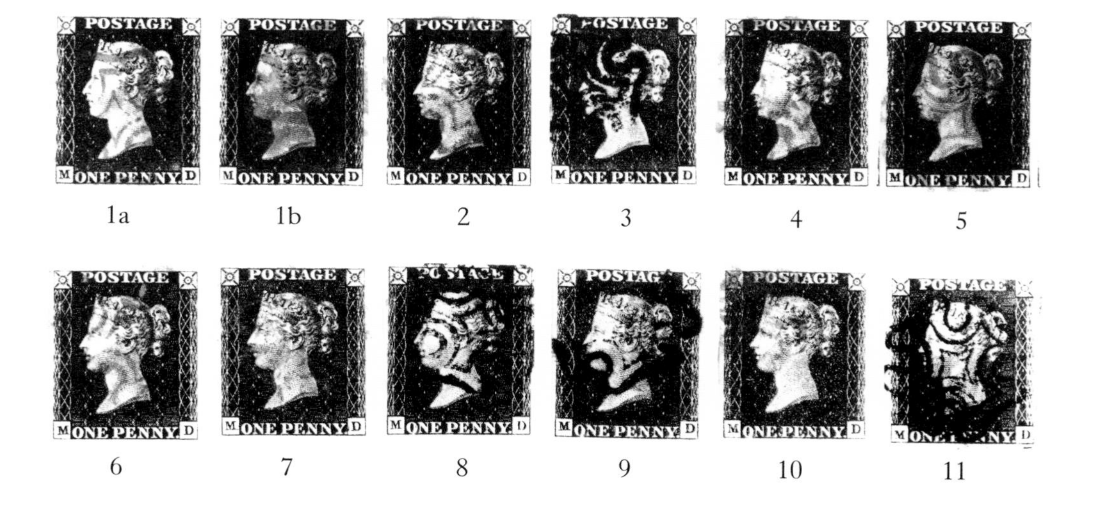
1a
1b
2
3
4
5
6
7
8
9
10
11

Plate.	Position of Corner-letter		Further distinguishing characteristics.
	at left.	at right.	
		ME	
1a*	central	central, to right	bottom line extends slightly on right.
1b*	central	central, to right	bottom line extends slightly on right; left side strengthened; bottom line of "M" square thin.
2*	high, central	central, to right	irregular blur below "M", not always apparent; guide-line above N.W. square.
3	slightly high, central	very high, far to right	
4	high, to right	low, to left	side line of N.E. square thin; distinct dot below "N" of "ONE".
5	high, central	central, to left	bottom line extends slightly on right.
6	high, to right	high, to left	vertical guide-line N.E. square, wide of frame.
7	high, to right	high, to left	
8†	high, central	central, slightly to left	bottom line extends slightly on right.
9†	high, to left	central	vertical guide-line N.E. square.
10†	low, to right	low, central	
11	high, to right	very high, to right	
		MF	
1a*	central	central	"M" double; vertical guide-line N.E. square and above, close to frame.
1b*	central	central	"M" double; right side line weak towards top.
2*	very high, to left	central, to right	top line extends on right; horizontal guide-line N.W. square and above, very close to frame.
3	central	very low, central	bottom line of "M" square, thin.
4	central	low, to left	two faint marks right side of "M"; scratches top and lower margin.
5	high, to right	central, to right	right line extends beyond bottom; lower part of right side line of N.E. square faint.
6	low, central	low, central	vertical guide-line N.E. square.
7	high, central	central, to left	trace of vertical guide-line N.E. square, close to frame.
8†	high, central	central	bottom line extends on right.
9†	central, to right	central, to left	vertical guide-line N.E. square; and in "F" square, very close to frame.
10†	low, to right	central, to left	vertical guide-line in left of N.W. square, close to frame.
11	very low, central	very high, central	

**Shows the Ray-flaw.* *†Shows the "O"-flaw.*

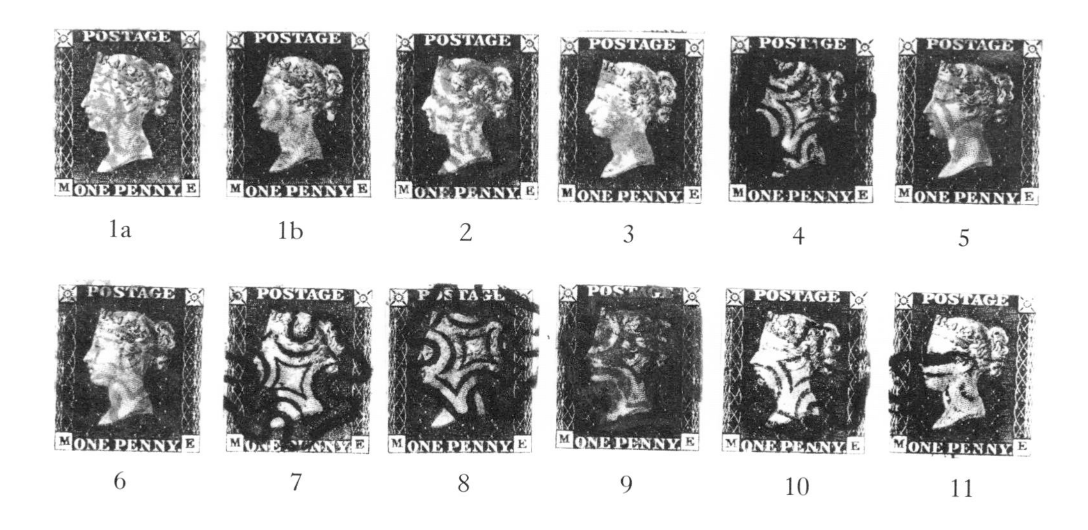
1a
1b
2
3
4
5
6
7
8
9
10
11

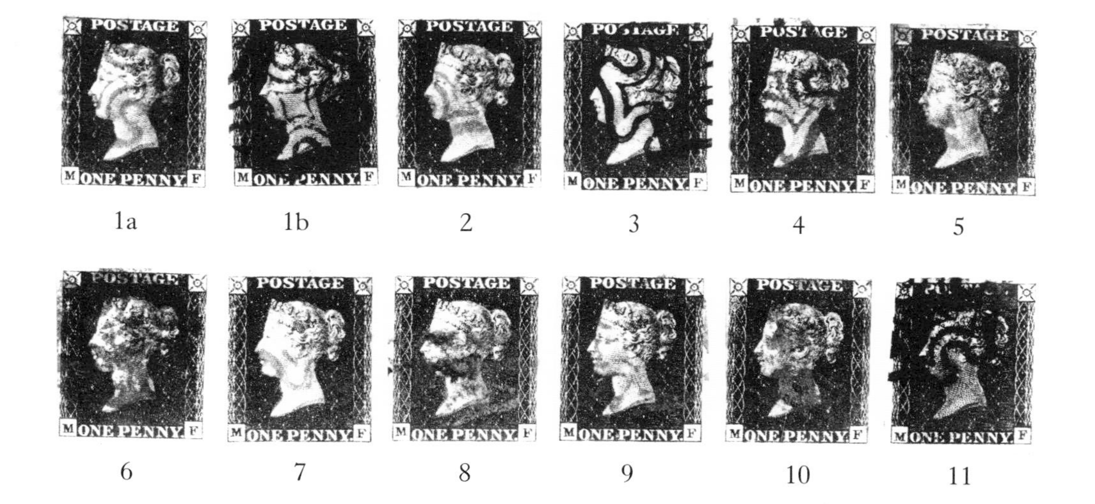
1a
1b
2
3
4
5
6
7
8
9
10
11

Plate.	Position of Corner-letter		Further distinguishing characteristics.
	at left.	at right.	
		MG	
1a*	high, slightly to right	central, to left	trace of horizontal guide-line through "M" square, very close to frame.
1b*	high, slightly to right	central, to left	distinct mark in "P" of "POSTAGE"; left side recut.
2*	low, central	high, central	trace of guide-line above N.W. square.
3	high, central	high, slightly to left	small blurred "M".
4	central—slopes up	slightly high, to left	
5	central—slopes down	very low, to left	
6	rather high, central—slopes up	central	mark attached to bottom line below "E" of "PENNY"; vertical guide-line N.E. square, close to frame.
7	high, to right	high, to left	
8†	high, to left	high, central	
9†	central	low, far to right	vertical guide-line N.E. square, wide of frame.
10†	high, to right	central, to left	
11	low, to right	high, central	
		MH	
1a*	high, central	rather low, central	
1b*	high, central	rather low, central	re-entry marks N.E. square.
2*	high, central—slopes up	high, to right	trace of horizontal guide-line above N.W. square, very close to frame.
3	high, to right.	high, central	trace of horizontal guide-line top of N.W. square, very close to frame.
4	central, to right	central, to left	dots above "M" and in "E" of "PENNY".
5	high, to right	high, to right	lower part of left side-line thin.
6	central	central, to right	dot in N.E. corner of "M" square; vertical guide-line N.E. square.
7	central	high, to left	
8†	high, central	high, central	scratches on lower margin.
9†	very high, to left	high, to left	vertical guide-line N.E. square, close to frame.
10†	high, to right	very low, central	squat "H".
11	very low, to right	high, central	blur below "H"; side line of N.E. square weak.

**Shows the Ray-flaw.* *†Shows the "O"-flaw.*

1a
1b
2
3
4
5
6
7
8
9
10
11

1a
1b
2
3
4
5
6
7
8
9
10
11

Plate.	Position of Corner-letter at left.	Position of Corner-letter at right.	Further distinguishing characteristics.
		MI	
1a*	central	low, to right	
1b*	central	low, to right	slight re-entry each upper square and "POSTAGE"; "I" with long top—re-cut.
2*	high, central	high, central	left side of "I" square slightly blurred.
3	high, central—slopes down	central	trace of horizontal guide-line in each upper square, and through "POSTAGE".
4	central, to right	central, to left	dot on margin to left of N.W. square; left side line irregular.
5	high, central	low, to right	top part of left side line irregular.
6	central, to right	central, to left	tiny dot to left of "I"; right side-line extends at top.
7	high, central	low, to left	right side line extends beyond bottom.
8†	high, central	central, slightly to left	top left portion of "M" slightly double.
9†	central, to right	high, to right	vertical guide-line N.E. square.
10†	central, to right	high, central	trace of horizontal guide-line through "I" square, close to frame; tall "I".
11	very low, to right	very high, to right	tall "I".
		MJ	
1a*	low, to right	central, to left	
1b*	low, to right	central, to left	slight trace of re-entry marks N.E. square, and in "Y" of "PENNY".
2*	slightly high, central	high, central	
3	high, to right	very high, to left	trace of horizontal guide-line in N.W. square, and through "POST" of "POSTAGE".
4	central	central, to left	slight blur before "J"; dot on margin below "P" of "PENNY".
5	central	high, to left	left side line thin.
6	central	slightly low, to left	small dot above "J"; vertical guide-line N.E. square, very close to frame.
7	slightly high, to right	slightly high, to left	
8†	high, central	high, central	
9†	very low, central	central	vertical guide-line N.E. square; horizontal guide-line through "M" square; "J" slightly square.
10†	low, to right	central, to left	trace of horizontal guide-line through "J" square, very close to frame; square-footed "J".
11	low, to right	high, central	"M" slightly defective on right; square "J".

**Shows the Ray-flaw.* *†Shows the "O"-flaw.*

1a
1b
2
3
4
5
6
7
8
9
10
11

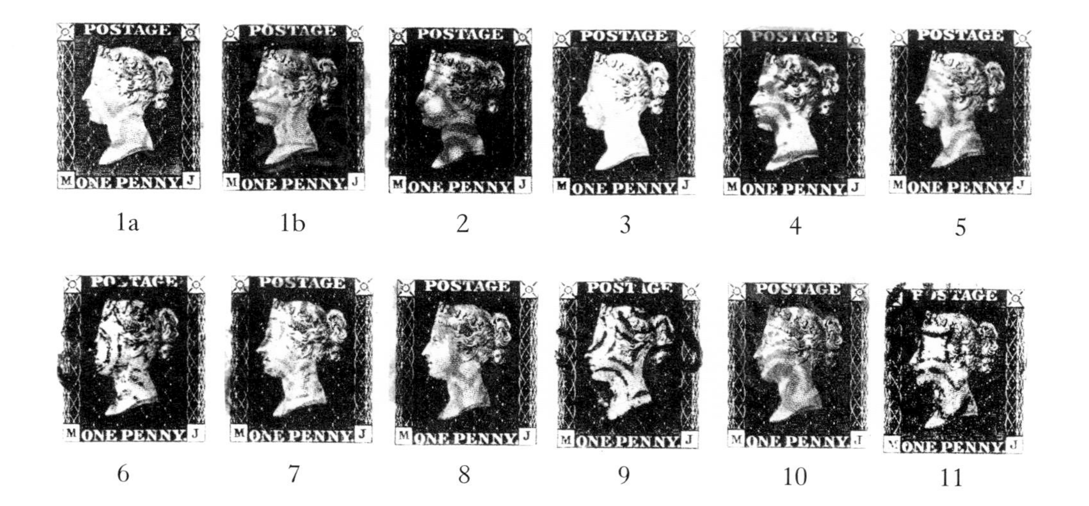
1a
1b
2
3
4
5
6
7
8
9
10
11

Plate.	Position of Corner-letter		Further distinguishing characteristics.
	at left.	at right.	
		MK	
1a*	central	slightly high, to right	
1b*	central	slightly high, to right	re-entry N.E. square.
2*	low, central	high, central	
3	high, to left	high, central	
4	high, to right	central	dot on right margin just above "K" square; right side line of N.E. square thin.
5	central	slightly low, to left	left side line weak; trace of extra line on left.
6	central	low, to left	"M" double; vertical guide-line N.E. square, very close to frame.
7	central, to right	slightly low, central	vertical guide-line N.E. square, close to frame.
8†	high, central	central, to left	
9†	low, to right	high, to right	right side of N.E. square absent; bottom line extends on left; vertical guide-line N.E. square, and very close to frame in "K" square.
10†	central	high, to right	very faint vertical guide-line N.E. square, very close to frame.
11	central, to right	central	blur on margin outside N.W. square.
		ML	
1a*	high, central	high, central	short horizontal stroke near top of "M" square on left.
1b*	high, central	high, central	stroke absent.
2*	rather high, to right	central	top line of N.W. square thin; small dot on junction of frame-lines of N.E. square.
3	low, to left	slightly high, slightly to left	dot below corner of "L" square; trace of horizontal guide-line in each upper square and through "POSTAGE".
4	central, to right	central	side line on right extends slightly beyond bottom.
5	central—slopes down	low, to left	small dot on junction of frame-lines of "L" square.
6	high, central	high, slightly to left	minute dot just below "L".
7	central	low, to left	
8†	high, slightly to left	slightly high, central	dot below "L" square, near corner.
9†	central, to right	central	horizontal guide-line through "ONE".
10†	high, to right	high, to right	
11	very low, to right	high, to right	right line extends beyond bottom.

**Shows the Ray-flaw.* *†Shows the "O"-flaw.*

1a
1b
2
3
4
5
6
7
8
9
10
11

1a
1b
2
3
4
5
6
7
8
9
10
11

Plate.	Position of Corner-letter at left.	Position of Corner-letter at right.	Further distinguishing characteristics.
		NA	
1a*	high, central	low, to right	
1b*	high, central	low, to right	"NE" of "ONE" joined.
2*	high, central	low, central	left vertical stroke of "N" faint.
3	central, to right	central, to right	
4	central, to right	low, central	top stroke of "N" extended; tiny dot in "A" square on right, near top of margin.
5	high, to right	low, central	"N" appears recut.
6	very low, central	central	left side and bottom lines cross.
7	central	low, slightly to right	line on left margin, above middle.
8†	high, to left	central	"N" with long foot; side and top lines of N.E. square thin; faint vertical guide-line same square, close to frame.
9†	high, to right	low, to left	vertical guide-line N.E. square, close to frame; horizontal guide-line through letter-squares and value.
10†	very low, central	very high, to right	vertical guide-line N.E. square, very close to frame.
11	central	high, to right	top line of N.E. square absent.
		NB	
1a	central, to left	high, central	
1b	central, to left	high, central	trace of horizontal guide-line through "B" square.
2	high, to right	high, to right	left vertical stroke of "N" faint at foot.
3	high, to right	high, to right	
4	central	slightly low, to right	two dots on margin at side of N.W. square, second dot some distance away; left side extends slightly beyond bottom.
5	high, to right	low, to left	top curved part of "B" defective; left side defective; side line of N.E. square weak.
6	very low, to right	low, central	left vertical of "N" appears double on some.
7	central	high, slightly to right	top stroke of "N" appears slightly double; scratches bottom margin.
8†	high, central	central	trace of horizontal guide-line through value and "B" square.
9†	high, to right	central	several blurred lines at left side; vertical guide-line N.E. square, wide of frame.
10†	central, to left	high, to right	
11	high, to left	high, central	trace of vertical guide-line N.E. square, very close to frame, with top line thin.

**Shows the Ray-flaw.* *†Shows the "O"-flaw.*

1a 1b 2 3 4 5
6 7 8 9 10 11

1a 1b 2 3 4 5
6 7 8 9 10 11

Plate.	Position of Corner-letter at left.	Position of Corner-letter at right.	Further distinguishing characteristics.
		NC	
1a*	central	central	diagonal stroke of letter "N" short.
1b*	central	central	"N" recut; distinct trace of missing ray.
2*	central, to left	slightly low, to left	corner of "C" square defective; "E" of "PENNY" runs nearly into bottom margin.
3	slightly low, slightly to right	central, slightly to left	top line of N.W. square thin.
4	low, to right	central, slightly to left	several dots in and above N.W. square; horizontal guide-line through "C" square, close to frame.
5	central	high, to left—slopes down	side line of N.E. square weak.
6	central	low, slightly to left	bottom line of "N" square thin.
7	central	slightly high, to left	
8†	high, to left	high, slightly to left	bottom line extends on right; bottom line wavy.
9†	central	high, slightly to left	vertical guide-line N.E. square; also in "C" square, very close to frame.
10†	central, to left	high, slightly to left	
11	high, to left	high, slightly to left	
		ND	
1a*	high, to right	high, to left	diagonal stroke of letter "N" short.
1b*	high, to right	high, to left	recut "N"; side line of N.E. square thin.
2*	central	central	bottom line of "N" square thin.
3	central, to right	high, to right	
4	central	rather low, to right	mark in N.E. corner of "N" square; dot left side of "D"; scratches on margin below.
5	central, to right	high, to right	marks of re-entry through "ON" of "ONE"; left side very irregular.
6	low, to right	very low, central	blur outside N.W. square.
7	central	central	
8†	high, to left	central	top line of N.E. square thin; vertical guide-line in the same square.
9†	high, to right	very high, to right	faint vertical guide-line N.E. square.
10†	high, to left	high, to right	short stroke attached to lower part of curve of "D".
11	central, to left	central, to right	

*Shows the Ray-flaw. †Shows the "O"-flaw.

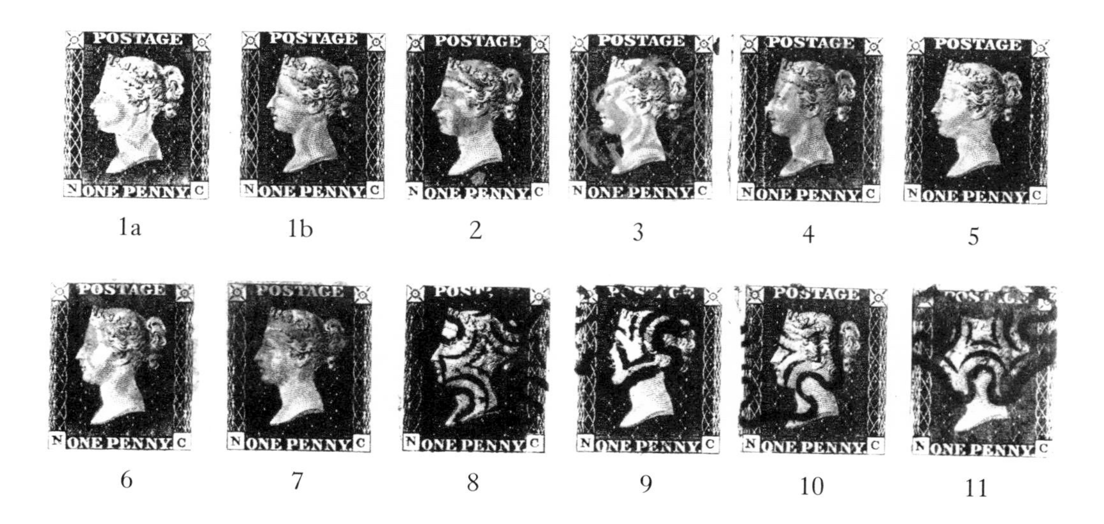
1a
1b
2
3
4
5
6
7
8
9
10
11

1a
1b
2
3
4
5
6
7
8
9
10
11

Plate.	Position of Corner-letter at left.	Position of Corner-letter at right.	Further distinguishing characteristics.
		NE	
1a*	central, to right	central, to right	diagonal stroke of letter "N" short.
1b*	central, to right	central, to right	"N" recut; corner of "N" square weak.
2*	low, to left	very high, to right	bottom line of "E" square thin.
3	low, to right	high, to right	
4	slightly low, to right	central	dot in middle of "N", and two others in square.
5	high, to left	high, central	side line of N.E. square thin.
6	very low, to right	high, to left	top line of N.W. square thin. In the second state, the frame-lines have been strengthened or recut
7	low, to right	high, slightly to right	right line extends beyond bottom.
8†	high, central	high, to left	top line of N.W. square thin.
9†	high, to right	central, far to right	vertical guide-line N.E. and "E" squares; diagonal stroke of letter "N" long.
10†	central	low, to left	letter "N" as in plate 9.
11	slightly low, central	very low, to right	
		NF	
1a*	high, central	central	diagonal stroke of letter "N" short.
1b*	high, central	central	left side and "N" recut.
2*	central, to left	central, to left	
3	central, to right	rather low, to right	faint horizontal guide-line N.E. square, very close to frame.
4	low, to right	low, to left	dot in N.E. corner of "F" square; horizontal guide-line through value.
5	high, to right	low, to right	top line of N.W. square and side line of N.E. square almost absent.
6	low, central	central, to left	
7	central	very low, to left	top serif of "N" double.
8†	high, central	central	top right ray in N.W. square very thin.
9†	high, to right	central	diagonal stroke of letter "N" long.
10†	high, central	central	letter "N" as in plate 9.
11	central, to left	very high, to right	letter "N" as in plate 9; bottom line extends slightly on right.

**Shows the Ray-flaw.* *†Shows the "O"-flaw.*

1a
1b
2
3
4
5
6
7
8
9
10
11

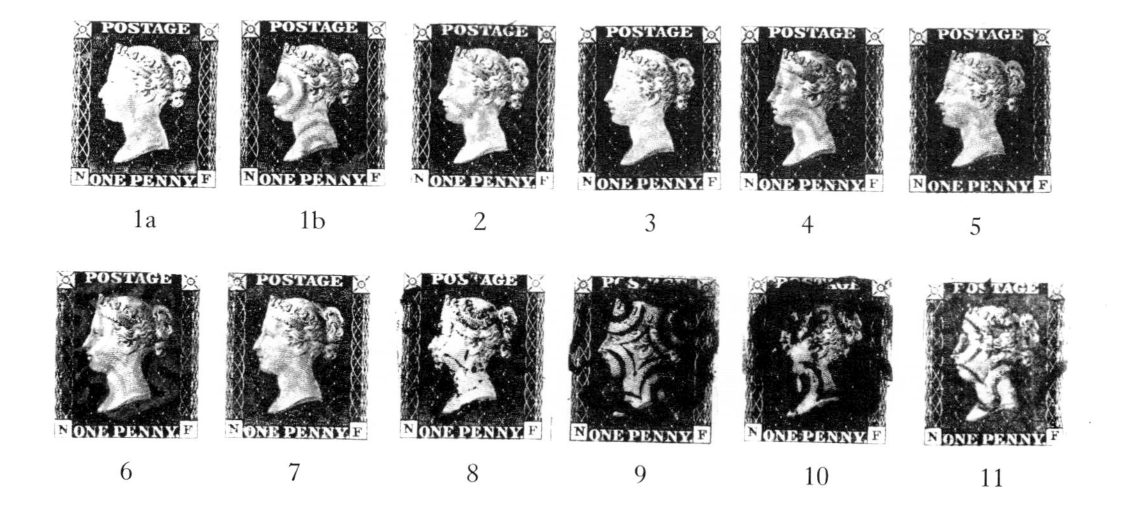
1a
1b
2
3
4
5
6
7
8
9
10
11

Plate.	Position of Corner-letter		Further distinguishing characteristics.
	at left.	at right.	
		NG	
1a*	central	high, central	diagonal stroke of letter "N" short.
1b*	central	high, central	"N" recut; slight re-entry N.E. square.
2*	low, to left	low, to left	left line extends slightly beyond bottom.
3	central, to right	rather high, central	
4	low, central	slightly high, to left	dot to right of foot of "G" (not always present); dot below first "N" of "PENNY"; horizontal guide-line each letter-square and value.
5	very high, to right	high, to left	left line extends beyond bottom; bottom line wavy.
6	low, to left	high, central	
7	very low, to left	high, slightly to left	
8†	high, central	low, to left	
9†	central, to right	low, to right	diagonal stroke of letter "N" long; vertical guide-line N.E. square, close to frame.
10†	central, to left	high, central	letter "N" as in plate 9.
11	high, central	high, central	letter "N" as in plate 9.
		NH	
1a*	high, to right	low, to left	diagonal stroke of "N" short.
1b*	high, to right	low, to left	recut "N"; left line extends beyond bottom.
2*	central	very high, to right	
3	high, to right	central, to right	mark through top left side of "O" of "POSTAGE".
4	low, slightly to left	rather high, central	dot on left margin, opposite top of diadem.
5	high, to right	low, central	"E" of "POSTAGE" runs nearly into top margin; bottom line wavy.
6	central	slightly high, to right	dot in "N" of "ONE".
7	high, to right	high, to left	
8†	high, central	high, central	
9†	high, central	high, central	tall "N"; "E" of "POSTAGE" runs nearly into top margin; faint vertical guide-line N.E. square.
10†	rather low, to left	slightly low, to right	tall "N"; squat "H"; vertical guide-line N.E. square, close to frame.
11	high, central	low, to left	tall "N"; first stroke of "H" double.

**Shows the Ray-flaw.* *†Shows the "O"-flaw.*

POSTAGE
N ONE PENNY G
1a
1b
2
3
4
5
6
7
8
9
10
11

POSTAGE
N ONE PENNY H
1a
1b
2
3
4
5
6
7
8
9
10
11

Plate.	Position of Corner-letter		Further distinguishing characteristics.
	at left.	at right.	
		NI	
1a*	low, to left	slightly low, to right	
1b*	low, to left	slightly low, to right	outer lines of N.E. square thin; "N" re-cut.
2*	high, to left	high, central	
3	high, central	central, far to right	
4	high, to left	slightly low, to left	left side line weak.
5	high, to right	low, to left	line below "ONE" wavy.
6	central, to right	central	vertical guide-line N.E. square, very close to frame; tiny dot after "I".
7	central	slightly low, to left	right side line extends slightly beyond bottom.
8†	high, slightly to left	central, to left	vertical guide-line N.E. square, close to frame; thin line extends from bottom line into right margin.
9†	very high, to right	low, to right	vertical guide-line N.E. square, close to frame; horizontal guide-line through letter-squares and value.
10†	high, to left	low, central	vertical guide-line N.E. square; horizontal guide-line through value and "I" square; tall "I".
11	central, slightly to left	rather high, to right	tall "I"; dot S.W. of and close to "I".
		NJ	
1a*	high, to right	high, central	diagonal stroke of letter "N" short.
1b*	high, to right	high, central	"N" recut; top line of N.W. square weak; scratches on lower margin.
2*	high, to left	central, to left	"E" of "PENNY" runs nearly into margin.
3	high, central	central, to left	stroke (re-entry) beside top left ray in N.W. square; distinct horizontal and vertical guide-lines through top of N.E. square.
4	central	central, to left	left side weak; blur before letter "J"; short horizontal stroke in left of "N" square, near foot; trace of horizontal guide-line through value.
5	high, to right	central, to left	line below "ONE" wavy.
6	very low, to right	low, to left	dots in "P" of "POSTAGE", in N.E. square and above.
7	central	central	Diagonal scratch N.E. square.
8†	very high, to left	high, central	
9†	high, to right	low, to left	vertical guide-line N.E. square, wide of frame; horizontal guide-line through value and letter-squares.
10†	high, to left	high, central	square "J", with stroke after it.
11	high, central	high, central	square "J", with full stop after it.

**Shows the Ray-flaw.* *†Shows the "O"-flaw.*

1a
1b
2
3
4
5
6
7
8
9
10
11

1a
1b
2
3
4
5
6
7
8
9
10
11

Plate.	Position of Corner-letter at left.	Position of Corner-letter at right.	Further distinguishing characteristics.
		NK	
1a*	high, to right	central	
1b*	high, to right	central	outer lines of N.E. square very weak.
2*	central	high, to right	"N" broken on left.
3	high, to right	central, far to right	
4	central	central	dot in "P" of "POSTAGE"; and two distinct dots after middle of "K".
5	high, to right	low, to left	bottom line wavy.
6	low, central	low, to left	right side line extends beyond bottom; left side very weak.
7	central	rather low, to right	
8†	high, slightly to left	central, to left	top right ray in N.W. square thin.
9†	high, to right	high, central	fine re-entry N.E. square, each letter-square and below "O" of "ONE".
10†	high, central	high, to right	tall "N"; right side line extends beyond bottom; trace of horizontal guide-line through value.
11	very high, central	low, central	tall "N".
		NL	
1a*	high, to right	high, to left	
1b*	high, to right	high, to left	horizontal guide-line through top of N.E. square.
2*	high, central	high, to left	dot above corner of N.E. square; vertical guide-line through that square, wide of frame.
3	high, to right	central	scratches on left side margin.
4	high, central	high, central	two dots above "L", one large and one small; also vertical mark close to frame.
5	very high, to right	central, to left	line on left side margin.
6	very low, to right	central, to left	
7	central	high, central	scratch in "N" square.
8†	high, central	high, central	right and bottom lines cross; letters of "POSTAGE" run nearly into margin.
9†	high, to right	central	trace of horizontal guide-line through "N" square and "ONE".
10†	high, to left	central, to right	tall "N".
11	central	low, to right	tall "N".

**Shows the Ray-flaw.* *†Shows the "O"-flaw.*

1a
1b
2
3
4
5
6
7
8
9
10
11

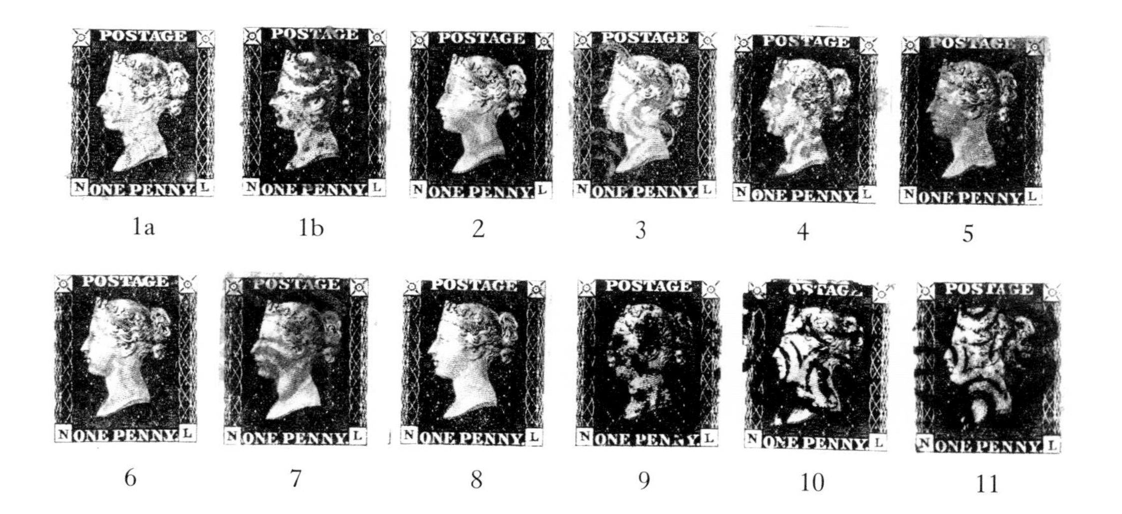
1a
1b
2
3
4
5
6
7
8
9
10
11

Plate.	Position of Corner-letter		Further distinguishing characteristics.
	at left.	at right.	
		OA	
1a*	slightly low, central	central	re-entry N.E. square with vertical guide-line; right side and bottom lines cross; line below "ONE"; dot in middle of "O".
1b*	slightly low, central	central	left side line recut; "E" of "PENNY" runs nearly into bottom margin; re-entry N.E. square; guide-line almost invisible; dot in middle of "O".
2*	central	central	
3	central	low, to left	
4	low, central	low, to right	tiny dot on top margin, above right corner of N.W. square.
5	central	central, to right—slopes up	vertical guide-line N.E. square, close to frame.
6	central	central, to right	right foot of "A" sometimes defective.
7	rather high, central	central	
8†	very high, slightly to left	low, to left	
9†	low, central	high, to left	vertical guide-line N.E. square, wide of frame; and horizontal guide-line through value; double "O"; bottom line extends on right.
10†	low, to right	high, to right	bottom line wavy; vertical guide-line N.E. square, close to frame.
11	low, to right	central	fine re-entry each upper square, "A" square and "POSTAGE".
		OB	
1a*	central, slightly to left	central, to right	trace of vertical guide-line N.E. square.
1b*	central—appears more to left	central, to right	left side line extends evidently beyond bottom; "NE" of "ONE" joined
2*	central, slightly to left	central, to right	mark on left side of "T".
3	central, to right	central, to right	bottom line extends on left.
4	high, to left	central, to right	dot in "Y" and below "P".
5	low, central	high, central	letters of "POSTAGE" run nearly into margin.
6	high, to right	central	fine re-entry N.W. square, "O" square and through value.
7	central, slightly to left	low, central	vertical guide-line N.E. square, very close to frame.
8†	high, to left	central, to left	sometimes without any trace of "O"-flaw.
9†	low, to left	slightly low, central	vertical guide-line N.E. square, wide of frame; trace of double "B".
10†	central, to left	high, to right	side line of N.E. square weak.
11	low, to right	high, central	bottom line extends evidently on right.

**Shows the Ray-flaw.* *†Shows the "O"-flaw.*

1a
1b
2
3
4
5
6
7
8
9
10
11

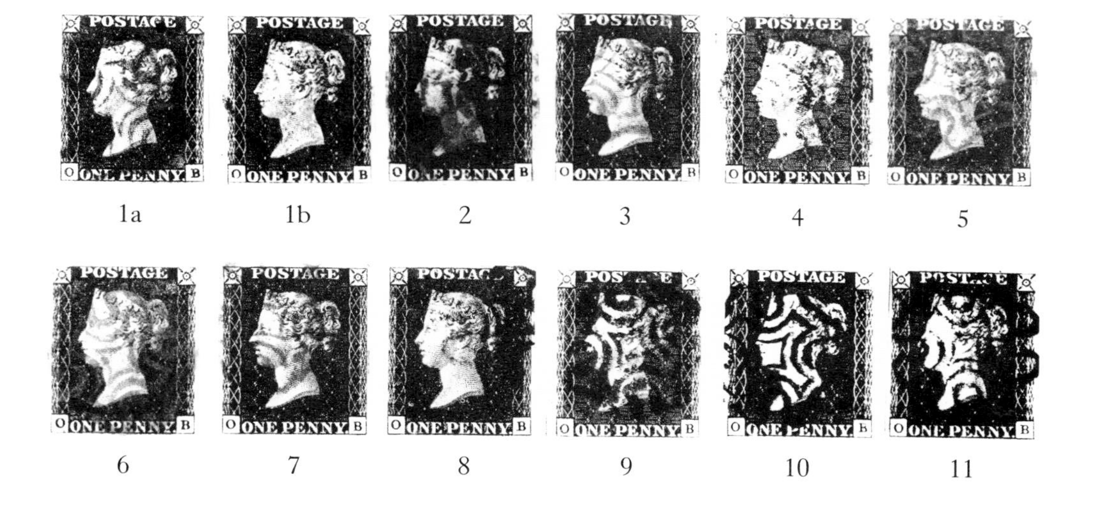
1a
1b
2
3
4
5
6
7
8
9
10
11

Plate.	Position of Corner-letter at left.	Position of Corner-letter at right.	Further distinguishing characteristics.
		OC	
1a*	central	central, to left	
1b*	central	central, to left	left side line recut.
2*	high, to left	low, to left	mark on top left serif of "T" of "POSTAGE".
3	central	central, to left	
4	central, to left	central, slightly to left	distinct dot N.E. of "O", and N.W. of "C".
5	high, to right	very high, to left	vertical line just outside N.W. square, on left.
6	central, to right	central, slightly to left	in second state, the left frame-line has been strengthened or recut.
7	slightly high, to left	high, central	vertical guide-line N.E. square, close to frame.
8†	central, to left	low, slightly to left	
9†	very low, central	high, central	vertical guide-line N.E. square.
10†	low, to left	central, to left	vertical guide-line N.E. square; top portion of "C" slightly defective.
11	low, central	slightly high, to left—slopes down	mark on left side of N.E. square; blur on line of "O" square.
		OD	
1a*	central	high, central	
1b*	central	high, central	left side recut; "NE" of "ONE" joined.
2*	high, to right	high, to right	trace of vertical guide-line in "D" square, close to frame; bottom line of "D" square thin.
3	central	rather high, slightly to right	
4	low, central	central	dot S.W. of "O"; dot before and after "D"; several dots on bottom margin.
5	high, to right	high, central	distinct horizontal line through N.W. square; left side line irregular.
6	high, to right	high, slightly to right	left side line thin. In second state, the left frame-line has been strengthened or recut.
7	rather high, central	central	
8†	central	central	vertical guide-line N.E. square; usually little trace of "O"-flaw.
9†	very low, central	very low, central	trace of vertical guide-line N.E. square.
10†	high, central	high, central	
11	central	high, to right	

**Shows the Ray-flaw.* *†Shows the "O"-flaw.*

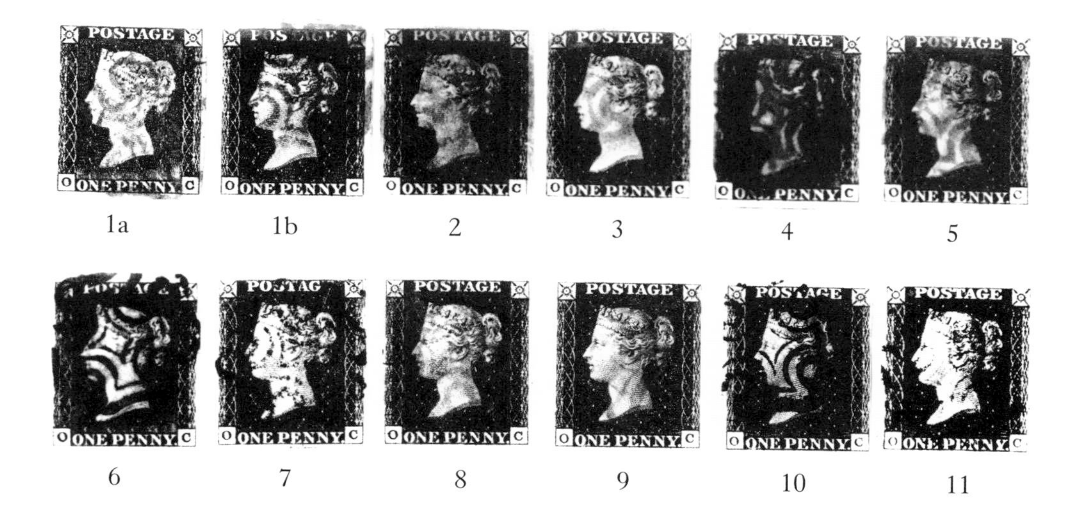
POSTAGE
ONE PENNY
1a
1b
2
3
4
5
6
7
8
9
10
11

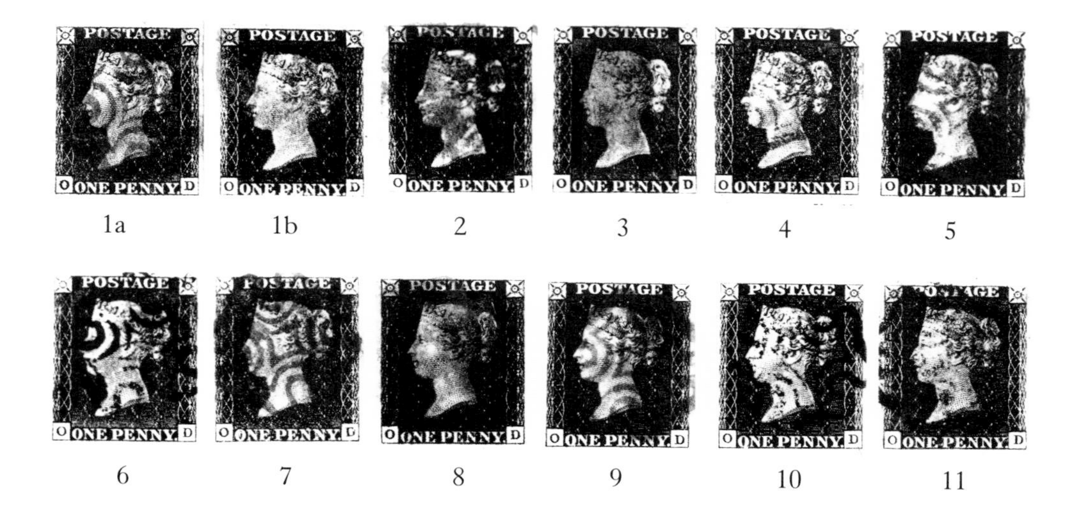
POSTAGE
ONE PENNY
1a
1b
2
3
4
5
6
7
8
9
10
11

Plate.	Position of Corner-letter		Further distinguishing characteristics.
	at left.	*at right.*	
		OE	
1a*	central	low, to right	
1b*	central	low, to right	"E" of "PENNY" runs nearly into margin.
2*	very low, to left	very high, to right	bottom serif of "E" faint.
3	central, to right	high, far to right	
4	central	central	two tiny dots in "O" of "ONE"; dot in "E" square touching top margin.
5	very high, to right	central, to left	
6	very low, to right	central, to right	left side line irregular. In second state, the left frame-line has been strengthened or recut.
7	high, central	high, central	faint vertical guide-line N.E. square.
8†	high, to left	central, close to left	faint vertical guide-line N.E. square.
9†	very low, to right	low, central	vertical guide-line N.E. square; and in "E" square, very close to frame; right side extends beyond bottom.
10†	high, to right	low, central	
11	central, to right	high, central	
		OF	
1a*	rather high, central	high, central	
1b*	rather high, central	high, central	left side recut; "NE" of "ONE" joined.
2*	central, to left	central	trace of vertical guide-line in "F" square, close to frame.
3	low, to right	central, to left	
4	central, to left	central	dot in "O" square, and in "O" of "ONE"; side line of N.E. square weak; right line extends beyond bottom.
5	central, to right	high, to right	left side very irregular.
6	central, to left	low, to left	trace of double side line on right margin.
7	high, central	central, to left	
8†	high, slightly to left	central, not so much to left	vertical guide-line N.E. square.
9†	low, central	very high, central	vertical guide-line N.E. square.
10†	very low, central	low, to left	trace of horizontal guide-line below "Y" and "F" square.
11	central, to right	central	top of N.E. square weak; blur on line of "O" square.

**Shows the Ray-flaw.* *†Shows the "O"-flaw.*

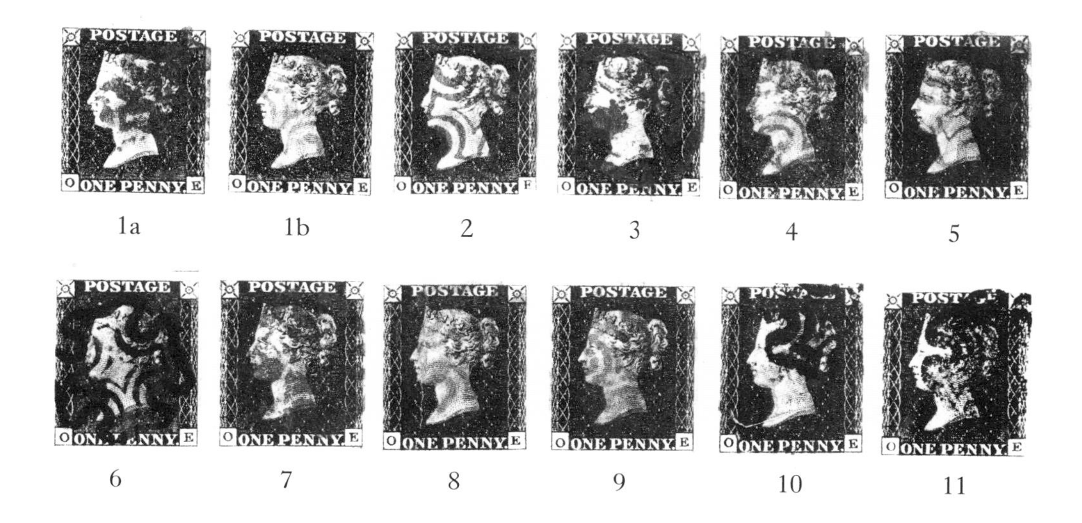
1a
1b
2
3
4
5
6
7
8
9
10
11

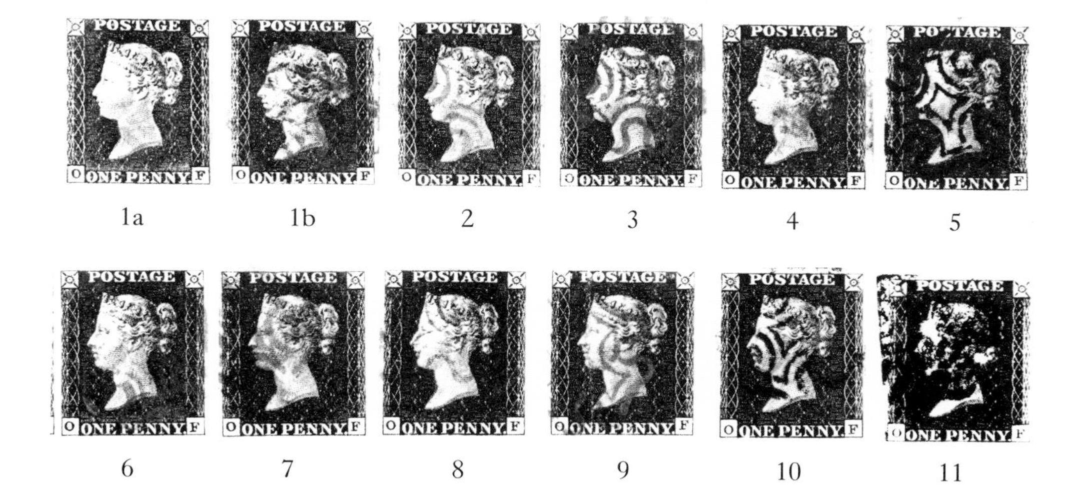
1a
1b
2
3
4
5
6
7
8
9
10
11

Plate.	Position of Corner-letter		Further distinguishing characteristics.
	at left.	*at right.*	
		OG	
1a*	high, to left	high, central	
1b*	high, to left	high, central	upper portion of right line incomplete.
2*	central	high, to left	bottom line thin.
3	central, to right	high, to left	
4	high, central	central, to left	two dots in "O" square; dot in curve of "G".
5	high, to right	low, to left	side line of N.E. square weak.
6	low, to right	central	very faint vertical guide-line N.E. square.
7	central, to left	high, to left	vertical guide-line N.E. square.
8†	central, to left	high, central	
9†	central, to left	slightly high, to left	vertical guide-line N.E. square.
10†	high, central	low, to left	
11	central	high, central	dot S.W. of "O".
		OH	
1a*	central	low, to left	top serifs of "H" join.
1b*	central	low, to left	thin "H"; serifs apart.
2*	central	slightly high, far to right	left corner of N.W. square weak.
3	central	central, slightly to right	
4	low, to right	central, to left	right side line extends beyond bottom.
5	very high, central	central	left side very irregular.
6	high, to right	high, central	distinct dot in middle of left side of N.E. square, and below "N" of "ONE".
7	central, to left	high, to left	
8†	high, to left	high, central	bottom line slightly wavy.
9†	central, to right	low, to left	vertical guide-line N.E. square, very close to frame; horizontal guide-line "H" square.
10†	high, central	low, central	squat "H".
11	central, to right	high, to left	blur on line of "O" square.

**Shows the Ray-flaw.* *†Shows the "O"-flaw.*

1a
1b
2
3
4
5
6
7
8
9
10
11

1a
1b
2
3
4
5
6
7
8
9
10
11

Plate.	Position of Corner-letter		Further distinguishing characteristics.
	at left.	at right.	
		OI	
1a*	central	low, central	right line extends beyond bottom.
1b*	central	low, central	right line extends beyond bottom; re-entry N.W. square.
2*	central, to right	central, to right	bottom line extends faintly on right; trace of vertical guide-line in "I" square.
3	central	central, to left	"E" of "PENNY" runs nearly into lower margin.
4	central	rather low, to left	horizontal guide-line through letter-squares and value.
5	central, to left	very low, to left	
6	central, to left	central, far to left	scratches through bottom line of "O" square; vertical line outside N.E. square.
7	very low, to left	high, central	
8†	high, central	central, slightly to left	vertical guide-line N.E. square, very close to frame.
9†	low, to left	rather low, well to right	vertical guide-line N.E. square, very close to frame; right side line extends slightly beyond bottom; faint guide-line through value.
10†	low, to right	high, to right	bottom line slightly wavy; tall "I".
11	low, to right	high, central	tall "I"; faint vertical guide-line N.E. square.
		OJ	
1a*	slightly high, to right	high, to left	
1b*	appears more central	high, to left	top line of N.W. square and bottom line of "O" square thin; "E" of "PENNY" runs nearly into margin.
2*	high, to right	high, to left	horizontal guide-line above N.E. and N.W. squares.
3	central, to right	high, central	horizontal scratches above.
4	central, to right	central, to left	left side very irregular.
5	high, to right	central, to left	right side line weak; trace of horizontal guide-line through "J" square.
6	central, to left	central	tiny dots in "O" square; left top ray in N.W. square distinctly short.
7	central	very low, to left	vertical guide-line N.E. square, close to frame.
8†	central	very high, central	bottom line extends slightly on right.
9†	very low, central	central	"J" slightly square.
10†	low, to right	very low, to right	"J" square and slightly double, with mark after it.
11	central, to right	very high, central	square "J"; side line of N.E. square nearly absent.

**Shows the Ray-flaw.* *†Shows the "O"-flaw.*

POSTAGE
O ONE PENNY I
1a 1b 2 3 4 5
6 7 8 9 10 11

POSTAGE
O ONE PENNY J
1a 1b 2 3 4 5
6 7 8 9 10 11

Plate.	Position of Corner-letter		Further distinguishing characteristics.
	at left.	at right.	
		OK	
1a*	central	high, slightly to right	
1b*	central	high, slightly to right	slight weakness at corner of "O" square; trace of missing ray.
2*	central	low, central	
3	central	central, to left	small blurred "K".
4	high, to right	central, to left	top line of N.W. square thin.
5	high, to right	central, far to left	left side line irregular.
6	high, to left	central, to left	
7	central	central	faint vertical guide-line N.E. square, close to frame.
8	high, slightly to left	central	vertical guide-line N.E. square.
9†	high, to right	high, to right	right side line of N.E. square thin.
10†	central, to right	very low, central	bottom line extends on right.
11	very low, central	low, to right	right side line of "K" square slopes inwards from top to bottom.
		OL	
1a*	high, central	central, to left	
1b*	high, central	central, to left	"E" of "PENNY" runs nearly into margin.
2*	high, to right	high, central	side line extends above N.E. square.
3	central	high, central	bottom line extends on left; top line of N.W. square thin.
4	low, to right	central, to left	distinct dot near top of N.E. square, and on margin above "E"; scratches through "O" square and below.
5	very high, to right	central, to left	scratches left side margin.
6	low, to right	central, slightly to left	tiny dot in left of "L" square, opposite foot of "L"; dot in "O" square.
7	low, to left	central, to left	left side line extends beyond bottom.
8	central, to left	slightly high, central	indistinct dot below corner of "L" square; "E" of "POSTAGE" runs nearly into top margin; faint vertical guide-line N.W. square, close to frame.
9†	very low, to left	central	trace of line or mark N.E. square, close to frame.
10†	very high, to right	low, to right	horizontal guide-line through letter-squares and value.
11	high, to right	slightly high, to right	dot above centre ray in N.W. square.

**Shows the Ray-flaw.* *†Shows the "O"-flaw.*

1a
1b
2
3
4
5
6
7
8
9
10
11

1a
1b
2
3
4
5
6
7
8
9
10
11

Plate.	Position of Corner-letter at left.	Position of Corner-letter at right.	Further distinguishing characteristics.
		PA	
1a*	high, to right	high, central	left side line extends beyond bottom.
1b*	central, to left	central, to left	letters in different position; squares show traces of original letters.
2*	high, to left	low, to right	trace of double "P" on right.
3	high, to right	high, slightly to left	"P" with small loop. "A" blind.
4	central, to right	central	trace of double "P" on left; scratches on lower margin.
5	central	central, to right	scratches on margin below; horizontal guide-line partly through value and "P" square.
6	low, central	high, central	left and bottom lines slightly cross; vertical guide-line N.E. square.
7	central, far to right	central	scratches on lower margin.
8	very high, to right	central, slightly to left	trace of vertical guide-line N.E. square.
9†	low, central—slopes up	high, central	
10†	central	high, central	trace of double "A".
11	central, to right	high, to right	
		PB	
1a*	central	rather low, slightly to right	recut "P" square showing the frame-line double.
1b*	central	rather low, slightly to right	"P" square normal.
2*	central, to right	high, to right	"P" square shows a line half-way up at right of "P"; "B" square shows a double line at base of "B"; both letter-squares recut.
3	central, to left	high, to right	"P" with small loop.
4	central, to right	high, central	dot in "A" of "POSTAGE", and in N.E. square.
5	low, to left	low, to left	horizontal guide-line in "B" square. In second state, the frame-lines have been strengthened or recut; third state shows re-entry through letter-squares and value.
6	high, central	high, to right	left side very irregular.
7	low, to right	high, to right	faint dot after "P"; horizontal guide-lines through value.
8	high, far to right	central	vertical guide-line N.E. square.
9†	central	high, central	
10†	very low, central	high, central	scratches on lower margin.
11	very low, central	very low, central—slopes down	

**Shows the Ray-flaw.* *†Shows the "O"-flaw.*

1a 1b 2 3 4 5
6 7 8 9 10 11

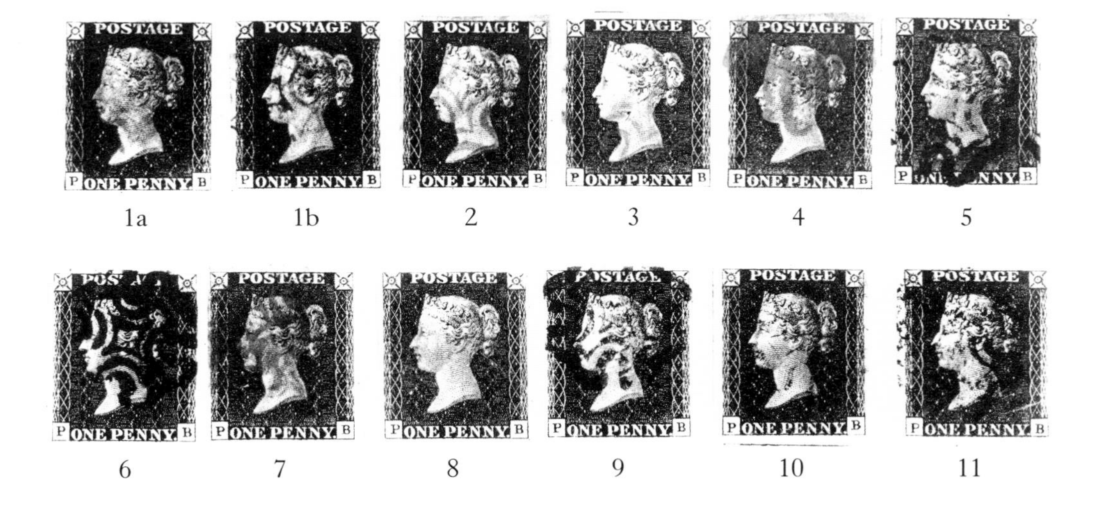
1a 1b 2 3 4 5
6 7 8 9 10 11

Plate.	Position of Corner-letter at left.	Position of Corner-letter at right.	Further distinguishing characteristics.
		PC	
1a*	slightly low, central	high, central	vertical guide-line N.E. square, wide of frame.
1b*	slightly low, central	high, central	no trace of guide-line.
2*	slightly low, central	high, slightly to left	trace of vertical guide-line N.E. square.
3	very high, central	high, to left	"P" with small loop.
4	central, to right	low, to left	dot in "P" of "POSTAGE", and two dots in "C" square.
5	central	central, slightly to left	distinct vertical scratches in "P" square; scratches on lower margin.
6	slightly low, central	slightly low, central	N.E. square, weak on right.
7	high, to right	high, to left	right side line extends slightly beyond bottom.
8	very high, slightly to left	central, to left	vertical guide-line N.E. square, close to frame.
9†	central, to left	slightly high, central	bottom line extends on left; vertical guide-line N.E. square.
10†	central	high, slightly to left	top line of each upper square thin.
11	high, central	very low, central	
		PD	
1a*	central, slightly to right	high, to left	upper portion of loop of "D" weak; sometimes shows vertical guide-line N.E. square.
1b*	central, slightly to right	high, to left	"D" complete; scratches on margin below "O" of "ONE"; "NE" of "ONE" joined.
2*	central	central	vertical guide-line N.E. square, very close to frame; "P" square recut.
3	slightly low, to right	slightly high, to right	"P" with narrow loop; left letter-square not rectangular, the line being partly double on right side.
4	central, to right	central, to right	dot in "D" square; upper portion of left side weak.
5	rather low, central	high, to right	left side weak; horizontal guide-line in "D" square, very close to frame.
6	high, to right	high, central	distinct dot on left margin opposite diadem; mark in "E" of "PENNY".
7	central, slightly to right	rather high, central	
8	very high, to left	very high, to right	vertical guide-line N.E. square.
9†	high, central	central, to right	
10†	central	very high, to right	
11	low, to left	high, far to right	bottom line wavy; sometimes shows trace of double bottom.

**Shows the Ray-flaw.* *†Shows the "O"-flaw.*

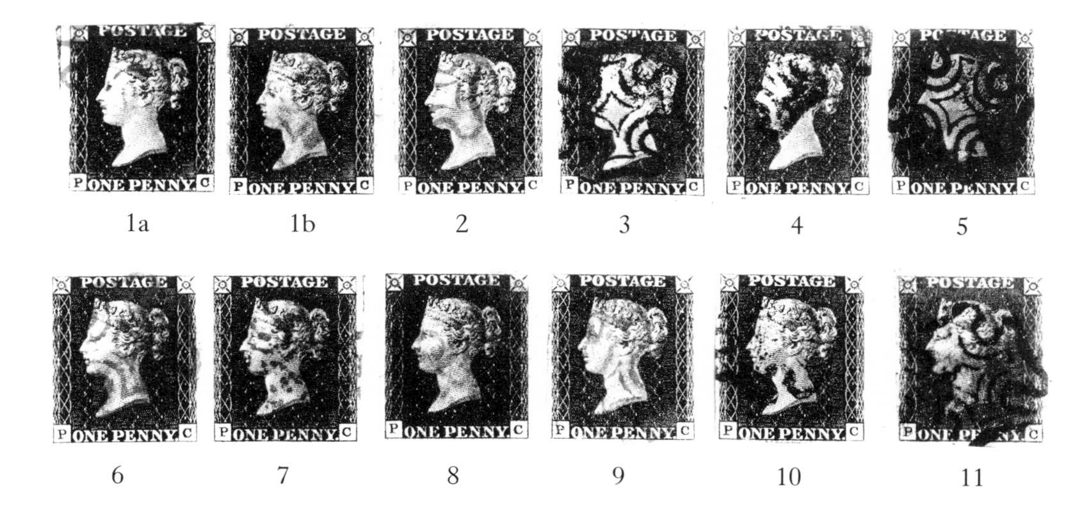
1a 1b 2 3 4 5
6 7 8 9 10 11

1a 1b 2 3 4 5
6 7 8 9 10 11

Plate.	Position of Corner-letter at left.	Position of Corner-letter at right.	Further distinguishing characteristics.
		PE	
1a*	central, to right	central, to right	
1b*	central, to right	central, to right	trace of missing ray; upper portion of right side weak.
2*	central, to right	high, to left	top lines of N.E. square cross.
3	slightly high, to right	high, central	"P" with small loop; short horizontal stroke attached to right side of "P" square, near frame.
4	central	slightly low, central	several dots in each letter-square and below, including a distinct dot in front of both "P" and "E".
5	slightly low, central	high, central	trace of horizontal guide-line through "E" square; scratches on top margin.
6	central, to right	rather high, far to right	left side line weak. In second state, the left frame-line has been strengthened or recut.
7	central, to right	rather high, slightly to left	top stroke of "E" double.
8	high, central	central	mark in N.E. corner of "P" square.
9†	central	very low, central	scratches on right side margin.
10†	high, to right	low, central	bottom line of "E" square thin.
11	central	high, central	bottom line extends on right.
		PF	
1a*	high, to right	high, slightly to left	bottom line extends on right.
1b*	high, to right	high, slightly to left	bottom line extends on right; left side line strengthened.
2*	high, to right	slightly low, central	vertical guide-line N.E. square, very close to frame.
3	slightly low, to right	central	right side line weak.
4	central	low, to left	vertical stroke attached to foot of "P"; several dots in "P" square, and one in "E" of "ONE" and in "P" of "PENNY".
5	low, to right	central	horizontal guide-line through letter-squares and value. Scratch above "OS" of "POSTAGE".
6	high, central	central	trace of double "P" on left.
7	low, to left	central, to left	
8	high, to left	central	
9†	central	very low, to left	vertical guide-line N.E. square, close to frame.
10†	very low, central	low, central	scratches on lower margin.
11	low, central	very high, slightly to right	

**Shows the Ray-flaw.* *†Shows the "O"-flaw.*

POSTAGE
ONE PENNY
P
E
1a
1b
2
3
4
5
6
7
8
9
10
11

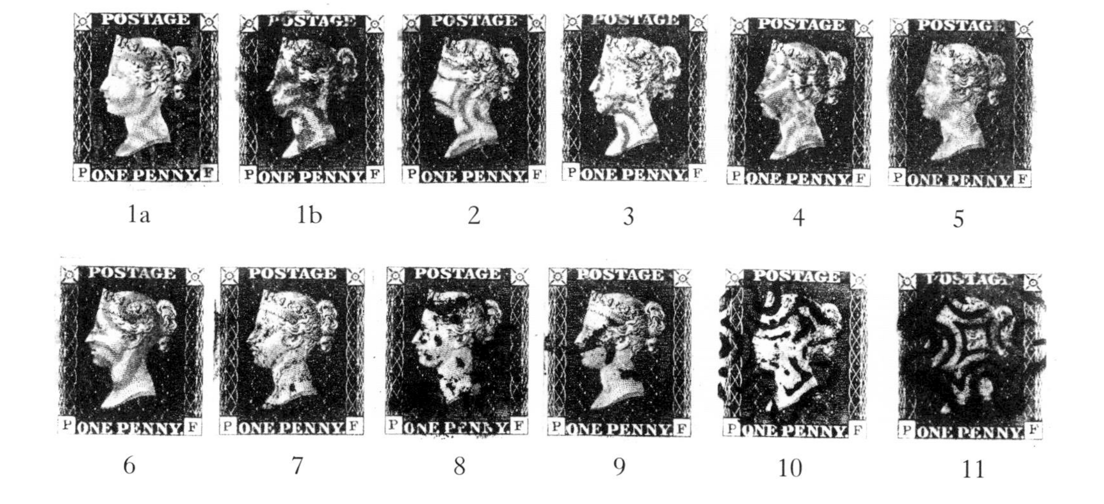
POSTAGE
ONE PENNY
P
F
1a
1b
2
3
4
5
6
7
8
9
10
11

Plate.	Position of Corner-letter		Further distinguishing characteristics.
	at left.	at right.	
		PG	
1a*	low, slightly to left	high, central	faint line on lower margin below value.
1b*	low, slightly to left	high, central	distinct dot in "O" of "ONE".
2*	central, to right	slightly high, to left	bottom line of "P" square slopes up.
3	central, to right	high, central	"P" with small loop; bottom line extends slightly on left.
4	high, to right	high, to right	dot on margin above "G" of "POSTAGE".
5	slightly low, central	low, to left	horizontal guide-line through "G" square; scratches on left side margin and in "P" square.
6	high, central	high, central	dot below "G"; side line of N.E. square thin. In second state, the side line has been strengthened or recut.
7	high, slightly to right	high, to left	scratches on left side margin, opposite Queen's neck.
8	very high, to left	high, central	vertical guide-line N.E. square.
9†	slightly low, central	very low, central	side line of N.E. square weak.
10†	high, to right	low, to left	marks of re-entry in N.E. square, "G" square and below.
11	low, central	low, to left	
		PH	
1a*	high, to right	low, slightly to left	
1b*	high, to right	low, slightly to left	cross-bar of "H" thinner.
2*	high, to right	central	
3	central	high, central	"P" with small loop; bottom line extends on left.
4	central, to right	high, to left	
5	low, to left	high, to left	first vertical stroke of "H" double; short line in margin below "E" of "ONE".
6	high, slightly to left	central, far to right	dot extending into margin above "T" of "POSTAGE"; horizontal guide-line through "ONE".
7	high, central	high, to left	
8	high, to left	high, to right	faint vertical guide-line N.E. square; bottom line extends slightly on left.
9†	central, to right	very high, slightly to right	
10†	low, to right	very low, to right	squat "H".
11	low, central	high, central	bottom serifs of "H" double.

**Shows the Ray-flaw.* *†Shows the "O"-flaw.*

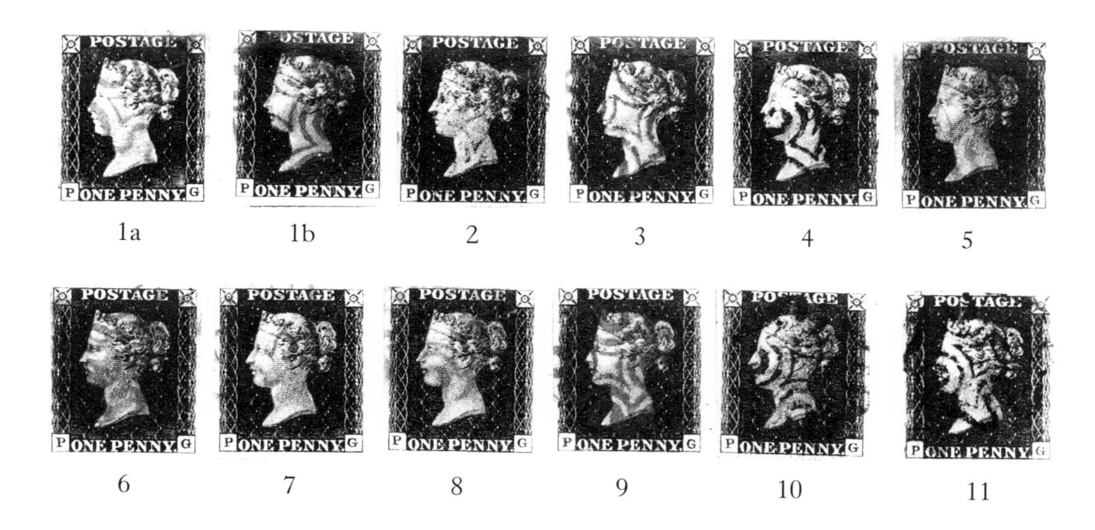
1a
1b
2
3
4
5
6
7
8
9
10
11

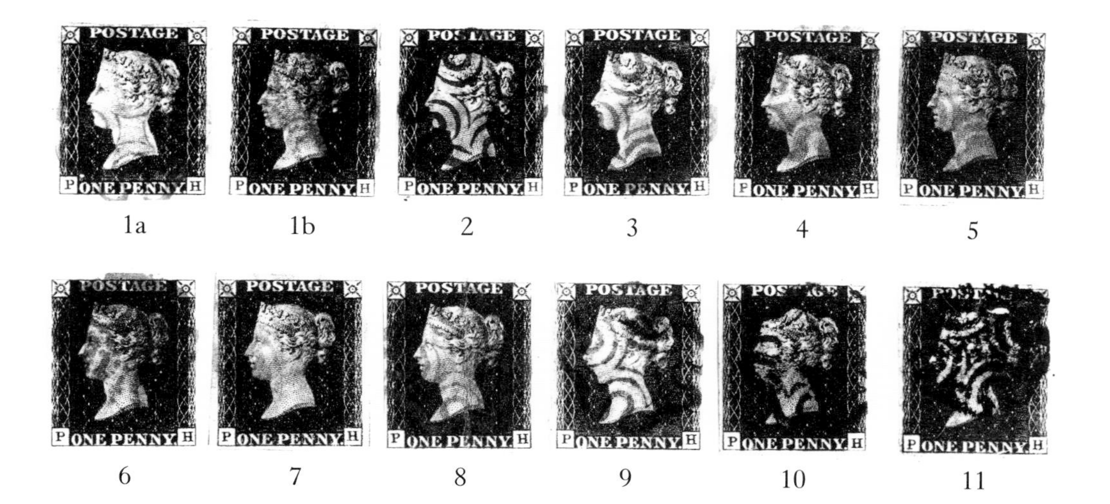
1a
1b
2
3
4
5
6
7
8
9
10
11

Plate.	Position of Corner-letter at left.	Position of Corner-letter at right.	Further distinguishing characteristics.
		PI	
1a*	high, to right	low, to right	
1b*	high, to right	low, to right	N.E. square weak on right.
2*	central, to right	high, to right	bottom line of "P" square not rectangular, lower line sloping up.
3	central	high, to left	"P" with small loop.
4	high, to right	central	
5	low, to right	very low, far to left	horizontal guide-line through "I" square, very close to frame.
6	high, to right	central, to left	indistinct horizontal stroke on margin below "Y" of "PENNY".
7	high, central	central, to left	
8	very high, to left	central, slightly to left	vertical guide-line N.E. square, and trace through "I" square.
9†	central, to right	central	vertical guide-line N.E. square, close to frame.
10†	high, central	high, central	tall "I".
11	very low, central	high, to right	top line of N.E. square double; "E" of "PENNY" runs nearly into margin; bottom line very thick; guide-line in "I" square; tall "I".
		PJ	
1a*	central, to right	high, to left	pin-point extension at lower left corner.
1b*	central, to right	slightly high, to left	both letters recut; bottom line extends slightly on left.
2*	central, to right	central, to left	dot on right margin, close to frame opposite middle of hair.
3	central	high, central	"P" with small loop.
4	low, to right	high, central	right side line extends beyond bottom.
5	central	central	two horizontal lines through "J" square more or less distinct and through "P" square and value; slight trace of double loop to "P".
6	central, to right	low, to left	
7	high, to right	central, to left	
8†	very high, central	high, slightly to right	vertical guide-line N.E. square; indistinct dot in S.E. corner of "J" square.
9†	high, central	high, central	bottom line extends on left; vertical guide-line N.E. square, close to frame; "J" slightly square.
10†	high, to right	low, to right	square "J" with dot after middle; distinct horizontal guide-line through "J" square; and vertical guide-line N.E. square, close to frame.
11	low, central	very high, central	square "J"; blur right side margin.

**Shows the Ray-flaw.* *†Shows the "O"-flaw.*

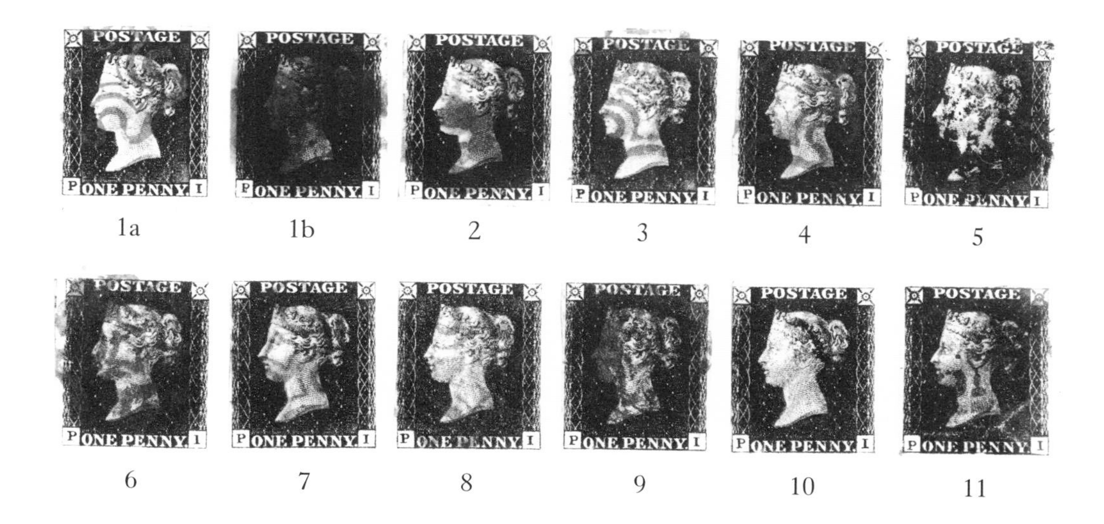
1a
1b
2
3
4
5
6
7
8
9
10
11

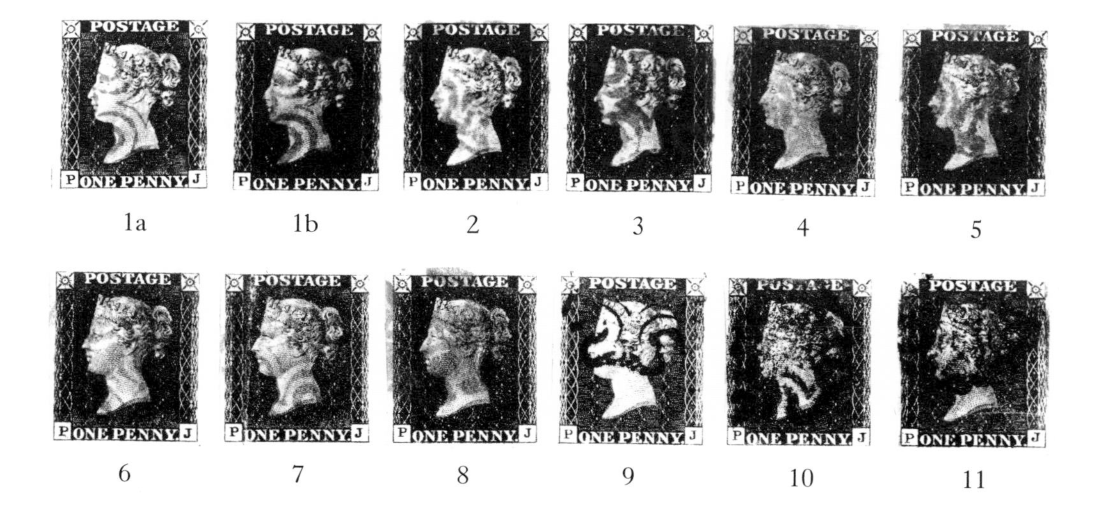
1a
1b
2
3
4
5
6
7
8
9
10
11

Plate.	Position of Corner-letter		Further distinguishing characteristics.
	at left.	at right.	
		PK	
1a*	central, to right	high, to left	
1b*	central, to right	high, to left	both letters recut; side line of N.E. square thin.
2*	central	low, central	top of N.E. square partly double.
3	central	central, to right	"P" with small loop; small blurred "K".
4	high, to right	high, to right	vertical mark at top left of N.W. star.
5	low, central	central, to right	horizontal guide-line through letter-squares and value.
6	very low, central	very low, to left	left side very weak.
7	slightly low, to left	slightly low, to right	
8	high, to left	high, central	mark on margin below "P" square; trace of faint vertical guide-line N.E. square, very close to frame.
9†	low, to left	low, to left	indistinct horizontal guide-line through "ONE" and letter-squares.
10†	very low, central	high, to right	re-entry showing in N.E. and both letter squares; and through "POSTAGE" and value.
11	central	very low, to right	
		PL	
1a*	central	high, central	horizontal guide-line through top portion of value and "L" square; and dot on margin at S.E. corner of "L" square.
1b*	central	high, central	similar; and also "PE" of "PENNY" runs nearly into bottom margin, and bottom line of "P" square thin.
2*	slightly low, central	central, to left	dot on margin above corner of N.E. square.
3	slightly low, to right	high, central	"P" with small loop; top line of N.W. square thin.
4	central, to right	central	indistinct dot before "L"; vertical line on left side margin.
5	slightly low, to right	central	small dot in corner of "L" square.
6	high, central	high, central	dot above "P".
7	central	central, to left	scratches on lower margin.
8	very high, to left	central	small dot below corner of "L" square; trace of vertical guide-line N.E. square.
9†	low, to left	low, central	
10†	central	low, to right	faint vertical guide-line N.E. square; very close to frame.
11	central	low, central	

**Shows the Ray-flaw.* *†Shows the "O"-flaw.*

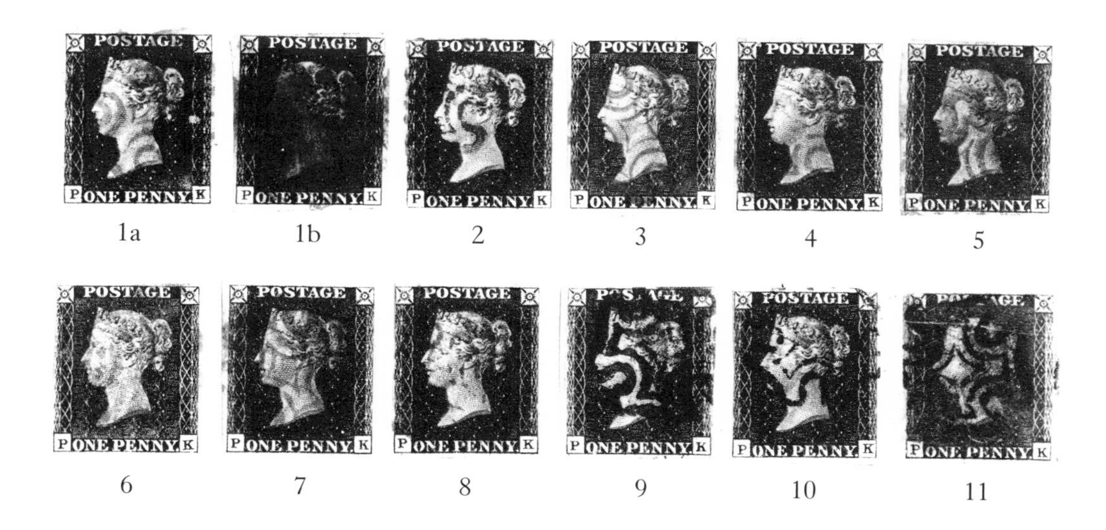
1a
1b
2
3
4
5
6
7
8
9
10
11

1a
1b
2
3
4
5
6
7
8
9
10
11

Plate.	Position of Corner-letter		Further distinguishing characteristics.
	at left.	at right.	
		QA	
1a*	high, to right	low, central	trace of double "Q"; "A" blurred.
1b*	high, to right	low, central	trace of double "Q"; "A" not blurred.
2*	central	central, to right	right side of "Q" faint. N.E. corner faint; vertical guide-line N.E. square.
3	high, to right	central, to right	top line of N.E. square weak.
4	central, to right	central	trace of double "Q"; both side lines extend beyond bottom.
5	rather high, central	central, slightly to right	mark on margin above "T" of "POSTAGE"; bottom part of circle of "Q" appears faint.
6	very high, central	high, to right	side line of N.E. square weak.
7	rather high, central	central	dot on left margin opposite diadem; faint horizontal guide-line through "NE" of "ONE" and "PE" of "PENNY", and scratches below.
8	central, to right	central, to left	vertical guide-line N.E. square.
9†	central, to left	slightly high, to left	trace of horizontal guide-line through each letter-square.
10†	high, central	high, central—slopes down	vertical guide-line N.E. square, close to frame.
11	central	very high, to right	bottom line extends slightly on right.
		QB	
1a*	high, central	central	right side of "Q" faint.
1b*	high, central	central	"Q" distinct; side line of N.E. square thin; faint mark below "B".
2*	very high, central	high, to right	lower portion of "Q" defective; vertical guide-line N.E. square, very close to frame.
3	central	central, to right	loop to "Q" blind, or closed.
4	central	central, to right	N.E. square broken at left corner.
5	central	low, central	top portion of left side irregular.
6	high, central	high, central	N.E. square weak on right; left side line irregular and extends slightly beyond bottom.
7	central	slightly high, to right	faint guide-line through value and "B" square.
8	high, to right	central, to left	vertical guide-line N.E. square.
9†	low, central	high, to left	lines of N.E. square weak; horizontal guide-line through "Q" square and value.
10†	very low, to right	high, to right	top curve of "B" faint; "Q" with short tail.
11	low, central	central—slopes down	bottom line extends on right.

**Shows the Ray-flaw.* *†Shows the "O"-flaw.*

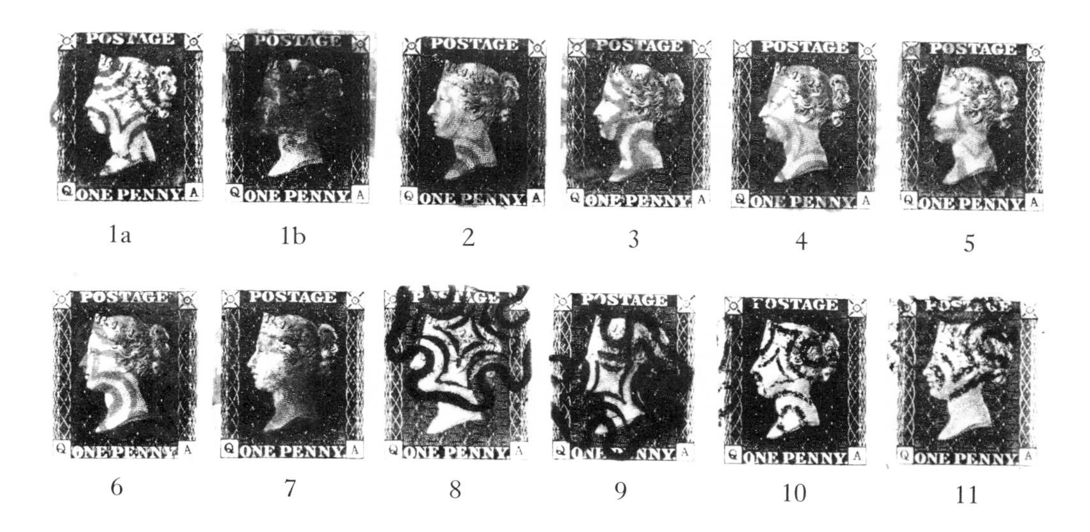
1a 1b 2 3 4 5
6 7 8 9 10 11

1a 1b 2 3 4 5
6 7 8 9 10 11

Plate.	Position of Corner-letter		Further distinguishing characteristics.
	at left.	*at right.*	
		QC	
1a*	high, central	low, slightly to left	
1b*	high, central	low, slightly to left	side line of N.E. square thin.
2*	central, to right	high, central	rays in each upper square thick; side line of "Q" square thin.
3	high, central	high, central	top line of N.W. square appears double.
4	central, to right	central	right line extends beyond bottom.
5	central, to left	central, to left	horizontal guide-line through "C" square; vertical scratch through N.W. square, and on left margin.
6	high, slightly to left	very high, slightly to left	dot below corner of "C" square.
7	central, to right	high, slightly to left	vertical guide-line N.E. square, very close to frame.
8	central	central, slightly to left	vertical guide-line N.E. square, wide of frame.
9†	central, to left	high, central	top line of N.E. square thin.
10†	central	high, to left	side line of N.E. square thin.
11	high, to right	central, to right	
		QD	
1a*	high, to left	high, central	side line of N.E. square thick.
1b*	high, to left	high, central	side line of N.E. square thin; "NE" of "ONE" joined.
2*	central	high, to right	corner of N.W. square weak.
3	central	central, to right	scratches on lower margin.
4	central, to right	central, well to right	
5	central, slightly to left	high, central	left side line very irregular; N.E. square; broken at left corner.
6	central, to right	rather high, far to right	in the second state the frame-lines have been strengthened or recut.
7	central, to right	very high, central	
8	low, central	low, to left	vertical guide-line N.E. square, wide of frame.
9†	very high, to left	very high, to right	horizontal guide-line through value and "D" square.
10†	very high, central	low, central	scratches on top margin.
11	high, central	high, far to right	

**Shows the Ray-flaw.* *†Shows the "O"-flaw.*

1a
1b
2
3
4
5
6
7
8
9
10
11

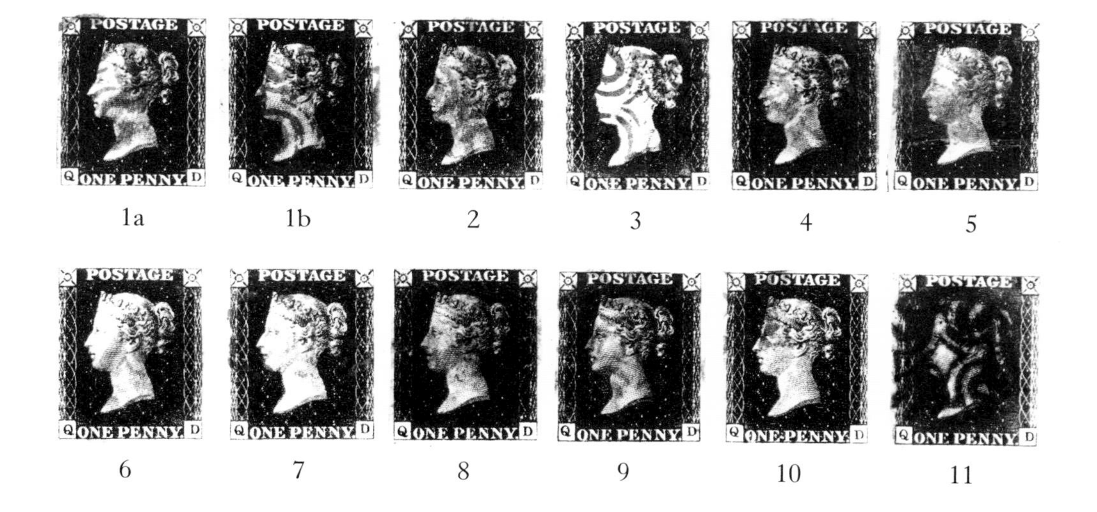
1a
1b
2
3
4
5
6
7
8
9
10
11

Plate.	Position of Corner-letter at left.	Position of Corner-letter at right.	Further distinguishing characteristics.
		QE	
1a*	low, central	low, to right	bottom line slightly wavy.
1b*	low, central	low, to right	bottom line slightly wavy; bottom line of "Q" square thin; scratch mark top margin.
2*	central, to right	high, well to right	broken frame under "E" of "PENNY".
3	high, central	high, well to left	top line of N.W. square thin.
4	central, to right	high, nearly touches left	left side line extends beyond bottom; dot on margin, near line of N.E. square.
5	central, to left	low, central	trace of vertical guide-line N.E. square, close to frame.
6	high, to right	central, to left	right side of N.E. square weak. In the second state the frame-lines have been strengthened or recut.
7	central	high, central	
8	low, central	central	vertical guide-line N.E. square.
9†	central, to right	very low, central	blur at side of N.W. square; scratches on lower margin.
10†	very high, to right	very low, to left	scratches on top and lower margins.
11	central, to right	low, central	right side line weak.
		QF	
1a*	high, central	high, slightly to left	
1b*	high, central	high, slightly to left	upper left ray in N.W. square short; top line of N.W. square thin.
2*	central	central	
3	central	high, slightly to left	side line of N.E. square thin; scratches on right side of top margin.
4	central, to right	central, to left	occasional dot in N.W. square; top line of N.W. square thin on right.
5	slightly high, to right	central	three or four small dots in N.E. square, near top line; horizontal scratch on lower margin.
6	rather high, to left	central	top line of N.W. square thin.
7	central	central	trace of horizontal guide-line through value and "F" square; dot on margin between "N" and "Y".
8	low, to right	central	right side of "F" square very thin; vertical guide-line in N.E. square.
9†	high, central	central	vertical guide-line N.E. square, and through "F" square, wide of frame.
10†	low, central	high, to right	"Q" with short tail.
11	central, to right	very high, central	

**Shows the Ray-flaw.* *†Shows the "O"-flaw.*

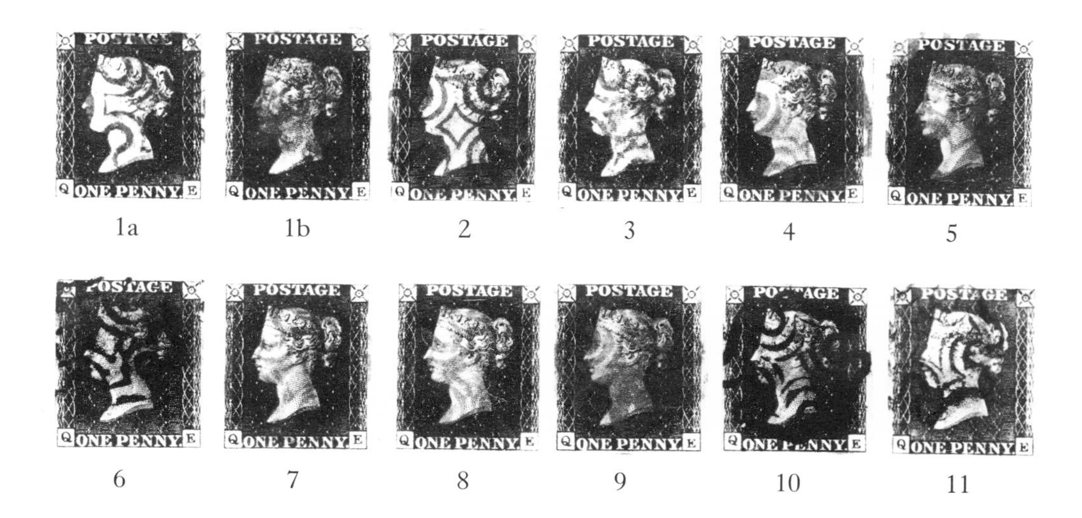
1a
1b
2
3
4
5
6
7
8
9
10
11

1a
1b
2
3
4
5
6
7
8
9
10
11

Plate.	Position of Corner-letter		Further distinguishing characteristics.
	at left.	at right.	
		QG	
1a*	low, central	high, to left	
1b*	low, central	high, to left	top line of N.W. square thin.
2*	very high, central	very high, slightly to right	
3	high, central	high, to left	
4	central, to right	high, to left	two dots on margin, one outside left corner of "Q" square, and the other on lower margin, just below right corner of "Q" square; scratches on left margin.
5	central	slightly high, well to left	slight extension of bottom line into left margin on each side of "P".
6	central, to left	high, central	right side of N.E. square weak.
7	central, to right	high, to left	
8	low, to right	very high, central	vertical guide-line N.E. square; right side of "G" square thin.
9†	central, to left	central	bottom line extends slightly on left; trace of horizontal guide-line through value.
10†	very low, central	high, to right	
11	very high, to right	high, to right	
		QH	
1a*	central	low, to left	bottom line wavy.
1b*	central	low, to left	bottom line wavy; "H" with thin centre bar.
2*	central	high, to right—slopes up	vertical guide-line "H" square, close to frame.
3	central	high, to right	
4	central, to right	high, central	mark above "O" of "POSTAGE", the letters of which run nearly into margin.
5	central, to right	central, to left	left side line, irregular; scratches on lower margin; short line in margin above "OS" of "POSTAGE".
6	central, slightly to left	slightly high, well to right	left side line weak.
7	central, to left	slightly high, slightly to left	
8	very low, to right	high, to left	vertical guide-line N.E. square.
9†	low, central	low, central	blur and scratches top left side margin; scratches on lower margin.
10†	high, central	central, to left	bottom line extends slightly on right; squat "H".
11	central, to right	high, central	

**Shows the Ray-flaw.* *†Shows the "O"-flaw.*

1a
1b
2
3
4
5
6
7
8
9
10
11

1a
1b
2
3
4
5
6
7
8
9
10
11

Plate.	*Position of Corner-letter*		*Further distinguishing characteristics.*
	at left.	*at right.*	
		QI	
1a*	central	slightly low, central	frame-line of "I" square strong.
1b*	central	slightly low, central	bottom line of "I" square double.
2*	low, to right	very high, central	right line extends below, and connects more or less to "R.I." stamp.
3	central	high, to left	left side line extends slightly beyond bottom; top side line of N.W. square weak at corner.
4	high, to left	central—slopes down	
5	central	low, to left	
6	high, to left	central, to left	
7	central, to right	central	marks of re-entry each upper square, and in "Q" square.
8	low, central	high, to right	vertical guide-line N.E. square.
9†	high, central	low, central	top line of N.E. square absent.
10†	low, to right	central, to right	vertical guide-line N.E. square, close to frame; bottom line extends on right; tall "I".
11	central, to right	high, to right	tall "I".
		QJ	
1a*	central	high, central	
1b*	central	high, central	trace of missing ray; "J" re-cut.
2*	low, to right	high, to right	
3	central	slightly high, central	line on margin above N.W. square to "P" of "POSTAGE".
4	central, to right	central	right side irregular; side line of N.E. square weak.
5	central, slightly to left	rather high, central	scratch on lower margin below "Y".
6	high, to left	low, central	re-entry each upper square and lower margin.
7	central, to right	rather high, central	trace of horizontal guide-line through "Q" square.
8	low, central	high, to left	vertical guide-line N.E. square, wide of frame.
9†	central	low, to left	"J" inclined to be square.
10†	low, central	low, to right	square "J" and stroke after it, vertical guide-line N.E. square, close to frame.
11	very high, central	high, central	square "J".

**Shows the Ray-flaw.* *†Shows the "O"-flaw.*

POSTAGE
ONE PENNY
1a
1b
2
3
4
5
6
7
8
9
10
11

POSTAGE
ONE PENNY
1a
1b
2
3
4
5
6
7
8
9
10
11

Plate.	Position of Corner-letter		Further distinguishing characteristics.
	at left.	at right.	
		QK	
1a*	low, to left	high, to right	top line of N.E. square strong.
1b*	low, to left	high, to right	top line of N.E. square weak.
2*	low, central	low, central	
3	high, to left	central, to left	narrow "K".
4	high, to right	high, to right	left side irregular; side line of N.E. square thin; horizontal line through N.E. square and "E" of "POSTAGE".
5	central	central	vertical guide-line N.E. square; horizontal guide-line through "E" of "PENNY"; scratches on lower margin.
6	central	central	re-entry through "POSTAGE", and each upper and "K" squares.
7	central	central	trace of horizontal guide-line through value; scratches on top margin.
8	rather low, central	central	vertical guide-line N.E. square, very close to frame.
9†	high, central	low, to left	bottom line extends on right; top and side lines of N.E. square weak.
10†	high, to right	high, to right	bottom line wavy.
11	high, slightly to left	very high, central	
		QL	
1a*	central	high, slightly to left	distinct dot below corner of "L" square.
1b*	central	high, slightly to right	dot much smaller; slight re-entry in N.E. square.
2*	low, to right	high, central	horizontal guide-line above N.E. square; bottom line of "Q" square thin.
3	low, to right	central	tiny dot in corner of "L" square.
4	central, to right	central, to left	mark on margin above "GE" of "POSTAGE".
5	rather low, to right	low, to left	right line extends slightly beyond bottom.
6	high, to left	central, to left	left side irregular; small stroke in circle of "Q"; dot below "L" square.
7	central	central, to left	dot in S.E. corner of "L" square.
8	very low, central	rather high, central	right line extends beyond bottom; vertical stroke on margin between "O" and "S" of "POSTAGE".
9†	high, to left	high, central	right side line thin.
10†	central, to right	central, to right	
11	central	very low, central	trace of guide-line below "L" square.

**Shows the Ray-flaw.* *†Shows the "O"-flaw.*

1a
1b
2
3
4
5
6
7
8
9
10
11

1a
1b
2
3
4
5
6
7
8
9
10
11

Plate.	Position of Corner-letter		Further distinguishing characteristics.
	at left.	at right.	
		RA	
1a*	high, to right	central	"R" sometimes blurred.
1b*	high, to right	central	side line of N.E. square weak.
2*	low, to right	central	vertical stroke of "R" faint; horizontal lines outside each upper square; vertical line on right side margin.
3	low, to left	central	trace of horizontal guide-line N.W. square; "A" blind or closed.
4	central, to right—slopes up	central, to right	
5	low, to right	central	horizontal guide-line through value and "A" square.
6	low, to right	slightly high, central	tiny dot in "P" of "POSTAGE"; left side extends beyond bottom; scratches on left and lower margins.
7	central	central	diagonal scratch below "NN" of "PENNY"; horizontal guide-line through "A" square, and N.E. square, close to frame.
8	central	central	vertical guide-line N.E. square, wide of frame; bottom line extends on right.
9†	central	central	vertical guide-line N.E. square, wide of frame.
10†	high, to right	central	tailed "R"; vertical guide-line N.E. square, wide of frame.
11	central, to right	rather high, central	lower part of right side line weak.
		RB	
1a*	central, to right	central	
1b*	central, to right	central	side line of N.E. square very weak.
2*	central	very high, to right	vertical guide-line through N.E. square, close to frame, and "B" square; horizontal guide-line N.W. square; lower portion of "B" faint.
3	high, central	central, to right	bottom line of "R" square thin.
4	slightly low, to right	central, to right	bottom line of "R" square thick.
5	low, central	slightly high, central	left side very irregular.
6	central	central	top line of N.W. square thin.
7	central, to right	high, to right	vertical guide-line N.E. square; bottom line extends on right.
8	central	central, to left	vertical guide-line N.E. square.
9†	very low, to left	central, to left	
10†	high, to right	high, central	tailed "R".
11	high, to right	high, central—slopes down	lower part of left and right side lines weak.

**Shows the Ray-flaw.* *†Shows the "O"-flaw.*

1a
1b
2
3
4
5
6
7
8
9
10
11

1a
1b
2
3
4
5
6
7
8
9
10
11

Plate.	Position of Corner-letter at left.	Position of Corner-letter at right.	Further distinguishing characteristics.
		RC	
1a*	slightly low, to right	central, slightly to left	bottom line wavy.
1b*	slightly low, to right	central, slightly to left	bottom line wavy; trace of missing ray.
2*	high, to right	low, to left	
3	central	central, to left	top line of N.W. square almost absent.
4	central, to right	central, to left	
5	central	slightly high, to left	short stroke below left star; trace of horizontal guide-line through value.
6	central, to right	low, to left	vertical guide-line N.E. square, wide of frame; right side line extends slightly beyond bottom.
7	low, to right	central, to left	indistinct blur or stroke before "C".
8	very low, to left	very high, to right	vertical guide-line N.E. square.
9†	high, to right	very high, to right	left side extends beyond bottom; horizontal guide-line through value and "C" square; scratches on lower margin.
10†	central, to right	central, to left	tailed "R"; dot in middle of "C".
11	high, to right	central	bottom line extends on right.
		RD	
1a*	central, to right	central, to left	bottom line of "R" square thick.
1b*	central, to right	central, to left	"E" of "PENNY" nearer bottom margin; bottom line of "R" square thinner.
2*	central	central, to right	horizontal guide-line above N.E. square; right side extends beyond bottom.
3	very high, to right	low, slightly to right	
4	central, to right	central, to right	small dot to right of "D" square.
5	central, slightly to right	rather high, central	upper portion of left side absent.
6	central, to right	high, central	horizontal guide-line, sloping down through "D" square.
7	central, to right	central	
8	slightly low, central	central	vertical guide-line N.E. square, wide of frame.
9†	central	high, to right	scratches through value and each letter-square; also scratches on top and lower margins.
10†	high, central	high, central	tailed "R"; trace of horizontal guide-line through value.
11	central, to right	central, to right	double "D".

**Shows the Ray-flaw.* *†Shows the "O"-flaw.*

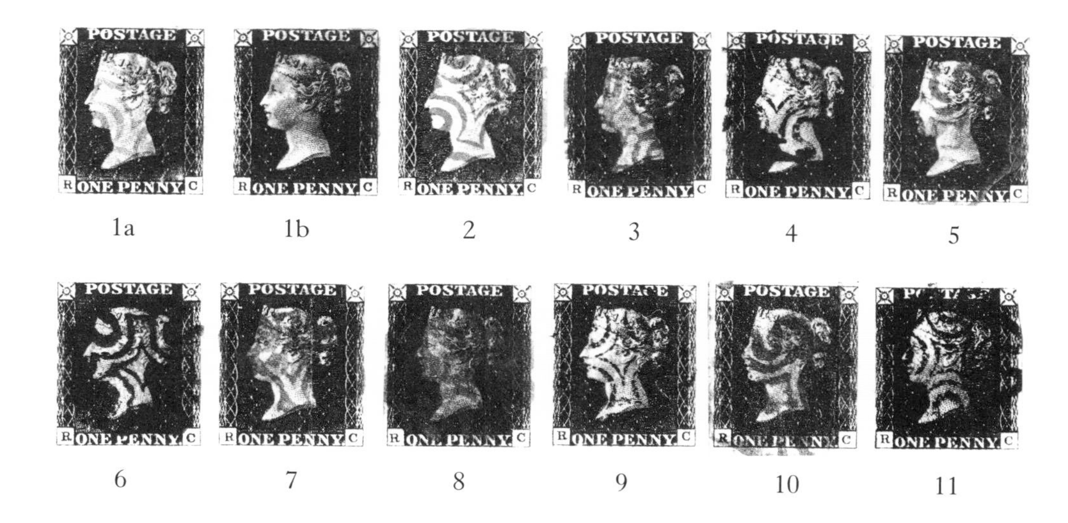
1a
1b
2
3
4
5
6
7
8
9
10
11

1a
1b
2
3
4
5
6
7
8
9
10
11

Plate.	*Position of Corner-letter*		*Further distinguishing characteristics.*
	at left.	*at right.*	
		RE	
1a*	high, central	central, to right	bottom limb of "E" faint.
1b*	high, central	central, to right	"NE" of "ONE" joined; side line N.E. square thin.
2*	high, to right	central, to right	trace of horizontal guide-line above each upper square.
3	high, to right	high, central	top line of N.E. square thin.
4	central	high, to right	left side irregular.
5	low, to right	central, far to left	left side irregular; trace of horizontal guide-line partly through value and "E" square.
6	central	central	left side irregular; side line of N.W. square weak.
7	central	high, central	N.W. square blurred.
8	central	rather high, central	vertical guide-line N.E. square.
9†	central, to left	low, central	left side line extends beyond bottom; vertical guide-line N.E. square, very close to frame.
10†	high, to right	high, to left	tailed "R".
11	central, to right	central	broad "E".
		RF	
1a*	high, to right	high, to left	
1b*	high, to right	high, to left	faint vertical line in "R" square.
2*	central	central	mark top of "F" square; line on left of "R" square is double or recut.
3	high, to right	central, to right	top line of N.W. square thin.
4	central, to right	central	each side line extends slightly beyond bottom.
5	high, to right	slightly low, central	top line of N.E. square thin; mark or scratches N.W. square.
6	central	central, to left	vertical scratches in "R" square, from letter to bottom margin, also top of N.W. square; faint dot on right of "F".
7	central, to right	central, to left	faint vertical guide-line N.E. square, very close to frame.
8	high, to left	central, to left	vertical guide-line N.E. square, wide of frame.
9†	slightly low, to left	low, to left	vertical guide-line N.E. square, very close to frame.
10†	high, central	central	tailed "R"; faint vertical guide-line N.E. square.
11	low, to right	low, to left	bottom line wavy; horizontal guide-line N.E. square, very close to frame.

**Shows the Ray-flaw.* *†Shows the "O"-flaw.*

1a 1b 2 3 4 5
6 7 8 9 10 11

1a 1b 2 3 4 5
6 7 8 9 10 11

Plate.	Position of Corner-letter at left.	Position of Corner-letter at right.	Further distinguishing characteristics.
		RG	
1a*	high, to right	high, to left	bottom line of "R" square thick.
1b*	high, to right	high, to left	bottom line of "R" square thin; left line extends beyond bottom.
2*	central, to right	central, to left	top and right side lines cross.
3	high, central	high, to left	
4	central, slightly to right	high, central	top serif of "R" double.
5	high, to right	central, well to left	large dot just outside "R" square.
6	central	rather high, slightly to left	left side irregular; scratches on margin; faint scratches N.E. square, and each letter-square.
7	central, to right	slightly low, to left	faint scratches left, top and lower margins.
8	central, to left	high, to right	vertical guide-line N.E. square; line on margin below "E" of "PENNY".
9†	high, to left	high, central	trace of vertical guide-line N.W. square; horizontal guide-line through value.
10†	central, to right	central	tailed "R"; faint vertical guide-line N.E. square.
11	low, to right	high, central	blur outside "R" square; bottom line extends beyond "R" square; frame lines do not quite join at N.W. square.
		RH	
1a*	central	central, slightly to left	right line extends beyond bottom.
1b*	central	central, slightly to left	no extension.
2*	central, to right	high, to right	right side line extends beyond top.
3	high, to right	central	
4	high, to right	very high, to left	right side line extends beyond bottom.
5	central	central, to left	trace of vertical guide-line N.E. square, very close to frame.
6	central	high, to right	trace of vertical scratches through and below "R" square.
7	central, to right	high, slightly to left	trace of vertical guide-line N.E. square.
8	slightly low, to left	high, to right	bottom line slightly wavy.
9†	low, to left	central	
10†	central	central, to left	tailed "R"; squat "H".
11	central, to right	high, central	trace of vertical guide-line N.E. square.

**Shows the Ray-flaw.* *†Shows the "O"-flaw.*

1a 1b 2 3 4 5
6 7 8 9 10 11

1a 1b 2 3 4 5
6 7 8 9 10 11

Plate.	Position of Corner-letter at left.	Position of Corner-letter at right.	Further distinguishing characteristics.
		RI	
1a*	low, central	low, to right	slight trace of top serif of "I" being double.
1b*	low, central	low, to right	"I" thinner.
2*	central, to right	high, to right	right side line extends beyond top; faint vertical guide-line in "I" square, very close to frame.
3	slightly low, central	low, to left	
4	central	high, central	right side line extends beyond bottom.
5	central	central, to left	vertical guide-line N.E. square, close to frame.
6	central	central, slightly to left	vertical guide-line N.E. square, close to frame; distinct dot above N.E. square, and one near N.W. square.
7	central, to right	central, slightly to left	bottom line extends slightly on right; scratches in N.E. square.
8	central	central	vertical guide-line N.E. square, close to frame.
9†	very high, to left	low, central	side line of N.E. square thin.
10†	high, to right	very high, to right	tailed "R"; re-entry N.E. square.
11	central	central, to right	tall "I".
		RJ	
1a*	central	high, central	top line of N.W. square thick.
1b*	central	high, central	"J" recut; horizontal guide-line in "R" square; top line N.W. square thinner.
2*	rather high, to right	low, central	faint vertical guide-line in "J" square, sometimes showing extension top right.
3	central, to right	rather high, central	bottom line of "R" square thin.
4	central, to right	central	blurred stroke before "J".
5	rather low, central	slightly low, central	right side line extends beyond bottom; horizontal guide-line through value; bottom line extends slightly on left.
6	very low, to right	central, to left	tiny dot on right margin outside N.E. square; N.E. square defective at left corner; dot in "O" of "POSTAGE".
7	central, to right	central, to right	faint vertical guide-line N.E. square, close to frame.
8	low, to left	central	diagonal stroke through "R".
9†	low, to left	low, central	"J" somewhat square-footed.
10†	central	central	tailed "R"; square "J".
11	high, to right	high, to left	square "J".

**Shows the Ray-flaw.* *†Shows the "O"-flaw.*

1a 1b 2 3 4 5
6 7 8 9 10 11

1a 1b 2 3 4 5
6 7 8 9 10 11

Plate.	Position of Corner-letter at left.	Position of Corner-letter at right.	Further distinguishing characteristics.
		RK	
1a*	high, to right	high, central	
1b*	high, to right	high, central	"K" recut; slight extension into bottom margin below "O"; faint mark on left of "K" square; line very close to frame under "Y" of "PENNY".
2*	central, to right	central, to right	bottom line of "R" square thin; "E" of "PENNY" runs nearly into margin; trace of horizontal line above N.E. square.
3	high, central	very high, to right	
4	central	central	right side line extends beyond bottom; trace of horizontal guide-line through value and "K" square.
5	central	central	trace of horizontal guide-line through value; mark or scratches top of N.W. square.
6	slightly low, slightly to left	central, to left	upper portion of left side irregular.
7	central, to right	central, slightly to left	trace of vertical guide-line N.E. square, very close to frame.
8	central, to left	central	vertical guide-line N.E. square, very close to frame.
9†	high, to left	central	
10†	central, to right	slightly high, to right	tailed "R"; double bottom.
11	high, central	central	top and side lines N.E. square thin.
		RL	
1a	high, central	slightly high, to left	tiny dot below corner of "L" square; long lower serif to "L".
1b	high, central	slightly high, to left	dot not so distinct; bottom line of "R" square thin; long lower serif to "L".
2*	central, to right	high, to left	defective "R"; horizontal line above N.E. square; mark below "L" square.
3	central, to right	rather high, central	bottom line extends slightly on left.
4	central, to right	central, to left	faint dot on right of "L". Dot below "O" of "ONE".
5	central	low, to left	dot on margin below S.E. corner of "L" square; left side line irregular.
6	low, central	central, to left	dot in S.E. corner of "L" square.
7	central, to right	central, to left	right and bottom lines cross.
8	central	high, to left	re-entry through N.E. square and "NN" of "PENNY"; pin-point extension on lower right.
9†	high, to left	very high, slightly to left	bottom line extends slightly on left.
10†	high, central	low central	tailed "R"; double bottom; vertical mark in N.W. square.
11	central, to right	very low, well to right	double tail to "R".

**Shows the Ray-flaw.* *†Shows the "O"-flaw.*

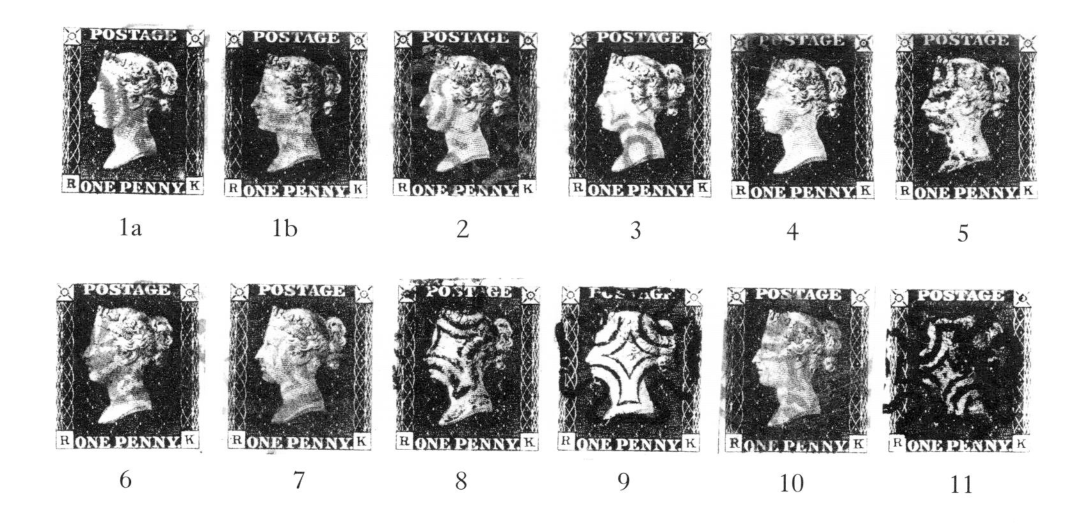
1a
1b
2
3
4
5
6
7
8
9
10
11

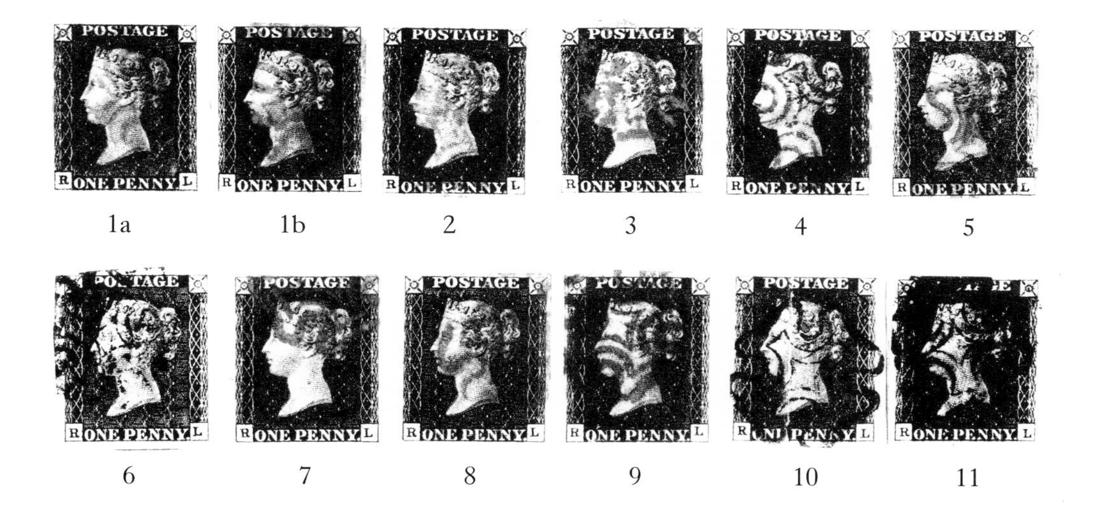
1a
1b
2
3
4
5
6
7
8
9
10
11

Plate.	*Position of Corner-letter*		*Further distinguishing characteristics.*
	at left.	*at right.*	
		SA	
1a*	high, central	low, central	
1b*	high, central	low, central	bottom line of "A" square double.
2*	high, slightly to right	central	re-entry each upper and "A" squares; right side line extends into margin at top.
3	central	central	top line of N.W. square weak; bottom line of N.E. square extends into margin.
4	high, to right	central	
5	low, to left	central	
6	high, to left	central, slightly to right	re-entry each upper square; bottom line extends on right.
7	high, to right	high, to left	vertical guide-line N.E. square, very close to frame.
8	high, to left	central	vertical guide-line N.E. square; bottom line extends on right.
9†	central	central	bottom line extends slightly on right.
10†	high, central	central	vertical guide-line N.E. square, wide of frame.
11	central—slopes down	low, to right	re-entry N.E. square; bottom line extends on right.
		SB	
1a*	high, central	central, to right	
1b*	high, central	central, to right	"E" of "PENNY" runs nearly into margin.
2*	high, to right	central, to right	traces of double line at top; right side line extends into margin at top.
3	central	central, well to right	
4	high, slightly to right	central, to right	top line of N.W. square thin.
5	high, slightly to left	low, central	top and side of N.E. square thin.
6	high, central	central	faint guide-line N.E. square.
7	central, slightly to left	high, slightly to right	trace of horizontal guide-line through "Y", and "B" square; marks on margin below the uprights of each letter "N".
8	high, to left	central, to right	vertical guide-line N.E. square.
9†	central	low, to left	faint line below "Y".
10†	central	high, to right	top line of N.W. square defective; vertical guide-line N.E. square, wide of frame.
11	very low, to left	low, to right	re-entry N.E. square.

**Shows the Ray-flaw.* *†Shows the "O"-flaw.*

1a
1b
2
3
4
5
6
7
8
9
10
11

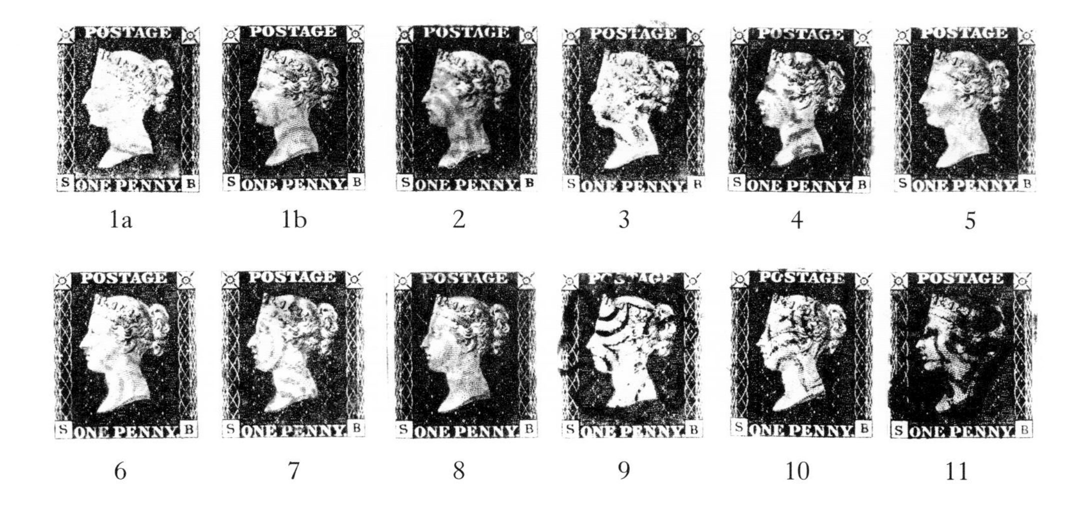
1a
1b
2
3
4
5
6
7
8
9
10
11

Plate.	Position of Corner-letter at left.	Position of Corner-letter at right.	Further distinguishing characteristics.
		SC	
1a*	low, to right	low, to left	
1b*	low, to right	low, to left	square-lines thinner; faint scratches through "POSTAGE".
2*	high, central	central, to left	traces of double top; dot or stroke below corner of "C" square.
3	high, to right	high, slightly to left	left and bottom lines cross.
4	high, to left	high, central	re-entry N.E. square.
5	high, central	low, to left	scratches on top margin; trace of vertical guide-line N.E. square, very close to frame, and N.W. square; bottom line extends slightly on right.
6	high, central	central	left line extends beyond bottom; dot on right margin, opposite middle of hair.
7	central	central, to left	scratches right side margin.
8	rather high, to left	high, to left	vertical guide-line N.E. square, close to frame; horizontal guide-line through "C" square.
9†	central, to left	very high, central	scratches right side and top margins.
10†	central	high, to left	vertical guide-line N.E. square, close to frame; horizontal guide-line through value and "C" square.
11	central, to right	low, to left	re-entry N.E. square; right and bottom lines cross.
		SD	
1a*	high, central	high, to right	
1b*	high, central	high, to right	"E" of "PENNY" runs nearly into bottom margin; side line of "S" square weak.
2*	central, to right	slightly high, central	trace of guide-line above top; right side line extends beyond top; vertical guide-line in "D" square.
3	low, central	high, to right	left line extends slightly beyond bottom.
4	central	low, central	re-entry N.W. and "S" squares, and through value.
5	central	high, to right	faint scratches in N.E. square; also on left side margin.
6	high, to right	central, slightly to right	trace of horizontal guide-line through value. In second state, the frame-lines have been strengthened or recut.
7	high, slightly to right	high, to right	
8	high, to left	central	vertical guide-line N.E. square.
9†	high, central	central, to right	trace of horizontal guide-line through "NY" and stop; scratches top and left side margins.
10†	central, to left	central, to right	right side line extends slightly beyond bottom.
11	high, to right	central, to right	re-entry N.E. square.

**Shows the Ray-flaw.* *†Shows the "O"-flaw.*

1a
1b
2
3
4
5
6
7
8
9
10
11

1a
1b
2
3
4
5
6
7
8
9
10
11

Plate.	Position of Corner-letter at left.	Position of Corner-letter at right.	Further distinguishing characteristics.
		SE	
1a*	central	central, to right	
1b*	central	central, to right	"E" of "PENNY" runs nearly into bottom margin.
2*	high, central	high, to right	double line at top; guide-line through N.E. square and above.
3	high, central	high, central	
4	central, to left	central, far to right	scratches on right side margin.
5	central—slopes up	central, slightly to left	bottom line extends on left; right and bottom lines cross.
6	central, to right	central, to left	bottom line extends on right; side line of N.E. square thin; trace of horizontal guide-line through value. In second state, the frame-lines have been strengthened or recut.
7	high, central	slightly high, central	
8	high, to left—slopes up	central	bottom line extends slightly on left.
9†	high, central—slopes up	high, central	horizontal guide-line through "S" square and value.
10†	low, central—slopes up	central, to left	
11	central, to right	low, to left	re-entry N.E. square.
		SF	
1a*	high, central	high, central	side line of N.E. square thick; bottom line wavy.
1b*	high, central	high, central	bottom line of "S" square thin; side line of N.E. square defective.
2*	central, to left	central, to right	trace of double line outside N.E. square.
3	high, central	high, central	"F" is higher than in any other of this lettering.
4	high, to left	central, to right	upper portion of left side irregular; scratches on margin below.
5	high, to right	low, to left	
6	high, central	central, to left	side line of N.E. square weak.
7	high, slightly to left	central	
8	low, slightly to left	central	mark on margin below "N" of "ONE".
9†	central	low, to left	
10†	central, to right—slopes down	central	trace of guide-line through value.
11	high, to right—slopes down	high, to right	re-entry N.E. square; bottom line wavy.

*Shows the Ray-flaw. †Shows the "O"-flaw.

1a
1b
2
3
4
5
6
7
8
9
10
11

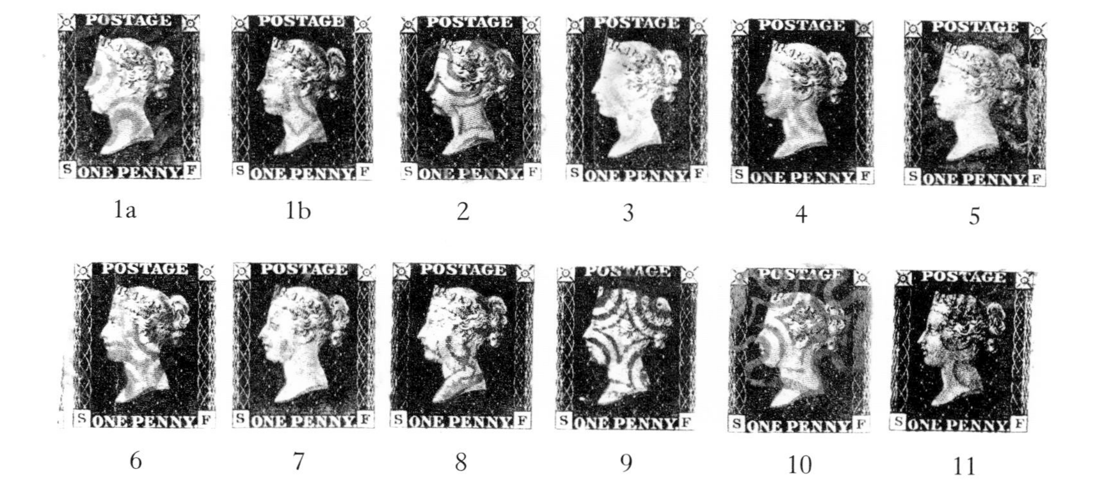
1a
1b
2
3
4
5
6
7
8
9
10
11

Plate.	Position of Corner-letter at left.	Position of Corner-letter at right.	Further distinguishing characteristics.
		SG	
1a*	high, central	high, central	
1b*	high, central	high, central	top line of N.W. square thinner.
2*	high, central	very high, central	distinct dot below "G" square; top line of N.W. and side line of N.E. squares double.
3	central, to right	high, to left	
4	high, central	high, central	
5	very high, central	slightly high, close to left	scratches on left and right margins.
6	very high, central—slopes up	high, central	scratches below "NNY"; dot S.W. corner of "G" square.
7	low, slightly to left	slightly high, close to left	
8	slightly high, to left	high, slightly to left	scratches on lower margin; blur outside N.W. square.
9†	low, to left—slopes up	low, central	trace of horizontal guide-line through value and "G" square.
10†	low, to right	low, to left	vertical guide-line N.E. square; bottom line extends slightly on left.
11	central, to right—slopes down	central, slightly to right	re-entry N.E. square.
		SH	
1a*	low, to left	low, to left	
1b*	low, to left	low, to left	side line N.E. square thin; cross-bar of "H" thinner.
2*	high, to right	central—slopes up	trace of horizontal guide-line, or scratch, above N.W. square.
3	high, to right	high, to right	
4	high, central	high, to left	
5	high, to left—slopes up	central	upper portion of left side line thin.
6	high, central	central	left side irregular; traces of vertical lines through each upper square.
7	high, central	high, to left	left side line extends slightly beyond bottom; trace of guide-line through "Y"; mark above "S" of "POSTAGE".
8	high, to left	high, central	bottom line slightly wavy.
9†	high, to left	central, to left	
10†	central—slopes down	low, central	squat "H".
11	central—slopes down	very high, to right	re-entry N.E. square.

**Shows the Ray-flaw.* *†Shows the "O"-flaw.*

1a
1b
2
3
4
5
6
7
8
9
10
11

1a
1b
2
3
4
5
6
7
8
9
10
11

Plate.	*Position of Corner-letter*		*Further distinguishing characteristics.*
	at left.	*at right.*	
		SI	
1a*	central, to left	low, central	mark through "OS" of "POSTAGE".
1b*	central, to left	low, central	right side line weaker; mark as in plate 1a.
2*	high, to right	central, to right	trace of vertical line in "I" square.
3	central	rather high, central	lower part of side line of N.E. square thin.
4	high, to left	slightly low, to left	side line N.E. square thin.
5	central, to right	low, close to left	top line of N.E. square weak; "E" of "POSTAGE" runs nearly into top margin.
6	high, to right—slopes up	central	left side line irregular; line below "ON" of "ONE".
7	high, slightly to left	central	
8	high, to left	central, to right	left side line weak.
9†	high, to left	high, central	horizontal guide-line through each letter-square and value.
10†	low, central	very high, to right	re-entry through N.E. and letter-squares, and value; tall "I".
11	low, to right	slightly low, slightly to right	re-entry N.E. square, bottom line wavy; tall "I".
		SJ	
1a*	central	high, central	
1b*	central	high, central	trace of missing ray.
2*	high, to right	high, central	side line of N.E. square extends into top margin.
3	high, to right	rather high, central	trace of vertical guide-line N.E. square, very close to frame.
4	high, to left	high, to left	side line of N.E. square weak.
5	low, central	central, to left	diagonal scratch in "J" square; scratch or line in N.W. square.
6	high, central	central, to left	
7	high, to left	central, slightly to left	
8	high, to left	central	extension at foot of N.E. square into margin.
9†	low, to right	low, to left	
10†	low, central	low, central	square "J" with stroke after it.
11	low, central	low, to left	square "J"; re-entry N.E. square.

**Shows the Ray-flaw.* *†Shows the "O"-flaw.*

1a
1b
2
3
4
5
6
7
8
9
10
11

1a
1b
2
3
4
5
6
7
8
9
10
11

Plate.	Position of Corner-letter		Further distinguishing characteristics.
	at left.	at right.	
		SK	
1a*	high, central	high, to left	
1b*	high, central	high, to left	"K" recut.
2*	high, central	high, central	trace of double line above top.
3	central, to right	central, to left	"NE" of "ONE" joined.
4	very high, slightly to left	central	
5	high, central	low, to left	left side line very weak; side line of N.E. square thin.
6	high, to right	central, to left	distinct dot or mark above N.W. square.
7	high, to left	slightly low, to left	
8	high, to left—slopes down	central, to left	bottom line thick.
9†	low, to left	low, to left	faint scratches below "K" square.
10†	central, to left—slopes down	central, slightly to left	bottom line slightly wavy.
11	low, to right	high, central	re-entry N.E. square; bottom line thick below "ON" of "ONE" and "NNY" of "PENNY".
		SL	
1a	slightly low, central	high, to left	double bottom.
1b	slightly low, central	high, to left	"S" square weak at corner.
2	high, to right	slightly high, to left	double line at top and right side; dot below "L" square.
3	central	central	"NE" of "ONE" nearly joined.
4	very high, central	central, to left	upper portion of left side weak.
5	high, central	very low, close to left	
6	high, to right	central	in second state the frame-lines have been strengthened or recut.
7	high, central	central, to left	dot just outside corner of "L" square, on right.
8	central, to right	central	dot just outside corner of "L" square, below.
9†	low, to left	central, to left	"L" with long foot on left; dot below corner of "L" square.
10†	high, central—slopes down	low, central	tiny dot below corner of "L" square.
11	high, to right	central, well to right	re-entry N.E. square.

**Shows the Ray-flaw.* *†Shows the "O"-flaw.*

1a
1b
2
3
4
5
6
7
8
9
10
11

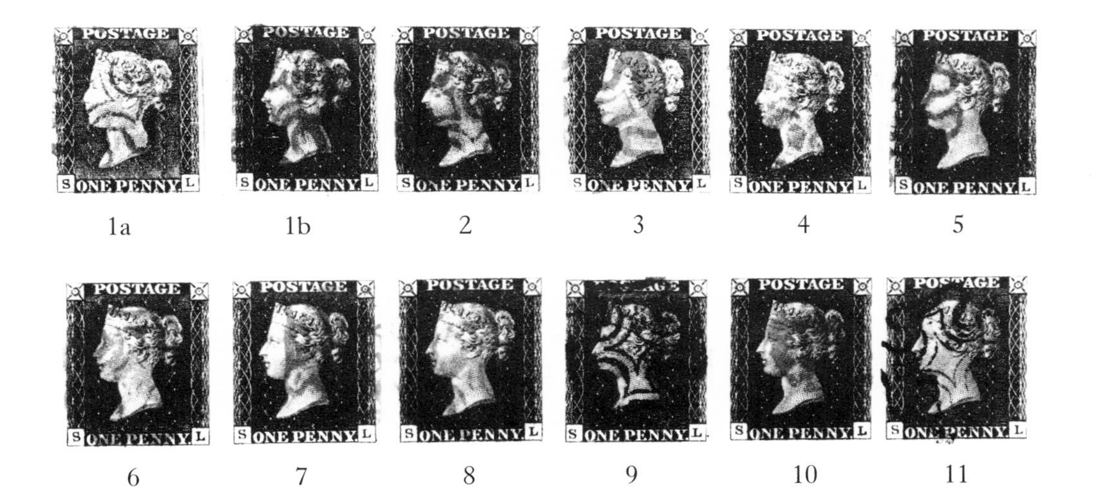
1a
1b
2
3
4
5
6
7
8
9
10
11

Plate.	*Position of Corner-letter*		*Further distinguishing characteristics.*
	at left.	*at right.*	
		TA	
1a*	central, to right	central	bottom line extends slightly on right; dot below corner of "T" square.
1b*	central, to right	central	dot below corner of "T" square not so distinct; bottom line extends slightly on right.
2*	central, to left	rather high, to right	vertical guide-line N.E. square, very close to frame; trace of horizontal guide-line N.W. square; top line of N.W. square nearly absent; dot some distance from corner of "T" square; faint dot at bottom of "A" square.
3	high, to right	central, to left	bottom line extends on left.
4	central, to right	central	trace of horizontal guide-line through "T" square.
5	central, to right	central, to left	vertical guide-line N.E. square, wide of frame. In second state the frame-lines have been strengthened or recut.
6	slightly high, to left	central	scratches in "T" square, close to frame.
7	central, to right	rather high, to left	
8	very high, to left	central	re-entry each upper square and below.
9†	high, central	central	dot in corner of "A" square; bottom line extends on right; trace of vertical guide-line N.E. square.
10†	low, to left	rather high, central	re-entry each upper square and through value; squat "T".
11	low, to right	high, to right—slopes down	bottom line wavy; squat "T".
		TB	
1a*	high, to right	low, central	
1b*	high, to right	low, central	top and side lines N.W. square, and bottom line of "B" square, thinner.
2*	central, to left	high, to right	bottom line of "T" square thin.
3	high, to right	rather high, to right	
4	high, to right	central, to right	
5	central, to right	central	left side, and outer lines of N.E. square, weak. In second state the frame-lines have been strengthened or recut.
6	low, to right	rather low, central	side line of N.E. square weak; some times scratches in each lower square and value. In second state, the frame lines have been strengthened or recut.
7	central, to right	high, to right	
8	slightly high, to left	central	vertical guide-line N.E. square, close to frame; bottom line extends on right.
9†	central, to left	high, central	trace of double "T"; vertical guide-line N.E. square, very close to frame.
10†	low, central	high, central	squat "T"; vertical guide-line N.E. square, wide of frame.
11	central, to right	high, central	dot below "B" square; squat "T".

**Shows the Ray-flaw.* *†Shows the "O"-flaw.*

1a
1b
2
3
4
5
6
7
8
9
10
11

1a
1b
2
3
4
5
6
7
8
9
10
11

Plate.	Position of Corner-letter		Further distinguishing characteristics.
	at left.	at right.	
		TC	
1a*	low, to left	high, to left	
1b*	low, to left	high, to left	trace of missing ray.
2*	central, to right	low, to left	right side line of N.E. square extends at top; dot below "C" square.
3	high, to right	central	faint horizontal guide-line N.W. square.
4	high, central	slightly high, central	left side line extends beyond bottom.
5	central, to right	very high, central	top line of N.W. square weak.
6	low, to right	low, to left	vertical guide-line N.E. square, close to frame; side line of N.E. square thin.
7	low, to right	central, to left	trace of guide-line through value and "C" square.
8	central, to left	central, slightly to left	vertical guide-line N.E. square, close to frame; two dots in corner of "C" square; one dot in "T" square.
9†	high, central	high, slightly to left	dot below corner of "C" square—sometimes nearly absent.
10†	very low, to right	high, slightly to left	squat "T"; vertical guide-line N.E. square, wide of frame; dot below "C" square.
11	high, to right	rather low, central	re-entry N.E. square; squat "T".
		TD	
1a*	central, to left	high, central	
1b*	central, to left	high, central	right side defective towards top.
2*	central, to right	central	vertical guide-line through "D" square; side line extends beyond top.
3	central, to right	central	
4	high, central	central	both sides irregular; trace of horizontal guide-line N.E. square.
5	central, to left	high, to right	left side irregular.
6	high, to right—slopes down	high, to right	short vertical stroke on left of "D" square, and also "T" square, joining top line. In second state, the frame-lines have been strengthened or re-cut.
7	central, to right	central	trace of horizontal guide-line through "T" square.
8	low, central	central	vertical guide-line N.E. square, close to frame; dot on left of "T"; dot in corner of "D" square.
9†	high, to left	slightly high, to right	trace of vertical guide-line N.E. square.
10†	low, central	high, central	squat "T".
11	high, to right	central, to right	re-entry N.W. and "T" squares, and through value; squat "T".

**Shows the Ray-flaw.* *†Shows the "O"-flaw.*

POSTAGE
T ONE PENNY C
1a
1b
2
3
4
5
6
7
8
9
10
11

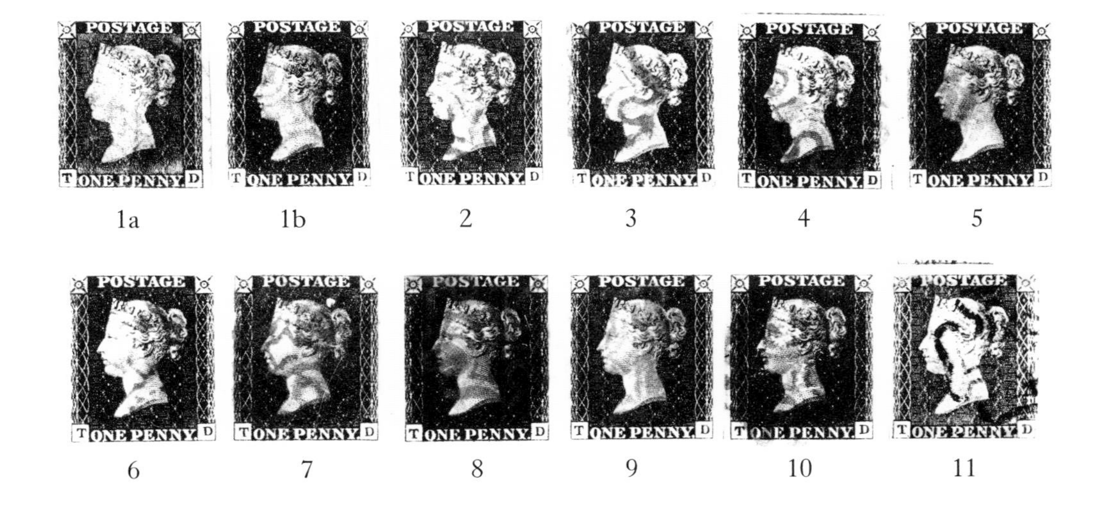
POSTAGE
T ONE PENNY D
1a
1b
2
3
4
5
6
7
8
9
10
11

Plate.	Position of Corner-letter		Further distinguishing characteristics.
	at left.	at right.	
		TE	
1a*	central, to right	low, far to right	
1b*	central, to right	low, far to right	right side weak towards top.
2*	low, to left	high, to left	dot below corner of "E" square.
3	high, to right	high, central	foot of "E" joined to left side of "E" square.
4	central	high, far to right	trace of horizontal guide-line through value and "E" square.
5	central, to right	low, to left	bottom line extends on right.
6	central, to right	central, to left	stroke through side of "E" square; side line of N.E. square thin. In second state, the frame-lines have been strengthened or recut.
7	central, slightly to right	central, slightly to left	two dots on top margin to left of N.E. square.
8	central, slightly to right	central	two dots in corner of "E" square; trace of horizontal guide-line N.E. square.
9†	central, slightly to left	central	
10†	central, to right	high, slightly to right	squat "T".
11	high, to right	low, central	two tiny dots below "E" square; squat "T".
		TF	
1a*	central, to right	high, to left	
1b*	central, to right	high, to left	
2*	central, to left	central	vertical guide-line N.E. square, very close to frame; two dots below "F" square; small dot top of N.E. square; top line of N.W. square nearly absent.
3	high, to right	high, central	dot on bottom line of "F" square; top serif of "T" is weak on left.
4	high, to right	rather high, to left	left side irregular.
5	central	central, to left	tiny dot below corner of "F" square.
6	central, to right	slightly low, well to left	left side irregular; top line of N.W. square thin.
7	central, to right	high, to left	
8	high, to left	central	right line extends beyond bottom; vertical guide-line N.E. square, close to frame.
9†	low, central	central, to left	
10†	very low, central	very high, to left	vertical guide-line N.E. square, wide of frame; tiny dot in corner of "F" square; squat "T".
11	central, to right	high, central	dot in corner of "F" square; squat "T".

**Shows the Ray-flaw.* *†Shows the "O"-flaw.*

1a
1b
2
3
4
5
6
7
8
9
10
11

1a
1b
2
3
4
5
6
7
8
9
10
11

Plate.	Position of Corner-letter		Further distinguishing characteristics.
	at left.	at right.	
		TG	
1a*	central	slightly high, central	bottom line extends slightly on right.
1b*	central	slightly high, central	top of N.W. square thin; bottom line extends slightly on right.
2*	slightly low, to left	central	vertical guide-line in N.E. square; upper portion of right side line double.
3	central	high, central	horizontal guide-line through "T" square.
4	central, to right	high, to left	right side line extends slightly beyond bottom; horizontal guide-line through "PENNY" running into "G" square.
5	slightly low, to right	central, to left	scratches left side margin; small dot below "G" square.
6	high, to right	central, to left	upper portion of left side line irregular, mark or stroke left side of "T" square, joining top frame-line.
7	central, to right	very high, central	similar mark in "T" square, as in plate 6; dot top margin near N.E. square.
8	low, to left	high, to left	long serif to "G"; dot on left margin, opposite lower part of neck.
9†	central, to left	central	
10†	low, central	low, central	squat "T".
11	high, to right	high, to left	squat "T".
		TH	
1a*	central, to left	low, central	
1b*	central, to left	low, central	bar in "H" thin; right side weak towards top.
2*	high, central	central	dot below "H" square.
3	high, to right	high, central	
4	central	very high, to left	vertical scratch in N.W. square.
5	central	high, central	"H" double.
6	high, to right	high, central	mark on right diagonal stroke of "Y"; bottom line just extends "H".
7	low, to right	high, to left	
8	high, to left	high, to right	dot outside "H" square.
9†	low, to left	low, slightly to left	vertical guide-line N.W. square.
10†	central, to right	central, far to right	squat "T" and "H".
11	central—slopes down	high, central	bottom line wavy; squat "T".

**Shows the Ray-flaw.* *†Shows the "O"-flaw.*

1a
1b
2
3
4
5
6
7
8
9
10
11

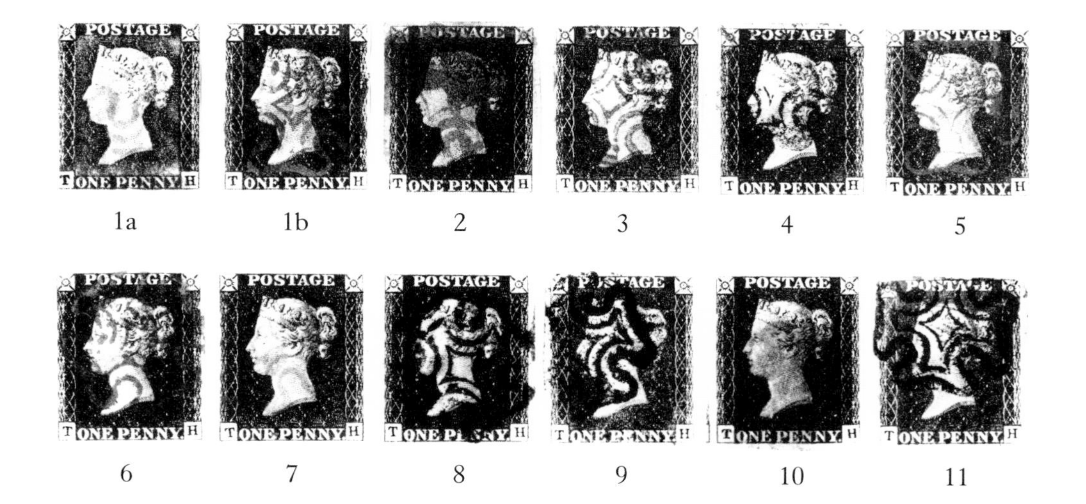
1a
1b
2
3
4
5
6
7
8
9
10
11

Plate.	Position of Corner-letter at left.	Position of Corner-letter at right.	Further distinguishing characteristics.
		TI	
1a*	high, to right	low, to right	dot outside corner of "I" square.
1b*	high, to right	low, central	dot outside corner of "I" square; N.E square weak at left corner.
2*	central	high, central—slopes down	guide-line above, N.E. square; "I" rather faint.
3	central	high, slightly to left	top line of N.E. square appears double; faint dot below "I".
4	central	high, central	two horizontal scratches upper right margin.
5	high, to right	central, slightly to left	bottom margin wavy below "O".
6	central, close to right—slopes up	low, central	trace of horizontal guide-line N.E. square.
7	central, to right	high, to left	faint scratches inside and outside "I" square.
8	high, central	high, to left	blur outside N.W. square.
9†	low, to left	low, central	left side irregular.
10†	very low, central	high, central	top line of N.W. square thin; squat "T"; tall "I".
11	high, to right	central, to right	squat "T"; tall "I".
		TJ	
1a*	central	central	side and bottom lines of "J" square strong.
1b*	central	central	side and bottom lines of "J" square thinner; "J" recut.
2*	central	high, slightly to left	guide-line N.E. square, and at top.
3	high, to right	very high, to left	
4	high, central	very high, to left	dot in extreme corner of "J" square.
5	central, to right	central, to left	left side line irregular; horizontal guide-line or scratches below "J". Stamps generally appear to be badly printed.
6	low, to right	central, to left	mark on left margin near upper square. In second state, the frame-lines have been strengthened or recut.
7	central, to right	central, to left	vertical guide-line N.E. square, very close to frame; faint mark on left side of "T" square, joining frame-line.
8	low, central	high, to right	re-entry N.E. square and below.
9†	low, to left	central	
10†	central	central, to left	vertical guide-line N.E. square; squat "T"; square "J".
11	high, to right	very low, central	dot below "J" square; squat "T"; square "J".

**Shows the Ray-flaw.* *†Shows the "O"-flaw.*

1a
1b
2
3
4
5
6
7
8
9
10
11

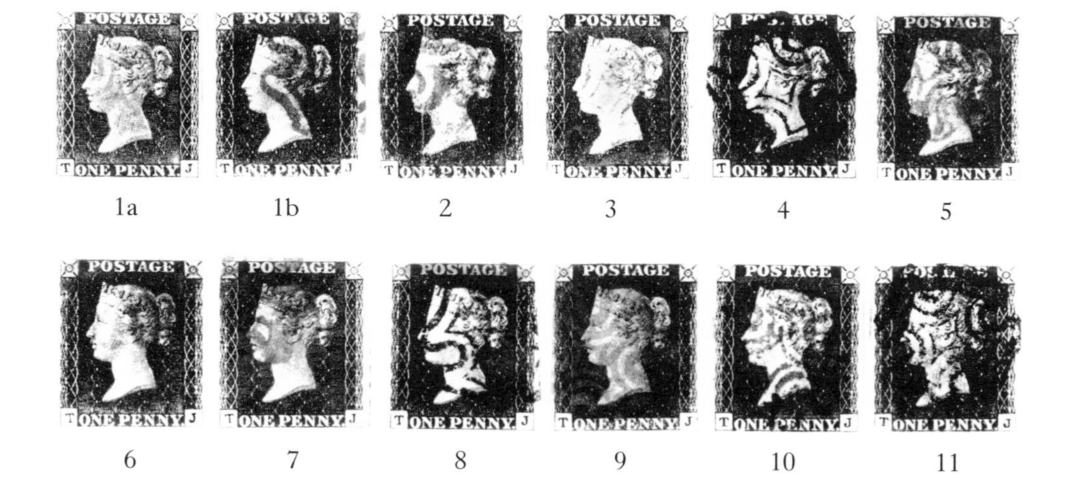
1a
1b
2
3
4
5
6
7
8
9
10
11

Plate.	Position of Corner-letter at left.	Position of Corner-letter at right.	Further distinguishing characteristics.
		TK	
1a	central, to left	central, to left	no ray-flaw; left side of "T" larger.
1b	central, to left	central, to left	no appreciable difference; dot to right of bun in frame.
2*	central	high, central	dot below corner of "K" square; horizontal guide-line N.W. square.
3	central, to left	central	dot after "T"; dot in front of foot of "T".
4	high, to left	low, central	right line extends beyond bottom.
5	low, central	central, to left	dot at right of corner of "K" square; trace of horizontal guide-line below "K".
6	high, to right	high, close to left	upper portion of left side rather irregular.
7	high, to right	high, to left	left side line complete.
8	high, central	high, to left	dot after middle of "K".
9†	high, to left	low, to left	
10†	central, to right	central, to left	vertical guide-line N.E. square, close to frame; dot below "K"; squat "T".
11	high, to right	low, to right	re-entry N.E. and "K" squares, and bottom margin; squat "T".
		TL	
1a	central, slightly to left	high, central	double bottom; no ray-flaw.
1b	central, slightly to left	high, central	bottom line slightly wavy; no ray-flaw. N.E. square broken at corner.
2*	high, to right	high, to left	double "T"; vertical and horizontal guide-lines outside N.E. square.
3	high, to left	high, central	dot in corner of "L" square, and two dots below.
4	central, to left	central, to left	dot inside N.E. square.
5	central, slightly to right	high, to left	
6	central, to right	central—slopes up	
7	central, to right	central, to left	dot in S.E. corner of "L" square.
8	high, to right	high, central	horizontal scratches top of N.E. square.
9†	high, to left	high, central	
10†	high, to right	low, central	squat "T".
11	high, to right	low, to left	dot below "L" square; squat "T".

**Shows the Ray-flaw.* *†Shows the "O"-flaw.*

1a
1b
2
3
4
5
6
7
8
9
10
11

1a
1b
2
3
4
5
6
7
8
9
10
11

APPENDIX.

DOUBLE LETTERS.

The two states of plate 1 in the following list are designated 1 A and 1 B respectively; and, where simply plate 1 is mentioned, it signifies that the double letter occurs in both states. The letters which are double are shown in heavier type.

Lettering.	Plate.	Remarks.
A **E**	1	Fine.
A **E**	9	Slight.
B **B**	11	Slight but fairly distinct.
B E	9	Slight.
B G	6	Very slight.
B L	9	Fine.
C A	7	Mark beside C, but perhaps not a double letter.
C **D**	1	Fine; often called "D over T".
C K	9	Fine.
D A	4	Sometimes clear but as a rule very faint.
D A	7	Very slight & often almost invisible.
D B	4	Slight.
D B	5	Very slight and usually does not show clearly.
D C	9	Fine.
D D	4	Very fine.
D D	11	Slight.
D G	2	Very fine; often called "D over I".
E A	2	Serif of foot double, fairly clear.
E B	5	Serif of foot double, distinct.
E **B**	9	Sometimes clear but usually faint.
E **E**	10	Slight.
F A	1	Very fine.
F A	7	Fine.
F D	3	Very slight.
F **G**	2	Fine; sometimes called "G over F".
F I	1	Very fine.
F **K**	6	Fine.
G **I**	1	Fine.
G **J**	10	Very slight.
H A	3	Slight and does not always show.
H A	10	Fine.
H B	5	Slight.
H B	9	Fair.
H E	5	Usually very fine.
H I	5	Very slight.
I F	2	Slight.
J E	11	Very fine.
J **L**	9	Slight.
K A	11	Slight but fairly distinct.
K C	3	Fine.
K **D**	1 B only	Slight.
K **E**	2	Very fine.
K **E**	5	Very fine. E more to left.
K **F**	1 B	Slight.
L B	6	Serif of foot double.
L **B**	9	Fine.
L **K**	2	Slight.
L L	9	Slight.
M A	9	Fine.
M E	2	Blur below M, perhaps not double: not constant.
M F	1	Fine.
M I	8	Fair.
M K	6	Fine.
N B	7	Slight.
N **D**	10	Slight.
N F	7	Slight.
N **H**	11	Fair.
O A	9	Usually faint, sometimes clear.
O **B**	9	Fine.
O **J**	10	Very slight.
P A	1 B only	Both double, shows traces of original letters of first state.
P A	2	Fine, letter double on right.
P A	4	Fine, letter double on left.
P **A**	10	Very fine.
P **E**	7	Slight but usually indistinct.
P F	6	Fine.
P **H**	5	Very fine.
P **H**	11	Fair.
P J	5	Slight.
Q A	1	Fine.
Q A	4	Very fine; often called "Q over S".
R **D**	11	Fine.
R G	4	Slight.
R **I**	1 A only	Slight but apparently constant.
T B	9	Fine, but perhaps not double.
T **H**	5	Fine, though does not always show.
T K	1	Top stroke of "T" prolonged on left.
T L	2	Very fine, probably the best.

RE-ENTRIES

In the following table N.W. represents top left, and N.E. top right corner-squares respectively.

Lettering.	Plate.	Position of re-entry marks.
A D	2	N.W. and N.E., letter squares and bottom margin.
A G	5	N.E.
B B	1B	N.E.
B C	11	N.W., N.E., B square, through "POSTAGE" and value, formerly called "double letter B over K".
C L	1B	N.W. and L square.
D L	8	N.E., D square and partly through value.
E H	1B	N.W. and N.E.
E H	9	N.E. and H square.
E J	1B	N.W. and N.E. and through value not very evident; both letters recut and enlarged.
E K	1B	N.E., and through "POSTAGE"; both letters recut.
E L	1B	N.W.
F C	5	N.E.
F D	9	Double bottom.
G A	1B	N.E.
G K	1B	N.W.
G L	1B	N.W. and each letter square.
H B	1	N.W. and N.E. and H square.
H D	1	N.W. and N.E., through value and bottom margin.
H K	1B	N.W. and N.E.
H L	2	N.W. and N.E., H square and through value.
I B	1B	N.W. and N.E.
I D	1B	N.W. and N.E. and through value.
I L	1B	N.W. and N.E. and I square; both letters recut and enlarged.
J C	1B	N.W., both letters recut.
J E	1B	N.E.
J F	2	N.W.
J I	1B	N.W. and N.E.
J K	1B	N.E.
K K	7	N.E., and each letter square and below.
L E	2	Through "NY" of "PENNY".
L F	2	Through "PENNY".
L H	1B	Diagonal lines N.W.; perhaps not a re-entry.
L L	5	Through "O" of "ONE".
M H	1B	N.E.
M I	1B	N.W. and N.E. and "POSTAGE".
M J	1B	N.W. and N.E. and "POSTAGE".
M K	1B	N.E.
N D	5	Through "ON" of "ONE".
N G	1B	N.E.
N J	3	N.W.
N K	9	N.E., each letter square and "O" of "ONE".
O A	1	N.E.
O A	11	N.W. and N.E., A square and through "POSTAGE".
O B	6	N.W., O square and through value.
O I	1B	N.W.
P B	5	Through value and B square; third state of plate only.
P D	11	Double bottom.
P G	10	N.E. and G square and bottom margin.
P K	10	N.E. and letter squares, "POSTAGE" and value.
Q I	7	N.W. and N.E. and Q square.
Q J	6	N.W. and N.E. and bottom margin, and in the hair at the top of the head above the diadem.
Q K	6	N.W. and N.E. and through "POSTAGE" and K square.
Q L	1B	N.E.
R I	10	N.E., through value and I square.
R K	10	Double bottom.
R L	8	N.E. and through value.
R L	10	Double bottom.
S A	2	N.W. and N.E. and A square.
S A	6	N.W. and N.E.
S A to S L	11	N.E.
S C	4	N.E.
S D	4	N.W., S square and through value.
S I	10	N.E.; letter squares, through value.
S L	1A	Double bottom.
T A	8	N.W. and N.E. and bottom margin.
T A	10	N.W. and N.E. and through value.
T C	11	N.E.
T D	11	N.W., T square and through value.
T J	8	N.E. and bottom margin.
T K	11	N.E., K square and bottom margin.
T L	1A	Double bottom.